D0081141

The Economic Growth of Brazil

The Economic Growth of Brazil

of Brazil

A SURVEY FROM COLONIAL TO MODERN TIMES

By Celso Furtado

Translated by Ricardo W. de Aguiar
and Eric Charles Drysdale

WITHDRAWN

GREENWOOD PRESS, PUBLISHERS
WESTPORT, CONNECTICUT

Library of Congress Cataloging in Publication Data

Furtado, Celso.
   The economic growth of Brazil.

   Translation of: Formação econômica do Brasil.
   Reprint. Originally published: Berkeley : University of
California Press, 1968.
   Bibliography: p.
   1. Brazil--Economic conditions.   I. Title.
HC187.F8133 1984   338.981   84-10782
ISBN 0-313-24448-0 (lib. bdg.)

ColRes
HC
187
.F8133
1984

© 1963 by The Regents of the University of California

Translated from *Formação Econômica Do Brasil*
(Rio de Janeiro, Editôra Fundo de Cultura, 1959)

Published with the assistance of a grant from the Rockefeller Foundation

Reprinted with the permission of the University of California Press

Reprinted in 1984 by Greenwood Press
A division of Congressional Information Service, Inc.
88 Post Road West, Westport, Connecticut 06881

Printed in the United States of America

10 9 8 7 6 5 4 3 2 1

This work is intended to be nothing more than a sketch of the historic process of Brazil's economic growth. The author's purpose has been to present an introductory text, accessible to the reader without a technical background in economics and of interest to the growing public desirous of getting acquainted in systematic fashion with the economic problems facing Brazil. His main concern has been with providing as broad a perspective as possible, feeling that without adequate depth of horizon there is no possibility of apprehending the interrelations and chains of causality that make up the texture of economic processes.

Though addressing a wider audience, the author had in mind, in preparing the present work, mainly students of social sciences, especially economics. Assimilation of economic theories at college level needs more and more to be completed by the application of those theories to the historic processes underlying the reality within which the student lives and upon which he may have to exert action. This book, which is in reality just an outline, suggests a series of themes which could serve as a basis for an introductory course in the study of the Brazilian economy.

The Brazilian historical bibliography has been almost completely omitted, as it goes beyond the specific field of the present study, which is more an analysis of economic processes than a reconstruction of the historical events underlying them. Nevertheless, bibliographical references included in the footnotes will undoubtedly be of some interest from the point of view of historical and comparative analysis.

In the last part (mainly from Chapter 31 through Chapter 35), the author has closely followed the textual analysis presented in a previous work (*A Economia Brasileira,* Rio de Janeiro, 1954). Data have been revised, however, and sources are now cited. Although there is no discrepancy between the two publications as regards fundamental conclusions, at various points the shift in focus or emphasis and the inclusion of new material are to be especially noted.

CELSO FURTADO

Contents

III. *The Slavery Economy of Mining (Eighteenth Century)*

IV. *The Economy of Transition to Paid Labor (Nineteenth Century)*

V. *The Economy of Transition to an
Industrial System* (*Twentieth Century*)

PART I

Economic Bases
of Territorial Occupation

1. FROM COMMERCIAL EXPANSION TO AGRICULTURAL ENTERPRISE

The economic occupation of land in the Americas was an aftermath of commercial expansion in Europe. There was no instance of a *Völkerwanderung* caused by population pressure —as in ancient Greece—or of great migrations of peoples determined by the disruption of a system of balance maintained by force, such as the Teutonic migrations toward western and southern Europe. European internal trade, having undergone intensive growth from the eleventh century, had reached a high level of expansion in the fifteenth century, when Ottoman invasions began to cause greater and greater difficulties on the lines of supply for high-quality products, including manufactures from the Orient. The rerouting of such lines, by making a detour around the Ottoman "roadblock," might indeed be considered as the major European accomplishment of the second half of that century.[1] The discovery of the West-

[1] The economic development of Portugal in the fifteenth century, with the exploration of the African coast and the agricultural expansion on the Atlantic islands and eventually the opening up of the maritime route to the East Indies, may be considered an autonomous feature of European commercial expansion, to some extent separate from the growing troubles in the eastern Mediterranean provoked by the Ottoman conquests. Sugar production on the islands of São Tomé and

ern Hemisphere was basically an episode in that strenuous effort. At the outset it had seemed to be a minor episode. In fact, it was so considered by the Portuguese for half a century. The first and most easily harvested fruits of the discoveries reverted in their entirety to the benefit of the Spaniards. The gold accumulated by long-settled civilizations on the Mexican *meseta* and Andean *altiplano* regions was the *raison d'être* of the Western Hemisphere and the main goal of the Europeans during the first stage of American history. The legend of unimaginable riches awaiting discovery spread throughout Europe, arousing enormous interest in the new lands. This interest led Spain and Portugal, as the "owners" of those lands, to defend them against all other European nations. Thereafter the occupation of the hemisphere was no longer a purely commercial matter; important political factors became involved. Spain, which had collected booty previously unknown in the world, had to make an effort to transform its dominions into a vast citadel. Other countries tried to build themselves into strongholds, either as a point of departure for new and rewarding discoveries or as bases for raids against the Spaniards. If

---

Madeira reached its highest levels in the latter half of the fifteenth century, at a time when the Venetians still preserved intact their sources of supply in the east Mediterranean. The same can be said of the spice trade from the Indies, since Turkish occupation of Egypt—the main entrepôt—occurred only a quarter of a century after the travels of Vasco da Gama. The immediate result of the opening up of the new route was a sudden fall in spice prices. The Venetians began to buy pepper in Lisbon for half as much as they paid the Arabs in Alexandria. On this subject, the reader is referred to Frédy Thiriet, *Histoire de Venise* (Paris, 1952), p. 104. The great Portuguese achievement of eliminating the Arab middlemen forestalling the Turkish threat, disrupting the Venetian monopoly and lowering the price of Oriental products, was of basic importance to the subsequent commercial development of Europe. On the causes of the outset of Portuguese maritime expansion, the illuminating study of Antônio Sérgio, "A Conquista de Ceuta," in *Ensaios* (2d ed., Coimbra, 1949), Vol. I, is recommended.

it had not been for the mirage evoked by such treasures—during the first two centuries of the history of the continents enjoyed only by the Spaniards—the exploration and occupation of the Western Hemisphere would have proceeded at a much slower pace.

The beginning of the economic occupation of Brazil was largely the result of political pressure exerted on Portugal and Spain by other European nations. Among the latter, the prevailing principle was that the Spanish and Portuguese should be entitled only to those tracts of land which they had effectively occupied. Thus, when for religious motives but with government support, the French organized their first expedition to promote a settlement for populating purposes* in the Western Hemisphere, which became the first permanent one on the American continents, their attention was directed toward the northern coast of Brazil. Portuguese statesmen watched these moves closely and even tried by means of bribery to divert attention from Brazil in the French court. Yet, with the passing of time, it became clearer that the Portuguese territories in the Western Hemisphere would be lost unless some major endeavor were directed toward the permanent occupation of those lands. Such an effort would mean diverting capital resources from far more productive enterprises in the Orient. The gold mirage hanging over inland Brazil (to which growing French pressure was not foreign) greatly influenced the Portuguese decision to make a strong effort to keep their territories in America, inasmuch as resources available to Portugal for unproductive

* Translators' note: Through the first few chapters of this book, the author stresses the difference between settlements for purposes of economic exploitation of resources and those created under state policies and aimed at establishing nuclei of population for the building of a potential manpower reserve against the event of continuing military operations. We have rendered the latter type as "settlements for populating purposes."

investment in Brazil were small. Furthermore, these would hardly be sufficient for the long-term defense of such possessions. Meanwhile, Spain, whose resources were incomparably greater than those of Portugal, was compelled to give way before the pressure of several invaders in a large part of the lands bestowed on Spain by the Treaty of Tordesillas. To promote a more effective defense of their territory, the Spanish had to shorten its perimeter. Moreover, it was essential for them to settle some areas of lesser economic significance— such as Cuba—for purposes of supply and defense. Outside the regions connected with large-scale Spanish military and mining undertakings, the Western Hemisphere could scarcely be of economic interest. To defend it effectively and permanently would involve a sheer waste of considerable resources. The fur and timber trade with the Indians, which developed during the sixteenth century along the entire eastern seaboard, was of small scope, and demanded no more than the establishment of provisional trading posts.

The most relevant features of the first century of the history of the Western Hemisphere are linked with the struggles over lands of little or no economic utility. Spain and Portugal took for granted their rights to all the newly discovered lands, but those rights were disputed by the European nations with the greatest rate of commercial growth at the time: the Netherlands, France, and England. Spain was in a position immediately to realize vast gains, making it possible to finance the defense of her rich holdings. Indeed, so great were those gains and so fruitless did many of the territories seem to the Spanish, that they decided to concentrate their defense system along the Mexico-Peru precious-metal-production axis. This line of defense ran from Florida to the mouth of the River Plate. Notwithstanding the enormous resources available to Spain, she could not prevent her enemies from driving a wedge into the heart of the Spanish defense line—the Caribbean islands. This Caribbean penetration marked the starting point of a basically military operation.[2] However, as we shall see later, in the following centuries this Caribbean military wedge was to become of enormous economic importance.

Portugal was faced with the task of finding a way of economic utilization of her territories in the Americas other than the easy extraction of precious metals. Only thus would it be possible to justify the costs of defending such possessions. The problem was widely discussed at top levels, with the participation of such statesmen as Damião de Góis, who managed to envisage the development of Europe at that time from a broad viewpoint. Portuguese policies drafted at the time led to the beginning of the agricultural utilization of Brazilian lands, an event of conspicuous importance in the history of the hemisphere. From mere plundering and mining ventures identical to those being undertaken simultaneously along the African seaboard and in the East Indies, the Western Hemisphere started to become an integrated part of the European reproductive economy, the technology and capital of which were thenceforth to be guided and invested in such a manner as to create a permanent flow of goods to the European market.

The economic utilization of the Western Hemisphere would have seemed a completely unfeasible undertaking in the sixteenth century. At the time, no agricultural product was the object of large-scale trade within Europe. Of wheat, the main farm product, abundant European supply sources were available. Freight costs were so high, because of the insecurity of long-distance transportation, that only manufactured products or Oriental spices were deemed profitable. In addition, the enormous costs to be faced by an agricultural undertaking in the distant Western Hemisphere can readily be imagined. It

---

[2] The settlement of the Caribbean islands by the French "was undertaken rather from the point of view of colonial defense and attack in Spanish America." Léon Vignols, "Les Antilles françaises sous l'ancien régime," *Revue d'Histoire Économique et Sociale* (Paris, 1928), p. 34.

is universally recognized that the first to attempt this undertaking was the Portuguese.[3] If their efforts had been unsuccessful, defense of the Brazilian territories would have been too costly, and excluding the hypothesis of gold discoveries at an earlier date Portugal could hardly have maintained her position as a great colonial power in the Western Hemisphere.

2. REASONS FOR THE SUCCESS OF THE AGRICULTURAL ENTERPRISE

A particularly favorable series of causes lay behind the success of the first large-scale colonial and agricultural enterprise in the Western Hemisphere. For a few score years the Portuguese had been engaged, in the Atlantic islands, in relatively large-scale production of one of the articles most appreciated in the European market: sugar. That experimental development was to acquire enormous importance. Besides providing a solution to technical problems related with sugar production, it was to spur the development of the Portuguese sugar-mill–equipment industry. In view of the difficulties prevailing at the time for the acquiring of any kind of production know-how, as well as of the prohibitive burdens hampering the export of equipment of any kind, the success of the Brazilian enterprise would have

[3] "Brazil was the first of the European settlements in America to attempt the cultivation of the soil." *Cambridge Modern History* (Cambridge, 1909), VI, 389. The Spanish attempted agricultural enterprises before the Portuguese. However, such enterprises did not progress beyond the experimental stage.

been far more difficult to attain or much longer in coming if it had not been for the technical progress achieved by the Portuguese in this sector.[1]

The greatest repercussions of the experimental work in the Atlantic islands were probably those felt in the commercial sector. All indications are that at the outset Portuguese sugar must have been routed over the traditional channels controlled by the merchants of the Italian seafaring cities.[2] The fall in prices which occurred in the last quarter of the fifteenth century would, however, lead to the supposition that those trade channels had not been broadened to the extent required by the expansion of sugar production. The problem of surpluses which made itself felt at that time seems to show that within the mercantile setup traditionally established by the Italian commercial cities sugar production could find only relatively limited markets. Nevertheless, one of the main consequences of the flow of Portuguese production into the European market

---

[1] Sugar-production know-how was relatively widespread in the Mediterranean region; sugar was produced all the way from Syria to Spain, although on a small scale. However, the making of top-quality sugar, such as that produced in Cyprus, involved trade secrets. References to a Genoese as being the main sugar producer on the island of Madeira would indicate that the Italians—who were at that time outstanding in sugar production and trade—were playing a part in the agricultural expansion of the Portuguese islands in the Atlantic. The secrets of sugar refining were jealously guarded. As late as 1612, the Council of Venice —a city which had long held a monopoly on all the sugar consumed in Europe—prohibited export of equipment, know-how, and capital connected with the industry. See Noel Deerr, *The History of Sugar* (London, 1949), I, 100, and II, 452.

[2] The fact that refineries were established outside Venice at the time of the expansion of Portuguese production—as at Bologna from 1470 onward—seems to show that the Venetian monopoly was broken at that time. The big price drop observed in the last decade of the century may perhaps have been due to the shift from a monopoly market to a competitive market.

was the disruption of the monopoly of access to sugar-producing areas heretofore exercised by the Venetians. Since early days, Portuguese products were shipped in vast quantities to the harbors of Flanders. When in 1496 the Portuguese government, under pressure from the decline in prices, decided to curtail production, one-third of the output was already being customarily routed to the Flemish ports.[3]

From the second half of the sixteenth century, Portuguese sugar production was being amalgamated to an increasing extent with Flemish and Dutch interests, first with those of Antwerp and later with those of Amsterdam. The production phase was in the hands of the Portuguese, whereas the Flemish would load the crude product in Lisbon, to be refined at home for distribution throughout Europe, especially in the Baltic area, France, and England.[4]

The Low Countries' contribution—chiefly that of the Dutch —to the great expansion of the sugar market in the latter half of the sixteenth century may be viewed as a basic cause of the success of agricultural settlement in Brazil. Experts in the inter-European trade—a large part of which was financed by the Dutch—they were at that time the only nation with an available commercial organization capable of providing a

[3] In 1496, Dom Manuel I, King of Portugal, set a production ceiling of 120,000 arrobas, including 40,000 for Flanders, 16,000 for Venice, 13,000 for Genoa, 15,000 for Chios, and 7,000 for England. Barros, *História da Administração Pública em Portugal* (Lisbon, 1777), IV, chap. v. Quoted by N. Deerr, *op. cit.* I, 101.

[4] "The date at which the first refinery was built [in Antwerp] is not on record, but it must have been soon after the beginning of the sixteenth century. . . . By 1550 there were thirteen refineries, increased by 1556 to nineteen . . . After the enforced closing down of the Antwerp refineries the Continental trade moved to Amsterdam. . . . By 1587 there is ample evidence that a number of refineries were working, of which some had been established by refugees from Antwerp." Deerr, *op. cit.*, II, 453.

huge market for such a new product as sugar. In view of the immense difficulties faced at the outset in marketing the small output of the island of Madeira, as well as the stupendous subsequent expansion of the market which absorbed at steady prices the great Brazilian production, the importance of the commercial phase for the success of the entire sugar enterprise at the time is clearly manifest.

It was not only through their trading experience that the Dutch engaged in the sugar business. A large part of the financing required by the undertaking had come from the Netherlands. There are many indications that Dutch capitalists did not restrict themselves to the financing of sugar refining and marketing, but that Flemish capital also shared in the financing of production facilities in Brazil and in the importing of slave manpower. Once the feasibility of the enterprise had been demonstrated, and its high profitability proved, financing of further expansion would not be faced with any major hindrance. Powerful Dutch financial groups, involved as they were in the sales promotion of the Brazilian product, would indeed be expected to have no objection to meeting the credit required for expansion of productive capacity.[5]

Still, neither Portuguese production skill nor the commercial ability and financial power of the Dutch was sufficient to guarantee the success of the agricultural colonization venture in Brazilian lands. Moreover, there was the manpower problem. The transportation of the necessary number of settlers from Europe would have required too large an investment, probably rendering the entire undertaking unprofitable. Working conditions overseas were such that only by paying much

[5] Since the Dutch controlled transportation (including a part of that between Brazil and Portugal), as well as refining and trade in sugar, the sugar trade was in their hands rather than in those of the Portuguese. Profit on refining alone amounted to approximately a third of the value of the crude sugar. On this point, see Deerr, *op. cit.*, II, 453.

higher wages than those prevailing in Europe would there be any possibility of enticing manpower from the Old World. The alternative of reducing costs by providing land grants to pay for the settler's work over a number of years had no attraction for him nor was it practicable, because without large amounts of capital the land was of no real economic value. Finally, the scarcity of manpower in Portugal, owing chiefly to the highly flourishing condition of the East Indies, had to be considered. Here too another circumstance arose that made solution of the problem much easier. At this juncture the Portuguese had already acquired a fairly thorough knowledge of the African slave traffic. Brigandage operations for the capture of Negroes, begun almost a century earlier in the days of Portuguese Prince Dom Henrique the Navigator (1394–1460), had evolved into a well-organized and prosperous trade for supplying slave manpower for some European areas. Once sufficient resources could be mustered, it would always be possible to expand this business and guide the transfer of low-cost manpower to the new agricultural settlement—without which the undertaking would have no economic feasibility.[6]

Each of the aforementioned problems—production skills, market development, financing, and manpower—had found a timely solution, independent of a general preconceived plan. Most importantly, there was a series of favorable circumstances, without which the undertaking could not have been blessed by the enormous success it achieved. Behind the entire enterprise undoubtedly were the desire and struggle of the Portuguese government to keep possession of its lands in the

---

[6] The idea of using native labor was underlying the first colonization projects. The volume of capital tied up in the importing of African slave labor was such that this alternative solution could be considered only at a stage when the business proved highly profitable. In places where the colonial centers had no chance for economic expansion, native labor was used.

Western Hemisphere, with the ever-present hope that some day gold would be extracted from them. Nevertheless, this desire could only be transformed into a working policy if some concrete support were forthcoming. If defense of the new lands had continued to be a heavy financial burden on the small kingdom, it would surely have been slackened. The success of the great agricultural enterprise of the sixteenth century—which was unique at the time—was therefore the reason for the continuing Portuguese hold over large parts of the Western Hemisphere. In the following century, when there was a change in the balance of power in Europe, with the hegemony of nations excluded from the Treaty of Tordesillas, Portugal had already gone far toward the effective occupation of its share.

3. REASONS FOR
THE MONOPOLY

The excellent financial results of the agricultural colonization of Brazil afforded alluring prospects of economic utilization of the new lands. In spite of all this, however, the Spanish continued to pursue their sole purpose of mining precious metals. Spain's reaction to the ever bolder challenge of her enemies was confined to a reinforcing of the chain of isolationist defenses ringing her wealthy possessions. The Western Hemisphere areas on which the Spaniards concentrated their attention were likewise unique in being densely populated. In fact, the basis of Spanish colonial enterprises was the exploitation of native manpower. Spain never showed any interest in promoting major interchange with her colonies, or even intercolonial relationships. Organized relationships between the homeland

and the colonies, in the form in which they existed, were a factor of permanent scarcity of means of transportation, which in turn led to exceedingly high freight rates.[1] Spain's policies were aimed at transforming her colonies into economic systems as self-sufficient as possible, producers of a high-grade net surplus in the form of precious metals for transfer to the parent country at regular intervals. This influx of precious metals attained enormous relative proportions and caused profound structural changes in the Spanish economy. The economic power of the state grew unbounded, and the huge income generated by public expenditures (or government-subsidized private ones) gave rise to chronic inflation in the form of an unremitting deficit in the country's commercial balance. Because Spain was the point of origin from which inflation spread throughout Europe, this was bound to make it only too evident that the general level of prices would be persistently higher there than elsewhere in the Old World. This in turn could lead to a rise in imports and declining exports.[2] Consequently, the precious metals which Spain collected from

[1] The laws of the Indies strictly prohibited the entry of non-Spanish ships into the ports of Spanish America, and limited traffic with Spain to the port of Seville. Only one fleet a year left the continent for that port, and it was difficult to get space in it. Even at the time when Portugal was linked with Spain, sugar-mill equipment manufactured in Lisbon had to be taken to Seville for shipment to the Spanish colonies at high freight rates. See Ramiro Guerra y Sánchez, *Azúcar y Población en las Antillas* (Havana, 1944), 3d ed., p. 50.

[2] Research by J. Hamilton on the supplying of the fleet in Seville brought out that this was largely done with imported manufactures and foodstuffs. Among other works by this author, see *American Treasure and the Price Revolution in Spain, 1501–1610* (Cambridge, Mass., 1934). The struggle for the conquest of the Spanish market became a common goal of the other European countries. Even Colbert wrote: "The more each state trades with the Spanish, the more money it has." See also E. Levasseur, *Histoire du Commerce de la France* (Paris, 1911), I, 413.

the Western Hemisphere as unilateral transfers caused an afflux of imports, with inhibitory effects on domestic production and at the same time a highly stimulating influence on the economy of other European countries. Further, the possibility of substantial profits from direct or indirect state subsidies led to a growing body of inactive persons, curtailing the relative importance in Spanish society of groups connected with productive activities as well as their influence on the drafting of state policies.

The economic decline of Spain created havoc in her Western Hemisphere colonies. Apart from mining operations, no major economic enterprise whatsoever had even been started. Agricultural exports from the immense territory at no time reached any meaningful figure for three entire centuries. The supply of manufactured goods for the great masses of the native populations was at all times based on local handicrafts, postponing any change in the already existing subsistence economies. Without the regression of the Spanish economy, which was greatly aggravated in the seventeenth century,[3] exports of manufactures from the home country to the colonies would necessarily have been made. This in turn would have led to economic ties far more complex than the mere periodic transfer of a production surplus in the form of precious metals. Consumption of European manufactures by the swarming populations of the Mexican meseta and the Andean altiplano would have created the need for a counterpart in local pro-

---

[3] This decadence may be seen from the fact that the population of the country declined 25 per cent between 1594 and 1694. "Almost all manufacturing cities suffered a catastrophic decline in population. . . . Valladolid, Toledo and Segovia, for example, lost more than half of their inhabitants." By mid-seventeenth century, Francisco Martínez Mata was observing that innumerable guilds, including the iron, steel, copper, tin, and sulphur workers had disappeared. See J. Hamilton, "The Decline of Spain," in *Essays in Economic History* (London, 1954), p. 218.

duction exports for Spanish consumption or reëxport. Such interchange would have necessarily introduced some transformations into the archaic structures of the native economies, permitting greater penetration by European capital and know-how.

If Spanish colonization had evolved in such a direction, the difficulties facing the Portuguese undertakings would have been much more difficult to overcome. It is likely that the Spanish could have dominated the entire tropical produce market, especially that of sugar,[4] from the sixteenth century on. Much of the finest sugar-growing land lay in their hands,[5] it was far closer to Europe, and they had cheap native manpower better acquainted with advanced farming practices, as well as enormous financial resources under Spanish control. The main reason this did not happen was most probably the decline of the Spanish economy itself. Inasmuch as there was no political factor in the background—as in Portugal—the development of Spanish lines of export for Western Hemisphere products had to be established by powerful economic groups interested in sales of their own products in colonial markets. As could be expected, leadership in such moves was to be taken by the manufacturers themselves, but for the deterioration of the manufacturing sector during the phase of

---

[4] Exports of sugar by the colonies on the American continent were prohibited to avoid competing on the Spanish domestic market with the small production of Andalusia.

[5] The most highly developed native populations, from the farming point of view, were those of the uplands of Mexico and the Andes. They did not readily accustom themselves to work on the sugar-cane plantations, situated in low-lying, humid regions. For this reason, Negro labor was also introduced at the sugar mills set up to supply the population in those regions. The dense population of the Antilles, which might have served as a basis for the farm development there, was largely transferred to mining activities, under different climatic conditions, and disappeared for the most part.

vast imports of precious metals and concentration of income in the hands of the Spanish state. Therefore, one of the reasons for the success of the Portuguese agricultural colonizing enterprises was the very decline of the Spanish economy, largely because of the early discoveries of precious metals.

4. BREAKDOWN
OF THE SYSTEM

The political and economic framework that favored the rise and fast growth of the agricultural enterprise, which was the foundation of settlement operations in Brazil, underwent a far-reaching change when Portugal was taken over by Spain. The war waged against Spain by the Dutch[1] from 1580 to 1640 had profound repercussions on Portuguese South America. From the beginning until the middle of the seventeenth

---

[1] The region today comprising Holland, Belgium, and a part of northern France was known at the beginning of modern times by the general name of Nederlanden, that is, the Low Countries. When the seven northern provinces—among which Holland and Zeeland were outstanding—won their independence at the end of the sixteenth century, the remainder came to be known as the *Spanish* Low Countries and from the eighteenth century onward as the *Austrian* Low Countries. The independent portion was then known as the United Provinces, and the name of Holland was later adopted. The independence of the United Provinces officially dates from 1579 (the Union of Utrecht), though war with Spain continued for the next thirty years, until the twelve-year truce signed in 1609. Thus the Flemish in the United Provinces, who had greatly developed their trade with Portugal while they were under Spanish rule, were obliged to relinquish it again when they won their independence, because in the following year Spain occupied Portugal.

century, the Dutch controlled nearly all the maritime trade of Europe.[2] Sugar marketing in Europe without the coöperation of Dutch merchants was clearly impracticable. They, in turn, were by no means prepared to give up their substantial share in the thriving sugar business, whose success had largely been due to their own efforts. Thus the struggle for control of the sugar trade became one of the main reasons for the relentless warfare carried on by the Dutch against Spain. One of the episodes of this war was the Dutch occupation of the Brazilian sugar-producing regions for a quarter of a century (1630–1654).[3] Nevertheless, the consequences of the breakdown in

---

[2] "It is now safe to assume that the practical monopoly of European transport and commerce which the Dutch established in the early seventeenth century by reason of their geographical position, their superior commercial organization and technique, and the economic backwardness of their neighbours, stood intact until about 1730." C. H. Wilson, "The Economic Decline of the Netherlands," in *Essays in Economic History* (London, 1954), p. 254.

[3] During the period preceding the treaty of 1609, the Dutch made extensive inroads into the Portuguese East Indies empire, while at the same time continuing to pull sugar into Lisbon, through the use of a number of subterfuges, mainly the conniving of the Portuguese themselves, who viewed the Flemish as enemies of the Spanish occupying powers. During the twelve-year truce, Dutch penetration increased and extended to trade directly carried on with Brazil. "It was during the truce of 1609–21 that their trade with Brazil expanded greatly, despite the Spanish crown's explicit and reiterated prohibitions of foreign trade with the colony. A representation of Dutch merchants concerned in this business, which was submitted to the Estates General in 1622, explains how this enviable position had been achieved. Dutch trade with Brazil had always been driven through the intermediary of 'many good and honest Portuguese mostly living in Vienna and Oporto,' who, after the first formal prohibition of Dutch participation in this trade in 1594, had spontaneously offered to continue it under cover of their names and flag . . . The magistrate of Vianna do Castelo, in particular, had always 'tipped off' the local Dutch factors and their agents as to 'how they could guard themselves against damage from the Spaniards.' . . . The Dutch merchants estimated that they had secured between one-

the coöperative system which had previously been in existence were far more enduring than military occupation itself. While they occupied northeastern Brazil the invaders acquainted themselves with every angle, both technical and organizational, of the sugar industry. This know-how was to serve as a basis for installing and developing a large-scale competitive sugar industry in the Caribbean region. From that time onward the monopoly which had by then existed for three-quarters of a century, based on identity of interests between Portuguese producers and Dutch financial groups controlling European trade, was broken. In the third quarter of the seventeenth century, prices of sugar fell to half their former level, and remained at this relatively low figure throughout the next century.

The period of maximum profitability for the Portuguese agricultural colonial enterprise had passed. In the second half of the seventeenth century, the volume of average annual exports attained barely 50 per cent of the highest points reached about 1650. And even those dwindling exports were to be sold at prices less than half as high as those prevailing in the previous phase. Real income from sugar production declined to a quarter of what it had been at its best. The depreciation of the Portuguese currency in relation to gold, as recorded at that time, was in nearly the same proportion, clearly revealing the enormous importance of Brazilian sugar in the Portuguese balance of payment. Portugal had been the chief source of supply for Brazil, and such a depreciation might have entailed massive transfer of real income to the benefit of the colony. However, the same manufactures which comprised the bulk of the commodities brought to Brazil by the Portuguese were also produced elsewhere in Europe. Moreover, as commodities

---

half and two-thirds of the carrying-trade between Brazil and Europe."
C. R. Boxer, *The Dutch in Brazil* (Oxford, 1957), p. 20. When war with Spain started again, the Dutch occupied by force the sugar colony which in many respects was financially and economically integrated with the United Provinces.

of domestic production exported by Portugal to Brazil were commonly the same as those exported to other countries, most probably their prices would have been established in terms of gold. Hence, income transfers resulting from the depreciation of the currency would revert mainly to the benefit of the Portuguese metropolitan exporters.[4]

5. SETTLEMENT COLONIES IN THE NORTHERN PART OF THE WESTERN HEMISPHERE

Insofar as Brazil is concerned, the main event in the history of the Western Hemisphere during the seventeenth century was the upsurge of a powerful competing economy for the tropical-product market. The advent of that economy resulted to a great extent from the weakening of Spanish military power in the first half of the seventeenth century. This decline in power was closely watched by the three powers whose might underwent almost simultaneous growth: the Netherlands, France, and England. The idea of seizing so rich a booty as the Spanish parts of the Americas was ever present in the minds of the statesmen of those countries. The idea never came to genuine fruition because of the growing rivalry between France and

[4] The depreciation of the Portuguese currency against gold was a natural consequence of the substantial reduction in the real value of exports, resulting from the decline in prices and contraction in the volume of sugar sales. The depreciation curtailed the losses of those traders who had capital tied up in the sugar business, and made it possible for this business to continue to operate. Had other factors (such as the discovery of gold half a century previously) prevented depreciation, the decadence of the sugar regions during the second half of the seventeenth century would have been much more far-reaching.

England. Those two countries endeavored to get a foothold in the strategic Caribbean islands so as to develop settlement colonies there for military purposes. According to a French historian, "At first there was but a single master policy: the conquest of precious-metal–producing lands or, failing that, lands providing access to the same." [1] The French and English were therefore engaged in the early seventeenth century in concentrating, at some desirable Caribbean islands, strong nuclei of European population, in preparation for a large-scale assault on the rich domains of the great "sick" power of that century. Describing Cardinal Richelieu's motives in the settlement of Martinique, another French historian says: "It was becoming a matter of urgency to create as soon as possible a strong and permanent militia. This was the basic policy to be upheld; the islands were in need of a great number of settlers, farmers, and soldiers." [2] In view of its political purposes, this settlement was to be based on the small holding system. Settlers were seduced by propaganda and various enticements, recruited from among condemned criminals, or simply kidnapped.[3] Each settler would receive the grant of a small landholding to be paid for with the fruits of his future labors.

The British Caribbean possessions were populated more rapidly than the French territories, and with small government

[1] Léon Vignols, "Les Antilles françaises sous l'ancien régime," *Revue d'Histoire Économique et Sociale* (Paris, 1928), p. 34.

[2] M. Delawarde, *Les Défricheurs et les Petits Colons de la Martinique au XVIIe siècle* (Paris, 1935), p. 30.

[3] Sometimes mass transfers of rebellious populations took place. Cromwell issued the following orders in regard to the Irish rebels: "When they submitted, these officers were knocked on the head, and every tenth man of the soldiers killed, and the rest shipped for Barbados"; see also V. T. Harlow, *A History of Barbados* (Oxford, 1926), p. 295. "Political criminals, prisoners of war, vagabonds, children of vagabonds were carried to America by merchants under contract with the government. Others were kidnapped, or induced to go under false pretences." Julius Isaac, *Economics of Migration* (London, 1947), p. 17.

financial aid, probably because of the easier task of recruiting in the British Isles. The seventeenth century was a period of great social change and deep-seated political and religious unrest in Britain. During the three-quarters of a century preceding the Toleration Act of 1689, political intolerance brought about sizable shifts in population within the islands and outward from them.[4] Although closely linked with the great British colonizing expansion drive in the first half of the seventeenth century, the migrations caused by religious and political motives should not be deemed to account, by themselves, for the whole of such expansion. Large-scale transportation of people across the Atlantic, especially at that time, required huge investments. However, the fact that considerable population groups were ready to accept the most severe traveling conditions in order to emigrate made it possible to utilize European manpower under relatively favorable conditions. Important companies were organized for financing the transfer of those population groups, which were granted extensive economic privileges in any settlements to be founded by them. Only in exceptional instances and for explicit military purposes —as in Georgia later in the eighteenth century—did the British government take upon itself the cost of financing the transfer of settlers.

Colonization for settlement purposes, as begun in America in the seventeenth century, might therefore be defined either as an operation for political purposes or as a form of exploita-

---

[4] "The English settlements developed in the course of the seventeenth century owe their existence mainly to the immigration of refugees from religious or political intolerance who left Britain before the Toleration Act of 1689. Puritans founded the first successful settlement in New England in 1620. English Dissenters established settlements in Massachusetts, where the Massachusett Bay Company had been granted a charter in 1629. Refugee immigration brought about the founding of Connecticut in 1633 and of Rhode Island in 1636. At about the same time discontented Catholics turned to the West Indies, where the Earl of Carlisle had received a charter." Isaac, *op. cit.,* p. 16.

tion of European manpower, which, owing to a particular set of circumstances, had turned out to be relatively cheap in the British Isles. As opposed to Spain and Portugal, harassed by a permanent manpower scarcity when starting to occupy the Western Hemisphere, seventeenth-century England had an abundant population surplus, owing to the far-reaching changes affecting the country's agriculture since the previous century.[5] Excess population was leaving the rural areas to the extent that the old system of communal farming was becoming extinct and farmlands were being transformed into sheep pastures. This population, faced with precarious living conditions, might better itself by accepting a regime of servitude for a limited period, in order to amass some savings. Interested persons would sign contracts in England whereby they were committed to work for others, for a term varying from five to seven years, in return for payment of passage, sustenance, and, at the end of the contract, a landholding or cash indemnity. Indications are that these persons received no better treatment than that offered African slaves.[6]

The beginning of settlement colonization in the seventeenth

[5] "Britain could afford to send so many emigrants overseas without endangering the ample supply of cheap labour for her home industry. The changes in agricultural organization, particularly enclosures, had created in England a surplus rural population which brought wages down to subsistence level, and provided a large reserve in the labour market." Isaac, *op. cit.,* p. 17. The idea that Spain was impoverished by mass emigration to the American continent is unfounded, because the type of colony which the Spanish created in the Western Hemisphere did not call for sizable transfers of European population. It is estimated that between 1509 and 1790 about 150,000 persons emigrated from Spain to the American continents, whereas in the seventeenth century alone 500,000 left the British Isles. See Irme Ferencz, in "Migrations," *Encyclopædia of Social Sciences* (New York, 1936).

[6] "The most significant feature of this question of treatment is the general agreement among contemporary writers that the European servant was in a less favoured position than the negro slave." Harlow, *op. cit.,* p. 302.

century opens a new chapter in the history of the Western Hemisphere. At first, the settlement ventures caused heavy losses to the colonizing companies, especially in North America.[7] The success of Portuguese agricultural colonization had been based on the production of an article whose market had grown considerably. The search for products capable of finding expanding markets was the main concern of the new colonial nuclei. There was also a need for turning out products which could be produced on small farms, without which the recruitment of European manpower would come to a halt. Under such conditions, settlements in the higher latitudes of North America faced serious trouble in finding a stable economic basis. From the viewpoint of companies financing the initial costs of immigration and settlement, colonization of that part of the continent was definitely a failure. It had not been possible to find any product adapted to the region under conditions capable of providing a line of exports which could pay for the investment. In fact, what could be produced in New England was exactly what was already being produced in Europe, where wages were on a subsistence level—extremely

[7] The first company to undertake the colonization of Virginia did not pay its shareholders one cent of income, and closed out its books with a loss of 100,000 pounds. See Edward C. Kirkland, *Historía Económica de los Estados Unidos* (México). Referring to the fact that Canada was a burden on France, and that the loss of it was in some respects a relief, E. Levasseur writes: "In France, the statesmen and men of letters were not impressed with the seriousness of this loss. . . . The population in question, it is true, was not wealthy; it subsisted by farming and hunting . . . Abbot Raynal reports that in 1715 exports from Canada to France reached a value of but 300,000 pounds, that during the most flourishing period they did not exceed 1,300,000 pounds, and that between 1750 and 1760 the government had spent 127½ millions there: all of this did not tend to make Canada popular with the French government." *Histoire du Commerce de la France* (Paris, 1911), I, 484.

low at the time. Then too, transportation costs were so high in relation to the cost of production of articles of basic necessity that even a substantial difference in real wages would have had little significance. Thus the slow initial rate of development of the colonies in North America is understandable. These would have remained in the background for a long time, had not certain events—to which I shall refer later in this work—brought about a transformation in the various factors involved.

Climatic conditions in the Caribbean area favored production of such articles as cotton, indigo, coffee, and especially tobacco, with promising prospects in European markets. Production of these articles was consistent with the small-farm system, and afforded the colonizing enterprises substantial profits while the governments of the expansionist European powers—France and England—watched their military might grow.

Efforts to recruit manpower under the prevailing regime of temporary servitude, chiefly in England, were intensified with colonial business prosperity. All possible means were used to persuade persons who had committed crimes—no matter how insignificant—to sell themselves for work in America instead of going to prison. Manpower supply must still have been insufficient, however, because the practice of kidnapping adults and children became a public calamity in England.[8] By these and other means the European population in the Caribbean area increased; in 1634, in Barbados alone, it numbered 37,200.

[8] See Harlow, *op. cit., passim.*

6. CONSEQUENCES OF THE PENETRATION OF SUGAR INTO THE CARIBBEAN AREA

As tropical agriculture—especially tobacco growing—became a commercial success, difficulties were bound to increase from the point of view of the supply of European manpower. For companies engaged in business with new colonies the natural solution for the problem was in the introduction of African slave manpower. In Virginia, where the land was not wholly divided up among small farmers, formation of large agricultural units quickly developed. An entirely new situation developed in the market for tropical products, with intense competition between regions utilizing slave manpower in large production units and those where small farms and European population prevailed. The resultant decline in prices in the international markets created serious difficulties for the populations in the Caribbean, evidencing the precarious nature of the whole colonization system there.[1] In fact, settlement colonies in the Caribbean islands proved to be nothing more than experimental stations for the production of commodities of still uncertain economic potentialities. When the stage of uncertainty was overcome, the massive investments involved in the large slave-plantation operations were seen to be much better business.

From that time, the course of Caribbean colonization changed, and this fact was to be of fundamental importance

---

[1] "No further profit was possible, whereas the British colonial settlers came to replace white labor by Negro slaves purchased at a good price or on credit." Louis Philippe May, *Histoire Économique de la Martinique 1635–1763* (Paris, 1930), p. 89.

to Brazil. The original idea of colonizing American tropical regions on a small farm basis would per se exclude any thought of sugar production. To the Caribbean colonies there remained all the other tropical products. The reason for this division of work stemmed from the political purposes behind Caribbean colonization, where the French and British intended to gather strong nuclei of European population. Nevertheless, those political objectives had to be abandoned under strong pressure from economic factors.

It is probable, however, that changes bearing upon the Caribbean economy would have occurred much more slowly except for an external occurrence at the end of the first half of the seventeenth century—the final expulsion of the Dutch invaders from northeastern Brazil. Having mastered production techniques and being most probably outfitted to produce equipment[2] for the sugar industry, the Dutch showed themselves altogether disposed to establish an important sugar-producing center outside Brazil. So favorable was the situation they found in the French Antilles and British West Indies that they preferred coöperating with the settlers in those regions rather than trying to occupy new lands and install such an industry on their own account. In Martinique there were great difficulties caused by falling prices of tobacco, a circumstance which would make it easier to set up any new business tending to restore the island's prosperity. In the British Caribbean territories, economic troubles had been aggravated by the civil war still being waged in the British Isles. Isolated from the home-

[2] The question as to whether the Dutch did or did not themselves master the techniques of sugar production or whether they allowed Antilles experts to come to Brazil so as to develop their know-how is of no real significance. On this subject, see A. P. Canabrava, "A Influência do Brasil na técnica do fabrico de açucar nas Antilhas francesas e inglêsas no meado do século XVII," in *Anuário da Faculdade de Ciências Econômicas e Administrativas, 1946–47* (São Paulo, 1947).

land, the settlers enthusiastically welcomed the possibility of intensive trade with the Dutch. The latter, in turn, not only provided the necessary technical assistance but also afforded easy credit for buying equipment, slaves, and land.[3] Powerful financial groups soon appeared in the islands, controlling great tracts of land and owning large sugar-mill installations. Thus, less than ten years after being expelled from Brazil, the Dutch were operating in the Caribbean area a sugar economy of large proportions, with new equipment and in a better geographical position vis-à-vis the European markets.

The results of such an authentic outburst of one economic system within another were deeply felt. The population of European origin decreased promptly, in both the French and British West Indies, whereas the number of African slaves rose sharply. In Barbados, the white population was reduced by half, and the number of Negro inhabitants increased more than tenfold within twenty years; meanwhile, the island became forty times richer.[4] In France, where trading companies had

[3] "It was thanks to Dutch refugees from Brazil, which was now being reconquered by the Portuguese, that the technique of sugar cultivation and manufacture came to Barbados. Dutch capital helped the planters to buy the necessary machinery. Dutch credit provided them with Negro slaves to work on the sugar estates, and Dutch ships bought their sugar and supplied them with food and other goods which England could no longer supply owing to internal troubles." Alan Burns, *History of the British West Indies* (London, 1954), p. 232.

[4] "Already, in 1667, this substitution of the negro slave for the white servant had reached an advanced stage. In that year Major Scott stated that after examining all the Barbarians' records he found that since 1643 no less than 12,000 'good men' had left the island for other plantations, and that the number of landowners had decreased from 11,200 small-holders in 1645 to 745 owners of large estates in 1667: while during the same period the negroes had increased from 5,680 to 82,023. Finally, he summed up the situation by saying that in 1667 the island was not half so strong, and forty times as rich as in the year 1645." V. T. Harlow, *A History of Barbados* (Oxford, 1926), p. 310.

less influence on the government, there was a strong reaction to the sudden economic and social changes in the Caribbean islands. A number of measures were taken to prevent emigration of the white population and transformation of the small-holding system into large sugar estates. Endeavors were even made, contrary to the prevailing colonial policy at the time, to introduce manufacturing activities into the islands. Taking the matter into his own hands, Prime Minister Colbert suggested several solutions and even sent technical missions of skilled workers to survey the islands' resources, but all in vain. Real estate prices skyrocketed with the introduction of sugar, and soon undermined this early attempt at population settling in tropical America.[5]

Although on the one hand the flourishing of the sugar economy in the Caribbean area caused the extinction of settlement economies in the islands, on the other it made a great contribution toward providing a sounder economic basis for other colonies of the kind the British had established in more northern latitudes of the Western Hemisphere. As already mentioned,

[5] There is on record an extensive exchange of correspondence which took place between Colbert and the governor of Martinique. A number of plans were set under way, to protect the small holders who were rapidly being eliminated by the large sugar plantations. "In 1683 expert male and female workers were transported to Martinique, and grain was distributed along with trees, by the initiative of the central government alone. In 1685, the King repeated his desire, and sent more grain, aspiring for manufacturing activities to be set up." Adrien Dessalles, *Histoire Générale des Antilles* (Paris, 1847–1848), II, p. 59. In 1687, Colbert wrote the governor of the island: "They must be obligated to engage in farming their land with indigo, rocou, cocoa, cassia, ginger, cotton, and other viable crops . . . The inevitable loss of the islands will otherwise be caused by the excessive quantity of sugar cane . . ." See also Lucien Peytrand, *L'Esclavage aux Antilles Françaises avant 1789* (Paris, 1897). However, the policy of the French government was not always a coherent one, which is explainable by the fact that the sugar interests were powerful ones.

the British colonies were far from being an economic success for the companies financing their installation, because the only products capable of entering the transatlantic trade at the time could not be produced there. Nevertheless, the communities in those colonies which did survive the vicissitudes of the early stages began to create a self-sufficient economy, supplemented by various commercial activities which guaranteed them the essential minimum of imports. Such colonies seemed to be doomed to slow development—as was true of the French groups settled in Canada—but the advent of the Caribbean sugar economy, in the second half of the seventeenth century, opened up unexpected prospects for North American colonies.

Sugar penetration into the Caribbean islands resulted in the departure of a substantial part of the white population settled there, through migrations toward the north. Most of the migrants were small landowners compelled to dispose of their holdings, usually taking some capital with them. On the other hand, subsistence agriculture was disorganized or even eliminated in some of the islands. Thus the Caribbean area became a large food-importing region. The northern colonies, which not long before had no disposition for their wheat surpluses, were transformed into the main source of supply for the prosperous sugar colonies. As an English historian has acutely observed, "Starting with fish, timber and meat, the New Englander by a clever, complex system of sale and barter in which the West Indies . . . formed the connecting link, drew to themselves any sort of commodity from the Old World of which they had need." [6]

Consumption goods were not the only articles of export in the trade between the two groups of English colonies. Since the islands had no water power available, they were dependent on draft animals to operate treadmills; they also had no lumber

[6] Harlow, *op. cit.*, p. 281.

to manufacture the boxes for packing sugar. Both these re-sources were provided by the north.[7] This important trade was carried on mainly by ships chartered or owned by New Eng-land colonists, a circumstance which favored the development of the shipbuilding industry in that colony. Having encountered exceptionally favorable conditions because of the plentiful for-ests, this industry achieved a high degree of development and became one of the main exporting activities of the New Eng-land communities. Mention should also be made of the instal-lation of another industry as an offshoot of the sugar-cane economy—the distilling of alcoholic beverages—in this in-stance by integration with the French West Indies. The latter were forbidden to utilize their own raw materials, so as to avoid competition with the metropolitan beverage industry, and hence sold these at extremely low prices. Northern settlers took advantage of these low prices to compete successfully with the British West Indies in this highly profitable business. Thus, in the latter half of the seventeenth and first half of the eighteenth centuries, the colonies in the northeastern seaboard area of the present-day United States developed as a compo-nent part of a major economic system within which the dynamic element was provided by the West Indies as producers of trop-ical commodities. The fact that the two main parts of the sys-tem—the region producing the basic export article, and its main supplying area—had developed separately is of funda-mental importance in accounting for the further development of each. Owing to this separation, capital generated by the whole system was not channeled exclusively into sugar making,

---

[7] "Sugar mills had sprung up for crushing the canes, but Barbados possessed no water power to drive them. The alternative was to use tread-mills worked by horses; and horses were accordingly obtained from New England. Casks and barrels too were needed in which to pack the sugar. These were provided from the abundant forests of Massachusetts and Connecticut." Harlow, *op. cit.*, p. 274.

although this was actually the most profitable activity. By making possible the development of a kind of farming not specialized in the export of tropical products, this separation marked the emergence of a new phase in the economic occupation of Western Hemisphere lands. The first phase had consisted basically of the exploitation of native manpower with a view to creating a net production surplus of precious metals; the second was concentrated on production of tropical farm products by large companies intensively utilizing native slave manpower.

In the third phase, a new kind of economy was arising, similar to that of Europe at that time, producing chiefly for the internal market, with no basic division of labor between activities producing for export and those connected with the internal market. An economy of this kind was in glaring contradiction to the prevailing principles of colonial policy, and it was only the result of a series of favorable conditions that such an economic development could take place. In fact, without the protracted civil war which afflicted England in the seventeenth century, it would have been much more difficult for the colonists of New England to gain a firm foothold in the markets of the thriving West Indies. Moreover, the famous British navigation act of 1751, excluding the Dutch from colonial trade, was another strong incentive not only for New England's exports but also for her shipbuilding industry. Finally, the long period of warfare between England and France made the supply of European commodities to the West Indies precarious, placing the northern colonists in a dominant position as regular suppliers of the British Caribbean islands and occasionally of the French Antilles.[8]

The almost invariably frustrated attempts of the British to

[8] The problem of supplies of food was less serious in the French Antilles, inasmuch as the French government, recognizing its inability to control the lines of trade during prolonged periods of warfare, had set up rules for the production of such supplies on each island.

cut off commercial relations between the North American colonists and the Antilles were to be the first stage in a period of friction and conflicting interests destined to become more and more manifest with the passing of time. As a matter of fact, once British supremacy was achieved in the latter half of the eighteenth century, with the French ousted from their main positions in the Americas, England had every intention of putting a stop to the growing competition by the North American colonies with the economy of the homeland. A series of legislative measures was enacted by the British Parliament for this purpose, but they were found only to aggravate tensions and bring into sharper focus the conflict of interests already prevailing, which culminated in the independence of the United States.

From the macroeconomic viewpoint, the New England colonies (as well as New York and Pennsylvania) constituted economies of relatively low productivity far into the eighteenth century. Production per inhabitant there might be expected to be substantially below that of the farming economies based on great plantations. Nevertheless, the kind of economic activity prevalent in those colonies was compatible with family-based small production units with no need for making huge investments. On the other hand, the abundance of land was attractive to European immigration under the regime of temporary servitude. With the small landowner provided with a chance of regularly selling a part of his farm production, it became possible for him to pay the fare of an immigrant laborer who would be redeemed from forced service after a four-year term. It has been estimated that at least half the European immigrants to what is today the United States before 1700 were persons bound to some form of temporary servitude.[9]

---

[9] "It has been estimated that at least half of the white immigrants before 1700 were redemptioners or had their fares paid by others." F. A. Shannon, *America's Economic Growth* (New York, 1951), p. 64.

The main advantages of this system to the small landowner were the much smaller involvement of capital than would have been necessary in the purchase of a slave, and the lesser risk in the event of the laborer's death. African slaves were a highly profitable business for the large capitalists, but as a rule were not within the financial capability of the small producer. Then too, farming activities in the northern colonies would hardly justify any large investments. This may explain why importing European manpower for temporary servitude had been maintained in the poorer colonies whereas it was being eliminated in the more prosperous ones, despite the fact that slave labor was widely recognized as being cheaper. Transition to African slavery occurred only in instances in which it was possible to engage in specialized agriculture for large-scale production of an exportable crop.

Small-farm colonies, largely self-sufficient, comprised communities quite different from those of the richer exporting agricultural colonies. In the former, there was much small concentration of income, and they were much less subject to sudden economic recessions. In addition, the proportion of that income that reverted to the gain of foreign capitalists was almost insignificant. Consequently, the average standard of consumption was high in relation to per capita production levels. In the great plantation colonies, a substantial part of the consumption spending was concentrated among a small group of landlords whose needs were met by imports, whereas the contrary was true in the North American colonies, where consumption spending was distributed over the population as a whole and the market for articles of common use was relatively broad.

Such differences in economic structure were bound to be matched by great disparities in the behavior of the ruling classes in the two kinds of colonies. In the British West Indies, dominant social groups were closely linked to powerful financial cliques in the home country and had much influence in Parliament. This intermingling of interests influenced the leading groups of the economy of the West Indies to consider it exclusively part and parcel of important undertakings originating in England. The northern colonies, on the other hand, were under the leadership of groups some of which were connected with commercial interests having headquarters in Boston and New York—and often in conflict with the interests of the home country—whereas others represented rural populations with almost no affinity of interests with England. This independence of the ruling classes vis-à-vis the metropolis was to be a basic factor in the development of the North American colonies, since it meant they could rely on political organizations which could be true interpreters of their own interests rather than being mere sounding boards for events occurring in some dominating but distant economic center.

7. THE END OF
THE COLONIAL PHASE

The evolution of the Portuguese colony in the Western Hemisphere, from the latter half of the seventeenth century on, was conspicuously influenced by the course taken by Portugal as a colonial power. Under Spanish rule, Portugal had lost the finest of its possessions in the Orient, and the best part of its territory in the Western Hemisphere was occupied by the Dutch. On regaining its independence, the small kingdom was in an extremely weak position, inasmuch as the threat of Spain (which for more than a quarter of a century did not acknowledge any separation) hung ominously over the Portuguese. Further, with the loss of its Oriental trade and the breakdown of the sugar market, Portugal had no resources available for defending what was left of its colonies at a time of growing imperialistic activities. Neutrality before the great powers was inadmissible. Portuguese statesmen therefore decided that in order to survive as a colonial power the country should link its destiny with that of one of the great powers, which would necessarily mean giving up a part of its own sovereignty. Treaties signed with England successively in 1642, 1654, and 1661 gave shape to an alliance which was to leave an indelible mark on the economic and political life of Portugal and Brazil for the next two centuries.[1]

Just as it would have been difficult to explain the astonishing success of the sugar undertakings without taking into due account the commercial and financial coöperation between Portuguese producers and Dutch financiers and merchants, so also the survival of Portugal as a power with extensive colonial possessions can be explained only if note is taken of the peculiar situation of semidependence which the Portuguese government came to accept as a form of sovereignty. Thus Portugal managed to keep its dominions during the latter half of the seventeenth century, and retained possession, without further contestation, of the most lucrative colony in the eighteenth century, to which the country owed its economic recovery. Such were

[1] When Portugal regained its independence in 1640, the Portuguese government strove to reach an agreement with Holland, then the main enemy of Spain on the seas. The numerous offers made, including partition of Brazil, were nevertheless rejected by the Dutch, excessively confident in their outstanding sea power and at the same time lacking in general policy guidance because of deep-seated internal disagreements. As the state of war continued to prevail, the Portuguese resorted more and more to British ships in order to avoid the Flemish blockade. Under conditions thus rendered favorable, British penetration proceeded rapidly. The 1654 agreement was imposed after an attack by the British squadron against Portugal, at a time when the latter was at war with Holland and Spain. On the British aggression, see C. R. Boxer, "Blake and the Brazilian Fleets in 1650," *Mariner's Mirror*, XXXIV (1950).

the privileges secured by British merchants in Portugal—including broad extraterritorial jurisdiction, freedom of trade with Portuguese colonies, and control over customs duties on merchandise imported from England—that they became a powerful and overbearing group exercising increasing influence over the Portuguese government. According to a student of the subject, "Portugal became virtually England's commercial vassal." [2] The spirit of the various treaties signed between the two countries during the first twenty years after the so-called Portuguese Restoration (1640) was always the same: Portugal was bound to make economic concessions, whereas England would be committed to political promises or guarantees. In the East Indies, for example, Portugal yielded Bombay permanently whereas England promised to use her fleet to defend Portuguese possessions. Moreover, England was granted the privilege of maintaining resident merchants in nearly every Portuguese colony. The Treaty of 1661 even included a secret clause whereby the British were committed to defend the Portuguese colonies against all enemies. If it is considered that at the time Spain had not yet acknowledged her separation from Portugal, and that in the same year negotiations were still under way for peace with the Dutch, it is easy to understand how much an alliance permitting the country's survival as a colonial power really meant to the Portuguese government.

Nevertheless, pledges obtained for mere survival could not solve the fundamental problem of the decline of Brazil because

---

[2] Alan K. Manchester, *British Pre-eminence in Brazil: Its Rise and Decline* (Chapel Hill, 1933), p. 9. "The treaty thus finally ratified was a diplomatic triumph for the Commonwealth for by it great commercial and religious advantages were secured from Portugal . . . It gave a convincing proof of the ascendancy of England, whose subjects trading with or residing in Portugal, were for the future in a better situation than the Portuguese themselves. Britain here laid the foundations of its privileged position in Portugal's overseas dominions" (pp. 11–12).

of the disorganization of the sugar market. Portugal's economic troubles continued to be aggravated, and successive devaluations of the currency took place. In the last quarter of the sixteenth century, Portuguese statesmen became conscious of the need for reframing the country's economic policy. The idea of finding a solution for deficits in the commercial balance by exporting colonial products did not seem satisfactory. Thinking was toward the reduction of imports and the development of internal production through the manufacturing sector. That policy bore some fruit, and for twenty years imports of wood textiles—which had been the chief imported manufactures—were prohibited. This policy, however, was not certain of reaching fruition. Rapid development of gold production in Brazil, from the beginning of the eighteenth century, was destined to change the limits of the problem radically. As we shall see in detail in subsequent chapters, a commercial treaty signed between Portugal and England in 1703 determined the basic course of events. To Portugal this treaty meant the renunciation of any industrial development; and it resulted in the transfer to England of the dynamic impulse generated by gold mining in Brazil. Thanks to the treaty of 1703, however, Portugal was able to maintain a firm political position through a period which proved to be fundamental to the definitive territorial consolidation of Brazil. John Methuen, who negotiated the commercial treaty of 1703, was also in charge of discussing conditions for the entry of Portugal into the War of the Spanish Succession on the side of England, which placed the Portuguese in a favorable position at the Utrecht peace negotiations. In the course of the discussions the Portuguese succeeded in having France refrain from any claims over the mouth of the Amazon as well as over navigation on that river; from Spain, Portugal secured acknowledgment of her rights over the colony of Sacramento (present-day Uruguay). Both agreements were signed under a direct pledge from England and came to be the true foundations of territorial stability for Portuguese America.

Broadly viewed, the Portuguese-Brazilian economy of the eighteenth century resembles an affiliation—and a basic one at that—with the most rapidly growing economic system of the time: the British. The so-called gold cycle might be considered as a more or less integrated system, within which Portugal played the role of a mere supply station. In Brazil, gold production permitted the financing of great population expansion, which introduced fundamental changes into the structure of the population, so that African slaves became the minority and Europeans the majority. In England, the Brazilian gold cycle brought vigorous stimulus to the development of manufacturing and great flexibility in importing capacity, and resulted in an accumulation of reserves which transformed the British banking system into the principal European financial center. From Portugal's point of view, however, the gold economy bore only an appearance of wealth, reënacting in the small kingdom the experience of seventeenth-century Spain. As was keenly observed by the great Portuguese statesman the Marquis of Pombal in the latter half of the eighteenth century, gold meant nothing more than fictitious riches for Portugal: even Negroes working in the mines had to get their loincloths from the British. Pombal had a lucid view of the position of his country as a political dependency and was endowed with an iron will; yet not even he could bring about any basic change in his country's relationships with England.[3] As a matter of fact, without those relationships it would be difficult to account for the survival of the little kingdom as the metropolis of one of the richest colonial empires of that century. There was only too much truth in some opinions expressed at the time in England, according to which trade with Portugal was "at the pres-

[3] In his memoirs, the Marquis of Pombal categorically states that England had reduced Portugal to a state of dependency, conquering the kingdom without the disadvantages of military victory, and that every act of the government was regulated in line with the desires of England.

ent the most advantageous that we drove anywhere," or the "very best branch of all our European commerce." [4]

The last quarter of the eighteenth century saw the decline of gold mining in Brazil. Meanwhile, England was already well advanced in the industrial revolution. The necessity for ever-widening markets for industries in the course of rapid mechanization led her to the progressive abandonment of protectionist mercantile policies. The so-called Methuen Treaty of 1703, which bestowed a privileged situation on Portuguese wines in the British market, was subject to strong criticism in England on the grounds of the new liberal economic ideology. The most pressing problem for England was the opening up of the great European markets for her manufactures, and for this purpose the elimination of restrictions carried over from the mercantile era was considered essential. In fact, when signing a treaty with France in 1789, England put an end for all practical purposes to customs privileges enjoyed by Portuguese wines in her market, the sole economic counterpart Portugal was granted in a century and a half of economic vassalage.[5] With the decline of

[4] Quoted by Manchester, *op. cit.*, p. 33.

[5] Even Adam Smith took it upon himself to demonstrate that the Methuen Treaty was harmful to England, arguing that it gave Portugal customs privileges, whereas England had to compete in the Portuguese market with other powers producing manufactured goods. See *The Wealth of Nations, passim.* In the commercial treaty signed with France in 1786, the British government endeavored to cover itself against any reaction in Portugal, by respecting the form of the Methuen agreement. Taxes on French wines were, in fact, reduced from eight shillings and three farthings to four shillings and sixpence per imperial gallon, but those on Portuguese wines were cut from four shillings and twopence to three shillings. It so happens, however, that when the relative rate of taxes was reduced, the differences actually became irrelevant, and imports of French wines increased tenfold in the year after the signing of the agreement. In this respect, see W. O. Henderson, "The Anglo-French Commercial Treaty of 1786," *Economic History Review*, X.

mining, the Portuguese-Brazilian market had shrunk, and there was no more excuse for maintaining a privilege which would serve as a hindrance to greater penetration into the main European Continental market as represented by France.

The remarkable way in which the independence of Portuguese America was won had long-term consequences on its future development. With the transfer of the Portuguese government to Brazil under British protection in 1808 and the declaration of independence in 1822 without discontinuity in government leadership, the economic privileges enjoyed by England in Portugal were automatically transferred to an independent Brazil. As a matter of fact, although Brazil had achieved independence from Portugal, the country had to wait a few score years to be rid of the tutelage of England, maintained through stringent international agreements. These had been signed at a difficult time and, in accordance with the tradition of Portuguese-English relationships, they followed the pattern of economic privileges bartered for political favors. Previously, in 1810, treaties had been signed between Portugal and England, the latter being committed to denying recognition of any government imposed by Napoleon on the former. Since Brazil had at that same time been advanced from a colony to a kingdom united with Portugal, every privilege bestowed on the British by the Portuguese was renewed, including those of extraterritorial rights, and the former additionally secured a preferential tariff.[6] Everything points to the fact that

---

[6] The Trade and Navigation Treaty, signed in 1810, though aimed at setting up a "liberal system of trade founded on the basis of reciprocity," actually created a series of privileges for England. The tariff on imports from the latter became 15 per cent ad valorem, compared with 24 per cent for the other countries and 16 per cent for Portugal. Errors in the translation from the English to the Portuguese text are of such a degree as to show clearly that the initiative was entirely in British hands and that the Portuguese signed the agreement without knowing

in negotiating such treaties the Portuguese government was aiming strictly at the continuity of the reigning house in Portugal, whereas the British were more intent on establishing a permanent foothold in the former colony, whose prospects were far more promising than those of Portugal.

Although from the military viewpoint Brazilian independence had been an operation without any major complexity, from the diplomatic standpoint it was to call for strenuous exertion. Portugal held a trump card: the country's political dependence on England. If Brazilian independence were to be interpreted as aggression against Portugal, England would be committed to come to the succor of her ally in distress. Negotiations opened in London by the Portuguese government for this purpose were fruitless, because to the British the reestablishment of their Portuguese supply station was not sound business. What really did matter to the British was to secure through the new Brazilian government the maintenance of the privileges obtained in the former colony. Thus from an exceptionally strong position the British government could negotiate for the recognition of an independent Portuguese America. By the treaty of 1827 the Brazilian government[7] recognized England as a privileged power, limiting Brazilian sovereignty in the economic field [8] of its own accord.

The first half of the nineteenth century was a period of transition, during which the country's territorial integrity was consolidated while political independence gained a firmer hold.

---

exactly what they were doing. Brazilian editor Hipólito José Soares da Costa, at that time publishing the *Correio Brasiliensis* in London, pointed out a number of these mistakes.

[7] The treaty was signed by the emperor, independent of any consultation with Congress.

[8] The new agreement did not, however, grant England a preferential tariff. Owing to the most favored nation clause, Brazil was later to grant a number of other countries the same 15 per cent ad valorem tariff.

The privileges enjoyed by England gave rise to serious economic difficulties, as we shall see in a later chapter. These economic troubles had the twofold effect of reducing the field of action of the central government authorities, while at the same time these very circumstances—by sowing seeds of discontent—created points of territorial disintegration. Only by mid-century did circumstances permit the country's definitive consolidation and set the course for its further development. As coffee increased in importance within the Brazilian economy, economic relationships with the United States were bound to become increasingly strong. As early as the first half of the nineteenth century the United States had come to be the chief market for Brazilian exports. These economic ties, as well as the rapidly developing ideology of continental solidarity, did much to solidify the sense of independence vis-à-vis England. Thus, when the treaty of 1827 expired in 1842, Brazil could find the strength to resist strong British pressure to sign another similar document.[9] Once the hindrances created by the treaty of 1827 were eliminated, the way was opened to higher tariffs and a resulting growth in the central government's financial capacity,[10] so that its authority could be definitely enforced throughout the country. Political liabilities inherited from colonial times were thus eliminated. Nevertheless, from the viewpoint of its economic structure, mid-nineteenth-century Brazil was not much different from what the country had been during the previous three centuries. The economic structure, based mainly on slave labor, had remained unchanged through the stages of expansion and decadence.

[9] The agreement expired in 1842, but the British succeeded in getting it maintained in force until 1844 by interpreting a certain clause in their favor. Negotiations for a new agreement took a number of years, with the Brazilians winning through patience and skill in deferring the issue.

[10] The central government's revenue remained stationary between 1829–1830 and 1842–1843, but doubled in the following decade.

The absence of internal tensions, as a result of this very change-lessness, was responsible for the relative lateness of Brazilian industrialization. Coffee expansion throughout the second half of the nineteenth century, which led to basic changes in the economic system, might be defined as a period of economic transition, just as the first half of the century had been a period of political transition. Internal tensions produced by the coffee economy in its periods of crisis gave rise to certain factors of an autonomous economic system capable of generating its own impulse for growth, thus ringing down the final curtain on the colonial stage of the Brazilian economy.

PART II

The Slavery Economy
of Tropical Agriculture
(Sixteenth and Seventeenth Centuries)

---

8. CAPITAL FORMATION AND
LEVEL OF INCOME
IN THE SUGAR COLONY

The rapid development of the sugar industry, in spite of enormous difficulties resulting from the physical environment, the hostility of the Indians, and the high freight rates, is a clear indication that the efforts of the Portuguese government had been concentrated on that sector. The privilege bestowed on the grantee, whereby he received exclusive rights to manufacture cane crushers and water mills, reveals that the specific purpose was to develop sugar-cane farming in the colony.[1] Later, special concessions[2] were made—such as tax exemptions, guarantees against court attachment of production facilities, honorary recognitions, titles, and so on—to those prepared to install sugar mills. The main difficulties encountered in the initial stage arose from manpower shortages. Utilization of native

---

[1] See João Lúcio de Azevedo, *Épocas de Portugal Econômico* (Lisbon, 1929), p. 235.

[2] Among the privileges received by the grantees was that of enslaving the Indians in unlimited numbers and the authorization to export to Portugal a certain number of native slaves a year. The success which the Spaniards had been achieving in the exploitation of native labor would seem to have influenced the Portuguese in their calculations in this respect.

slaves, on which plans were apparently based at the outset, was not feasible to the extent required by such large-scale agricultural undertakings as sugar-cane plantations.

Since early days, slavery had been shown to be a prerequisite for the survival of the European settler in the new land. According to the comment of one chronicler, without slaves colonists "cannot get sustenance from the land." [3] In fact, in order to dispense with slave labor, it would have been necessary for settlers to organize into communities engaged in production for self-consumption, which would in turn have required a completely different kind of settlement. Those groups of colonists who, because of shortages of capital or unsuitable choice of situation, were faced with greater difficulties in economic consolidation had to strive by all possible means to capture natives for sale into slavery. The capture and trading of Indian slaves therefore came to comprise the first stable economic activity of those population groups not engaged in producing sugar.

Broadly viewed, the colonization of sixteenth-century Brazil seems to have been fundamentally linked with sugar production. Wherever this activity failed—as it did in São Vicente— the small colonial nucleus managed to survive because of the relative abundance of native manpower. The natives not only engaged in forced labor for the settlers but were reduced to the state of being the sole exportable merchandise. However, except for the slave markets in the sugar regions and their small urban centers, the capture of natives would never have become an economic activity capable of justifying the existence of the São Vicente settlement. Therefore, even those communities that underwent apparently autonomous development

[3] Gandavo, *Tratado da Terra do Brasil* (1570 ?), as quoted by Roberto Simonsen, *História Econômica do Brasil*, 3d ed. (São Paulo, 1957), p. 127.

at this stage of Brazilian colonization actually owed their existence, albeit indirectly, to the success of the sugar economy.

The fact that since the early days of colonization some communities had specialized in capturing natives for slavery stresses the importance of native manpower in the first stage of Brazilian settlement. Almost always in the process of amassing wealth the initial effort is relatively the most exacting. African manpower came to expand an already established enterprise. The profitability of the sugar business was well ensured by the time African slaves began to arrive in the necessary numbers as the basis for a more efficient production system with a higher degree of capitalization.

Once the initial difficulties had been overcome, the sugar settlements underwent rapid development. By the end of the sixteenth century, sugar production probably exceeded two million arrobas a year (approximately sixty-five million pounds),[4] at least twenty times as much as the production quota established a century before by the Portuguese government for the Atlantic islands. Expansion was particularly rapid during the last quarter of the century, when a tenfold increase occurred.

The amount of capital invested in the new settlement was already considerable by that time. Assuming that only 120 sugar mills were in existence at the end of the sixteenth cen-

---

[4] The figures on sugar production in the colonial period, appearing in works by chroniclers, visitors, Portuguese and Dutch official reports, and books by both Brazilian and foreign students of the subject, were carefully scrutinized by Simonsen (*op. cit.*). The data taken as a basis for the calculations and estimates appearing in the text have all been taken from the work of this great researcher into the economic history of Brazil. However, we have not always followed in our selection the same criteria as Simonsen, who was always concerned with choosing merely the more conservative references. All values are given in gold pounds.

tury, with an average value of £15,000 per mill, the total amount of capital invested in the production phase of the industry would be equivalent to £1,800,000. On the other hand, the number of African slaves in the colony at the time is estimated to have been about 20,000. Surmising that three-quarters of the Africans were used in the sugar industry, and ascribing to them an average value of £25 each, investment in manpower may be assumed to have amounted to £375,000. Comparing data on total investments, it may be inferred that capital invested in slave manpower amounted to about 20 per cent of the total fixed assets of the business, a substantial part of which was comprised of imported equipment.

As to the amount of income generated by that economy, there seems to be no possibility of making much more than vague conjectures. The total value of the sugar exported in a favorable year probably amounted to about £2.5 million. Considering 60 per cent of this amount[5] as the net income produced in the colony by sugar working, and assuming that the sugar sector accounted for three-quarters of the total income, the latter would approach £2 million. Taking into account the fact that the European population was not more than 30,-000 persons, the small sugar colony must have been exceptionally rich.[6]

[5] Monetary replacement costs, which must be deducted to give total net revenue, may be estimated, *grosso modo*, at £110,000: £50,000 for slave replacement, assuming an effective average life of eight years and taking 15,000 slaves at £25 a head, and £60,000 for imported equipment, assuming that one-third of the tied-up capital (including slaves) was composed of imported equipment and that the latter had an effective duration of ten years.

[6] Although long-term comparisons of monetary incomes—based on gold value—are practically meaningless, for the sake of curiosity we would mention that the per capita income (of the population of European origin) at the turn of the sixteenth century amounted to about $350 in terms of values of today. This income per capita was evidently

Income produced in the colony was strongly concentrated in the hands of the sugar-mill and plantation owners. Of the value of sugar ready for shipment at port, only an insignificant part (not more than 5 per cent) came from services rendered outside the mills, such as transportation and warehousing. Plantations and mills undoubtedly maintained a number of salaried workers: sundry craftsmen and slave overseers. Even assuming that there was one salaried worker for each ten slaves—totaling 1,500 wage earners in the entire sugar industry—and ascribing to each worker an annual monetary salary of £15,[7] the total would be £22,500, or less than 2 per cent of the income produced in the sugar sector. Finally, it must be borne in mind that the mills and plantations involved a certain amount of monetary expenditure, mainly for the purchase of draft cattle and firewood (for the furnaces). These purchases were the main link between the sugar economy and other settlement nuclei in the country. It is estimated that the total number of oxen on plantations and mills may have been equivalent to the number of slaves. Further, the value of an ox is surmised to have been one-fifth of that of a slave, whereas the animal had a working life of only three years. Hence the investment in draft oxen would be about £75,000, with replacement costs amounting to £25,000 a year. Even ascribing to expenditures

---

far higher than that prevailing in Europe at the time, and at no other period of its history—even at the height of the gold cycle—did Brazil regain this level of income.

[7] £15 a year would be considered a very high salary at the time, inasmuch as the actual cost of slave labor would not be much more than £4 a year—assuming a price of £25, a useful life of 8 years, and that one-third of the slave's time was absorbed in producing food for his own sustenance. As a basis for comparison it might be mentioned that farm wages in the Northern United States in the second half of the eighteenth century were about £12, and about half as much in England. See F. A. Shannon, *America's Economic Growth* (New York, 1951), p. 64.

on firewood and other lesser items twice this figure, the payments made by the sugar economy to other population groups did not amount to much more than 3 per cent of the total income. Thus everything seems to indicate that at least 90 per cent of the income generated by the sugar economy within Brazil was concentrated in the hands of the sugar-mill and plantation owners.

The utilization of such a vast sum of income concentrated in so few hands seems to be a problem difficult to solve. The aforementioned data testify to the fact that income from productive investments—that is, the part in the hands of the sugar-mill and plantation-owner class—amounted to more than one million pounds in a favorable year in the early part of the seventeenth century. The proportion of such income spent on imports of consumption goods—mainly luxury articles—was indeed considerable. Data supplied by the Dutch administration, for instance, indicate that in 1639 about £ 160,000 was collected in import duties, one-third of which was levied on wines. Assuming an ad valorem duty of about 20 per cent, it may be inferred that the total imports amounted to no less than £ 800,000.[8] In that same year the value of sugar exported by Dutch Brazil was about £ 1.2 million. Due account must, however, be taken of the fact that consumption spending was increased considerably at the Dutch conquest, either by the need for keeping strong garrisons or by reason of government

[8] These estimates are based on data of Dutch origin at the time, transcribed by P. M. Netscher in *Les Hollandais au Brésil* (Paris, 1853). The list of products imported at that period is of interest, including as it does Spanish and French wines, olive oil, beer, vinegar, salted fish, tallow and leather, flour, crackers, butter, linseed and whale oil, spices, cloth, wool, silk, copper, iron, steel, tin, boards, and so on. See Simonsen, *op. cit.*, p. 119. For a balance of Dutch revenue and expenditure in Brazil in 1644, see C. R. Boxer, *The Dutch in Brazil* (Oxford, 1957), Appendix II.

pomp and pageantry during the administration of Prince Moritz of Nassau (1637–1644). It can hardly be supposed that the Portuguese colonists, confined to their estates and deprived of any kind of urban conviviality, could afford such consumption expenditures. Assuming, at a generous estimate, that their consumption expenditures may have been as high as £600,000, there remained in the hands of the landlords at least that much more unspent in the colony. These figures stress the wide capitalization margin afforded by the sugar economy, and at the same time explain how production could be increased tenfold in the last quarters of the sixteenth century as noted above.

The data in the previous paragraph suggest that the sugar industry was profitable enough to self-finance a doubling of productive capacity every two years,[9] which was apparently the rate of growth during the most thriving phases. The fact that such financial potentiality had been utilized only on exceptional occasions shows that the growth of the sugar industry was determined by the absorption capacity of the buying markets. Since there was no repetition of the trying experience of the Atlantic islands, with their surpluses, this fact seems to indicate that many precautions were taken in the marketing stage, and further that from the latter the basic decisions regarding the entire sugar business issued.

[9] Starting with a gross income of £1.5 million in the sugar sector, and assuming 10 per cent of this income went for payment of wages, purchases of livestock, lumber, and so on, and that the cost of replacement of imported factors was of the order of £120,000, it may be deduced that the net income of the sector was about £1.2 million. deducting £600,000 for the cost of imported consumer goods, this would leave £600,000, which represented the investment potentialities of the sector. Since tied-up capital amounted to £1.8 million and at least one-third of the latter was in buildings and facilities erected by the slaves themselves, it may be deduced that over a period of two years the capital could be doubled.

But if the full self-financing capacity of the industry was not being utilized, what was happening to the remaining financial resources? Obviously they were not being utilized within the colony, where economic activities other than sugar did not require large amounts of capital. Nor is there any record of investments elsewhere by sugar-cane planters or sugar-mill owners. The most plausible explanation is perhaps that a substantial part of the capital derived from sugar production eventually found its way into the hands of the merchants. Thus a part of the income ascribed above to the sugar-mill and plantation owners may have been what is now called nonresidents' income, remaining outside the colony. Hence the close connection between the production and marketing phases might easily be explained. Such coördination would prevent the natural tendency toward surpluses.

9. INCOME FLOW AND GROWTH

What effective possibilities for expansion and structural evolution did the slave economic system present, as a background for the occupation of the Brazilian territory? To shed some light on this question, there is a need for closer observation of the inner mechanism—that is, the processes of generation and utilization of income and capital formation within the system.

A unique feature of the Brazilian slave economy is clearly indicated in the way in which the process of capital formation had to operate. Sugar entrepreneurs in Brazil, since the beginning of their activities, were compelled to operate on a relatively large scale. Environmental conditions did not permit of their thinking in terms of small sugar mills, as had been true in the Atlantic islands. It may be fairly deduced, therefore, that starting capital was imported. In the beginning, imports took the form of equipment and skilled European manpower. Native labor must therefore have been utilized both for feeding the new community and in nonskilled tasks connected with installation work. In the early stages of operation, native labor most probably played an equally important role too. Once in operation, the value of the sugar mills at least doubled imported capital in the form of equipment and costs of transfer of skilled workers. Introduction of African labor did not entail any fundamental changes, since it came only to take the place of other slave manpower, less efficient and more risky to recruit. After its installation, the sugar industry followed a process of expansion always along the same lines: monetary expenditures for importing of equipment, some basic construction materials, and slave manpower. Skilled workers were already being brought in on a lesser scale, since the industry was trying to become self-sufficient in this area too by training those slaves who displayed greater skill in handicrafts. This did not occur, however, in the case of nonskilled manpower, inasmuch as the slave population showed a tendency to a diminishing life span. Throughout the entire period in which slavery was practiced, nothing was successfully accomplished to reverse this trend.[1]

[1] To the contrary of what occurred in the United States, where there were even some regions specializing in the breeding of slaves, in Brazil a short-term view was always taken of the matter, as though slavery were a business for just a single generation. For instance, Jesuit priest Antonil, in his wise council to the lords of the sugar-mills at the beginning of the eighteenth century, recommended that "overseers by no means be permitted to kick slaves, and especially not kick the pregnant women slaves, nor beat the slaves with wooden rods, because blows in anger are not dealt sparingly and might cause injury to the head of a valuable and serviceable slave, leading to his being lost. However, they may be rebuked and given a few lashes on the back with a switch, and

When the stage of importing equipment and slave manpower had come to an end, the next stage of investment—construction and installation work—was carried out practically without the possibility of creating a flow of monetary income. Some of the slaves were engaged in producing food for the population as a whole, and others were occupied on installation work and later in agricultural and processing tasks on the sugar plantations and mills.

In an industrial economy, investments lead to a constant growth of the community's income up to a figure identical to the investment itself. This occurs because investments are automatically transformed into payments for production factors. Thus an investment in a building consists of payments for construction materials and workers' payroll. On the other hand, purchases of construction materials are nothing more or less than remuneration for manpower and capital used in their production and transportation. These payments to factors give rise to an increase in monetary income[2] or buying power, and recompose directly in the aggregate the initial investment value.

But investments made in a slave and exporting economy follow an entirely different pattern. A part of them is transformed into payments abroad, as expressed by imports of manpower and equipment and building materials; nevertheless, the major part arises from the very utilization of the slave manpower itself. The difference between the replacement and maintenance costs and the value of the production by that manpower is profit for the entrepreneur. Thus, new investments

---

this should be allowed for disciplinary purposes." Quoted by Roberto Simonsen, *História Econômica do Brasil*, 3d ed. (São Paolo, 1957), p. 108.

[2] Monetary income is the same as real income when there is no modification in the general level of prices.

were bound to make real income grow only to an amount equivalent to the rise in profit to the entrepreneur.

Slave manpower may be compared to the equipment of a plant: investment consisted of the purchase of the slaves, and their maintenance was similar to fixed costs. Whether the plant or slave was working or not, the maintenance costs would have to be paid. Moreover, a lost hour of slave labor could not be recovered, as would be true with a machine to be discarded after a fixed number of years. It was only too obvious that, being unable to utilize slave manpower continuously in productive activities directly connected with exporting, the entrepreneur would have to find another series of tasks for this manpower during enforced interruptions in the main job. The tasks thus adopted took the form of building work, opening of new lands, local improvements, and so on. Investments of this kind accrued to the entrepreneur's assets, but they did not create a flow of monetary income as in the preceding example.

Consumption spending presented similar features. A substantial part of such expenditures went abroad for importing consumers' goods, as already mentioned. Another part consisted of the utilization of slave labor for rendering of personal services. In this instance the slave was being used as a durable consumer good. Services thus rendered were the counterpart of an initial disbursement for acquiring ownership of the slave. This might be compared with the service rendered by an automobile, which is the counterpart of its cost. Just as community income does not diminish when private automobiles are left in their garages, neither did that income undergo any change when slaves stopped rendering personal services to their masters.[3]

---

[3] The service rendered by a durable consumer good is the counterpart of its initial cost and of the current expenditure required for upkeep. A stoppage of automobiles, for instance, would react on the income

Let us now take an over-all look at the operation of the slave economy. Since production factors almost in their entirety belonged to the entrepreneur, monetary income generated by the productive process reverted almost wholly to him. Such income—the total payments for production factors in addition to replacement costs of equipment and imported slaves—was equivalent to the value of exports. It can readily be understood that if most monetary income came from export figures, most monetary expenditures had to be equivalent to the value of imports. The difference between total monetary expenditure and total imports would be equivalent to the monetary reserves plus net entry of capital, besides financial servicing of such production factors under the ownership of nonresidents of the colony. A flow of income was therefore established between the productive unit taken as a whole and its customers abroad. Since all production factors belonged to the same entrepreneur, income flow could evidently be reduced in the sugar economy to mere bookkeeping operations, either of a real or of a virtual kind. This does not mean that such an economy was of a nonmonetary nature. As the cost of each factor was expressed in monetary terms, which was also true of the final product, the entrepreneur knew somehow or other how to promote the best combination of factors in order to reduce production costs and increase his real income.

The purely bookkeeping nature of the income flow within the sugar sector has led many persons to ascribe to this economy a semifeudal nature. Feudalism may be considered as a

---

level of the collectivity to the extent that such current expenditures ceased to be incurred. In the instance of the slaves, the upkeep expenditures did not, as a general rule, create any flow of income. Since the slaves produced their own means of sustenance, with the exception of some coarse textiles which were imported, the concept of *net slave manpower* might be introduced—that is, excluding that part which was used for producing food for the slaves themselves.

regressive process, indicated in the atrophy of an economic structure.[4] This atrophy results from the isolation imposed upon an economy, engendering a great decline in productivity, with the system unable to benefit from the specialization and division of labor that would permit it to attain some already existent technological level. The slavery unit might be considered a typical instance of overspecialization. Opposing the feudal unit, the slave unit owes its existence entirely to the external market. The supposed similarity derives from the existence of payments in kind in both instances. Once again this proves to be quite misleading, because in the slave unit payments to factors are all monetary, due account being taken of the fact that payment to the slave is that made at the time of his acquisition. The *current* payment to the slave would be the cost of his mere maintenance, as with the maintenance of machines, cost of which may be implicit in book accounts without any loss of their monetary nature.[5]

Let us return to our opening question: what possibilities of expansion and structural evolution did the slave economic system afford? Undoubtedly, if the external market were able to absorb ever-increasing quantities of sugar, the system would

[4] See Celso Furtado, "O Desenvolvimento Econômico," *Econômica Brasileira*, I.

[5] The attempt at transposing feudal institutions into the commercial colonies on the American continent proved impracticable, even when there was the explicit intention of adapting them and where feudal traditions were strongest, as in the case of France. May, referring to this question, says: "Some writers have supposed that the feudal organization of the homeland was transposed en bloc, just as it stood, to the colonies; that baronial rights were carried over to them and head taxes instituted. Actually, nothing is further from the truth. The company endeavored to collect poll and sales dues at St. Christophe, but these dwindled more and more and it ended up by abandoning them. In Martinique we found no trace of them." Louis Philippe May, *Histoire Économique de la Martinique 1635–1736* (Paris, 1930), pp. 69–70.

grow—assuming an external manpower supply of a flexible nature—until all adequate land was occupied. Because such land was abundant, possibilities of unlimited expansion might be supposed to exist from such a point of view. As noted in the previous chapter, at the price levels prevailing in the latter half of the sixteenth and first half of the seventeenth centuries the profit picture was encouraging enough to support self-financing of the sugar industry at a rate of expansion far greater than what actually occurred. Everything seems to indicate, therefore, that the increase in productive capacity was regulated with a view to avoiding a collapse in prices, while at the same time a persistent effort was engaged in making the product well known so as to expand the area of consumption. Whatever the situation may have been, growth was in fact considerable—especially from the point of view of the colony—and continued for an entire century. Nevertheless, this growth occurred without any perceptible change in the inner structure of the economic system, nor did the òccasional regressions bring about any structural change. Even if the production unit were to cease operation, the entrepreneur would not undergo great losses, inasmuch as maintenance costs were dependent mainly on the utilization of the slave labor force itself. Further, the major part of the entrepreneur's consumption costs were met by the utilization of that same labor force. Hence, the slave enterprise had a tendency to grow in size only—that is, without undergoing any structural changes. Any breakdown or regression in this growth did not tend to generate tensions to the point of changing the structure. In this instance growth meant occupation of new land and increased imports, whereas decadence implied a decline in expenditures for imported goods and manpower replacements (also imported), with a progressive though slow decline in the enterprise's assets. The industry would undergo some shrinkage, but without structural transformations.

There was therefore no prospect of growth based on an outward impulse giving rise to a self-generated developmental process. Increase merely in size permitted the occupation of vast tracts of land in which a relatively dense population proceeded to settle. However, the workings of an economy that did not permit direct linkage between the producing and consuming systems nullified the advantages of such population growth as a dynamic factor of economic development. As already noted, the profits were the only type of income affected by changes in productivity, whether the latter was purely economic in nature (improvement in relative prices) or resulted from occasional technological improvements. In the event of a reduction in the rate of production for export, the entrepreneur's profits would be curtailed but at the same time a labor surplus was created which could be utilized for expanding production capacity. If there were no interest in expanding such productive capacity, the available potential investment could be channeled into construction work connected with the welfare of the proprietor class or into some other kind of nonreproductive activity.

Thus, the slave economy was dependent for all practical purposes on external demand. If there were a slackening of that demand, a process of decadence would commence with the atrophy of the monetary sector. This process would in no way, however, present the catastrophic character of modern economic depressions. Monetary income from the exporting unit was comprised almost entirely of the entrepreneur's profits, it being to his advantage at all times to go on operating, whatever occasional price declines might be. Inasmuch as costs were composed of almost nothing but fixed outlays, any reduction in utilization of productive capacity would lead to some losses to the entrepreneur and there would always be a certain advantage in full utilization of that capacity. If prices fell below a certain level, the sugar-mill operator or plantation owner would not be able to face replacement costs of either the labor force or the imported equipment. In such instances the unit tended to undergo a loss of capacity, which would, however, necessarily be a slow process for the reasons already mentioned. The exporting unit was therefore able to preserve its characteristic structure. The sugar economy in the Brazilian Northeast managed to resist the most protracted of depressions for more than three centuries, achieving some degree of recuperation, whenever conditions in the external market permitted, without being compelled to undergo any significant structural changes.

In the latter half of the seventeenth century, when the sugar market collapsed under vigorous West Indies competition, prices fell to half their former level. In spite of this fact, Brazilian entrepreneurs did their best to keep production at a relatively high level. The tendency toward falling prices persisted for the next century. Further, the mining economy then undergoing expansion in the Brazilian south-central region, by attracting skilled manpower and raising the price of slaves, reduced the profits of the sugar industry even more. Thus the system entered into a state of lethargy that was to last for ages, but its structure remained intact—so much so that when favorable conditions again occurred at the beginning of the nineteenth century it recommenced operations with full vigor.

10. CATTLE BREEDING

The formation of a highly productive, fast-growing economic system along the northeastern coast of Brazil was bound to have direct and indirect consequences on the other regions of the subcontinent claimed by the Portuguese. Generally speaking, resources for defending the colony and intensifying the development of other regions had been assured, and in particular a market had emerged capable of justifying the existence of other economic activities.

As already discussed, owing to its great profitability and high degree of specialization, the sugar economy became a relatively extensive market, or—to use a modern expression— it was an economy with a high import coefficient. Actually, in spite of the almost complete absence of monetary flow within the sugar economy, it displayed a high degree of commercialization. The profitability of the sugar business was inducive to specialization, and it is not surprising from the economic standpoint that the entrepreneurs avoided diverting production factors into secondary activities, at least at times when the prospects of the sugar market seemed favorable. At such times even the production of food for the sustenance of the slaves was anti-economic for the sugar-mill and plantation owners. Conversely speaking, the extreme degree of specialization of the sugar business is in itself proof that it was remarkably profitable.

In Chapter 6 it was shown that the extreme specialization of the Caribbean sugar economy in the latter half of the seventeenth century was an incentive to the development of settlements in the northeastern part of what is today the United States. The highly profitable sugar business led within a relatively short time to an entirely new market for a number of products, inasmuch as the West Indian colonists (mainly the British) utilized their land and slave labor exclusively for sugar production.

It may unquestionably be recognized that the Brazilian sugar economy afforded a relatively substantial market, capable of acting as a dynamic factor for the development of other regions of the country. Nevertheless, a series of circumstances contributed to the diversion abroad of almost the entire effects of that dynamic drive. First, there were the vested interests of the Portuguese and Dutch exporters, who could count on exceptionally low freight rates in sugar-carrying ships; second, there was the ever-present policy of avoiding the development in the colony of any activity capable of competing with the economy of the homeland.

If a comparison were made between the evolution of Brazil's São Vicente colony (a settlement project) and that of New England, vis-à-vis the two powerful sugar economies coexisting in those areas, the similarities and differences would be highly illustrative. In the former, as in the latter, the initial goals of colonization failed completely; colonists who held out through the early difficulties engaged in low-profit activities, and both nuclei were transformed from colonial enterprises into settlement colonies. For the New England colonists, fishing became not only a means of subsistence but also one of their first trading activities. Thus they turned to the sea from the beginning. Soon they were building their own ships, progressively developing this skill to the point where they became independent in those lines of business based on maritime transportation. When the great Caribbean market emerged, the New Englanders went there with their own vessels. Even so, it would be difficult to account for their remarkable success in the conquest of the West Indian market without remarking the fact that for lengthy periods England was unable to supply the Caribbean markets: in the latter half of the sixteenth century because of internal conflicts, and in the first half of the following century because of foreign wars.

The manpower shortage was greater in São Vicente than in New England, which could resort to importing population surpluses from the British Isles for enforced work on a temporary servitude basis. There being no other solution, the first economic activity of the São Vicente colonists was the capture of Indians. Thus they turned toward the interior and became professional hinterland explorers. Just as the Portuguese of the sixteenth century ranged far into Africa hunting Negro slaves, the São Vicente colonists were compelled to penetrate deep into the Brazilian hinterland in quest of Indian captives for slavery. Hence, the development of a high degree of exploratory and military skill became a decisive factor in the early occupation of vast areas in the heart of the South American continent.[1]

It is probable, however, that the main factor curtailing the dynamic impulse of the Brazilian sugar economy on the southern settlement had been the abundance of available land surrounding the sugar settlements. Farther to the north, on the other hand, the principal feature of the Caribbean sugar economy had been the extreme scarcity of land. For centuries after the advent of the sugar economy the economic and social evolution of the West Indies was strongly marked by this fact, whereas that of northeastern Brazil was influenced by the fluidity of its own frontiers. Owing to this abundance of land, a subsidiary economic system arose in the Northeast as an outgrowth of the sugar economy.

[1] It is not surprising that the Spanish did not occupy a large part of the land in South America granted them under the Treaty of Tordesillas, because they early realized that it was not practicable to defend everything they were entitled to in the New World under that treaty. Their line of defense was built up along the Mexico-Peru axis and around their two points of access: the Caribbean and the River Plate. The Amazon and the central regions of South America were of lesser interest to the Spanish than the region which is today the United States, because it was not easy to enter Peru through the former, whereas the latter provided a route into Mexico. Since the land not effectively occupied by the Spanish tended to fall into the power of the British and French in the seventeenth and eighteenth centuries, Portuguese expansion in South America was certainly not inconvenient from the point of view of the Spaniards. In other words, it at least avoided penetration by those powers whose declared objective was to grab the cream of the Spanish portion. It is nevertheless surprising that the South American continent —including the Amazon basin—was occupied and partitioned a century before the North American continent was. This was because of the exceptional boldness of the "Bandeirantes," as the descendants of the original colony of São Vicente came to be called.

In contrast to what was to happen in the West Indies, the part of the Brazilian sugar economy market to which other colonial producers could have access was relatively small. As to the consumption goods sector, imports consisted mainly of luxury articles, evidently incapable of being produced in the colony. The only article of consumption that could be supplied domestically was beef, which formed a part of the diet of even the slaves, according to the chronicler Antonil. It was in the producers' goods sector that local sources of supply found better chances of expansion. The two main sources of power for sugar mills—firewood and draft animals—could be supplied locally to great advantage. The same was true of the most widely used building material at the time—lumber.

With the expansion of the sugar economy the need for draft animals tended to grow disproportionately, inasmuch as the devastation of the forests along the seaboard made it necessary to haul firewood from ever-greater distances. Furthermore, the impracticability of cattle breeding along the seaboard—that is, on the sugar-producing estates themselves—soon became apparent. Quarrels between neighbors as a result of cattle trespassing must have been serious, because the Portuguese government eventually prohibited cattle breeding in the sugar-cane areas. This separation between the two economic activities was responsible for the development of a subsidiary economy within the Northeastern region. Cattle breeding, as developed in the Northeast and later in other Brazilian regions too, was an activity with economic characteristics completely different from those of the sugar-producing sector. Occupation of land was extensive and to some degree nomadic. Water availability and the distance from markets entailed periodic moving of herds, the proportion of permanently occupied land being insignificant. Investments in items other than livestock herds themselves were the smallest possible, because the economic density of the system was extremely low. Further, the process of capital accumulation within the cattle-breeding economy was conducive to perennial expansion, whenever there was land to be occupied, independent of the conditions of demand. These features account for the fact that stock breeding became a basic factor of the exploration and occupation of the Brazilian backlands.

Due note must, however, be taken of the fact that stock breeding—at least in the initial stages—was an economic process induced by the sugar economy and of relatively low profitability. The total income generated by the cattle economy of the Northeast cannot have exceeded 5 per cent of the value of sugar exports. This income was obtained from the sale of cattle in the seaboard areas and from exports of hides. The value of the latter in the eighteenth century, when stock breeding had already been greatly expanded in the south, was even then probably not much more than £100,000 a year.[2] Taking into account merely the region directly dependent on the sugar economy in the early eighteenth century, it can hardly be supposed that gross income was as much as £100,000 sterling,[3] at a time when the value of sugar exports was perhaps more than £2 million a year.

The population engaged in cattle-raising activities was evidently very small. According to Antonil, the corrals had capacities of from 200 to 1,000 head of cattle, although there were ranches with 20,000 head. Surmising a ratio of 1 to 50

[2] Roberto Simonsen, *História Econômica do Brasil,* 3d ed. (São Paolo, 1957), p. 171.

[3] Antonil estimated the number of head of cattle in the Northeast (Baía and Pernambuco) at the beginning of the eighteenth century to be 1,300,000. Even assuming that a hundred years before that time the cattle population stood at half the above figure (which would indicate an absurdly low rate of natural increase in view of the environment), the total amount of cattle sold could not have been far more than 50,000 head, inasmuch as it is not very likely that the rate of utilization of the herds would be more than 8 per cent. Assuming an average sale price of £2.5 per head, this would give a gross value of £125,000.

between the human and the livestock population, corresponding roughly to one actual cowhand for 250 head of cattle, the conclusion reached is that the total population supporting itself by stock breeding in the Northeast was not more than 13,-000, assuming a total of 650,000 head of cattle. Recruiting of manpower for such activities does not seem to have created a serious problem, because the Indians adapted easily to the work. Notwithstanding the resistance of the Indians in some areas where they were dislodged from their lands, all indications are that stock-breeding activities were expanded with the aid of local manpower.

What were the prospects of growth of this new economic system, an offshoot of the sugar economy? A fundamental condition of its existence and expansion was availability of land. Owing to peculiarities of local grazing land in the Northeast, on the prairies and tablelands, the livestock density those pasturelands could support was extremely low. Hence the speed with which the herds forged inland, fording the São Francisco River to reach the Tocantins River and moving north in the early seventeenth century into the present-day states of Maranhão and Piauí. It is easy to understand that the farther the pastures were from the seacoast, the more costs were bound to increase as cattle transportation became more expensive. The fact that such expansion was able to proceed for so long was due mainly to the fact that the stock-breeding economy underwent basic changes, as shall be discussed later.

From the point of view of manpower, expansion of cattle breeding does not seem to have faced any major obstacle. To the colonist without financial resources, this activity presented greater attractions than other available occupations in the sugar economy. Those who had no means of their own for starting ranches could build up a starting stake by working for some rancher. Similarly to the settlement system developed in the British and French colonies, a man who worked on a stock-breeding establishment for four or five years acquired rights over a share in the new herd (one calf of every four), and could thus start breeding on his own. There is every indication that this line of activity had much appeal to colonists with no capital, since many migrated not only from the sugar region but also from distant São Vicente for this purpose. In addition, as has already been mentioned, Indians were capable of accustoming themselves rapidly to subsidiary stock-breeding tasks.

From the point of view of supply, there were no inhibiting factors to the expansion of the stock-breeding economy. Such factors did, however, exist on the side of the demand. Since stock breeding in the Northeast was dependent on the sugar economy as a rule, development of the former was tied to the expansion of the latter. The stage of fast growth of the sugar industry to the mid-seventeenth century was matched by great pioneering drives into the backlands. Similarly, in the eighteenth century, expansion in the mining sector led to the substantial development of stock breeding in the south. In stock breeding, expansion consisted merely of increasing the herds along with recruiting of manpower to a limited extent. The possibilities of expanded development did not entail any concern with the improvement of output. Moreover, since the distances involved became greater and greater, the general trend was actually toward a decline of productivity. Hence, excluding the hypothesis of an improvement in relative prices to the extent that stock breeding in the Northeast developed, the average per capita income of those engaged in it actually declined. The situation of breeders with ranches at great distances from the seaboard was particularly unfavorable.

Unlike the sugar industry, stock breeding was a market of the smallest size, in spite of the fact that there was no predominance of slave manpower. The reason was that the average productivity in the subsidiary economy was many times smaller than in the main economic activity, the degree of specialization and marketing being much smaller. Generally speaking, the main sector of the stock-breeding economy was that linked with the subsistence of its population. To understand this fact, it must be realized that stock breeding was the only source of food as well as of a raw material (leather) utilized for practically every purpose. This relative importance of the subsistence sector in cattle breeding will be shown to have been a fundamental factor in the structural transformations undergone by the Northeastern economy throughout its protracted period of decline.

11. DEVELOPMENT OF THE ECONOMIC COMPLEX OF THE NORTHEAST

The characteristics acquired by the two economic systems in the Northeast—the sugar industry and stock breeding—during the slow process of decline, beginning in the latter half of the seventeenth century, were basic factors in the formation of what was to become the Brazilian economy of the twentieth century. It has already been noted how the production units, whether in the sugar economy or in stock breeding, tended to preserve their original form throughout the phases of contraction and expansion. Development in both groups of economic activity occurred merely in extension, through the accretion of land and manpower, without entailing structural changes affecting production costs and hence productivity. In addition, the small monetary costs—that is, the small amount paid out in the form of payrolls and payments for services from other productive units—rendered both types of economy highly resistant to the short-term effects of declining prices. It was still advantageous to stay in business, in spite of a decline in prices, inasmuch as production factors could not be put to alternative uses. To use a modern term, supply was quite inelastic on a short-term basis. But although the short-term effects of a contraction in demand were largely similar in both the sugar industry and in stock breeding, the differences on a long-term basis were substantial.

Quite to the contrary of what occurred in the production of sugar, the stock-breeding economy did not depend on monetary expenses for capital replacement and expansion of productive capacity. Thus in sugar-cane areas the economy was dependent on imports of manpower and equipment even for the maintenance of productive capacity alone, whereas in the cattle-breeding areas the assets were replaced automatically without any major monetary expenditures. Moreover, working conditions and diet in the cattle regions were such as to cause rapid natural growth of the labor force itself. The basic differences in the behavior of the two systems, during the long period of declining sugar prices, were due to these disparities.

When the dynamic effects of external stimuli were reduced, the sugar economy entered into a phase of relative stagnation. Even though profitability was affected, the results did not reach catastrophic proportions. The new prices were still high enough to make the sugar industry in the West Indies a first-rate business. Nevertheless, in Brazil there was a shift from a highly favorable situation, in which the sugar industry had been able to self-finance a doubling of productive capacity every two years, to a state of affairs in which the economy of the Northeast faced a period of relatively low profitability.[1] The situation

---

[1] We have seen how, in the preceding situation, for an export value of £ 2 million, the net investment potential—on a reasonable assumption regarding expenditures on imported consumer goods—might be as much as £ 600,000. Hence expenditures on replacement of manpower and equipment, and on important consumer goods, absorbed £ 1.4 million. With sugar prices falling to half their former level, it may be

deteriorated still further in the eighteenth century, owing to an upward trend in the prices of slaves and to migration of skilled manpower because of expanding gold production. Since sugar production in the Northeast throughout the eighteenth century remained consistently below the high points reached in previous centuries, probably some of the former producing units had become disorganized, to the benefit of those with more favorable soil and transportation facilities.

In stock breeding, the slackening of the external dynamic impulse apparently had different results. Internal expansion occurred because of the natural growth of the animal population; thus there would always be opportunities of employment for the labor force that grew as a result of the same natural process, and also for those who lost their jobs in the sugar system as the slow process of decline proceeded. Even if the demand for cattle in the seaboard areas did not increase rapidly enough, the stock-breeding system would still expand at a relatively rapid rate, keeping in step with the subsistence sector. In other words, the relative importance of monetary income in stock breeding tended to diminish, bringing about a concomitant reduction in economic productivity.[2] Relative reduction in monetary income affected the degree of specialization of the economy as well as the division of labor within the system. Many imported articles previously purchasable in seaboard cities must now be produced domestically. Such pro-

---

deduced that it would not even be possible to maintain the productive capacity unless consumption expenditures were curtailed. It is, however, probable that the substantial devaluation in the Portuguese currency contributed to maintaining the system in a position at least to preserve its productive capacity.

[2] Physical productivity—the number of head attended to by one man—could be kept stable; but as the total value of the herd diminished, since the number of head that could be sold was relatively lower, the value of output per man shrank and with it the economic productivity of the system.

duction was, however, purely local—merely a crude form of handicrafts. Leather could take the place of almost any other raw material, stressing the enormous rise of relative prices of nearly everything that could not be produced locally. The atrophy of the monetary economy was aggravated to the extent that distances from the coastline grew, inasmuch as cattle transportation costs and the closing of markets were transforming the more distant breeders into "submarginal" producers. Hides and leather now became their sole source of cash income.

There is every indication that during the long period between the last quarter of the seventeenth and the beginning of the nineteenth century, the economy of the Northeast underwent a slow process of atrophy, in the sense that the real per capita income of the population declined steadily with the passing of time. Nevertheless, it is of interest to note that such atrophy was in itself the formative process of what, in the nineteenth century, was to become the Brazilian Northeastern economic system, characteristics of which still prevail today. The stagnation of the sugar industry did not create a need for emigration, as it did in the West Indies, on the part of the surplus labor resulting from the natural growth of the free population. Since no adequate employment was available in the sugar region for the entire increased free population, part of the workers were attracted to the interior by the shifting stock-breeding frontier. Hence the more unfavorable conditions in sugar, the greater the tendency to migrate inland. Possibilities of stock breeding for the sustenance of new levies of population are known to be large wherever land is abundant, inasmuch as food supply in such an economy is highly elastic on a short-term basis. On the other hand, because the profit picture in the stock-breeding sector was largely dependent on the profitability of the sugar economy during its periods of depression, with a flow of population inland the process of the conversion of cattle breeding into a subsistence economy was speeded up. If it had not been for this process, the protracted depression of the sugar sector would have caused either emigration of factors or a stagnant population. Food supply being nearly inelastic in the regions along the coast, population growth would have been much smaller except for this connection with cattle breeding.

A decline in real income in an agricultural region with a scarcity of land would necessarily affect food supplies, either because of conversion of former food-producing land to export-crop production (to compensate for export losses) or because of an enforced reduction in food imports. In a cattle-breeding region, the staple food product being the export article itself, a reduction in exports has no effect whatsoever on domestic food supplies; hence its population can go on growing normally even during a long period of declining exports. In the Brazilian Northeast, because food conditions were better in the lower productivity economy—that is, the stock-breeding areas—the protracted periods of depression, in which migration from the seacoast inland was intensified, were marked by more rapid population increase. This may explain why the population in the Northeast continued to expand—possibly at an even more rapid rate—during the entire century and a half of stagnating sugar production.

In summary, it may be said that the expansion of the economy of the Northeast during this long period consisted of a process of retrograde economic evolution: the high-productivity sector was losing its relative importance, whereas productivity in the stock-breeding sector declined in proportion to its own expansion. Actually, such expansion represented only growth of the subsistence sector, within which an increasing proportion of the population was clustering. In this way the Brazilian Northeast became converted from a high-productivity economic system into an economy in which the major part of the population produced only what was necessary for its bare existence. Dispersion of a part of the population through extensive cattle breeding caused an involution in the division of labor and specialization, resulting in a reversion to primitive techniques, even in craftsmanship activities. The shaping of the population of the Northeast, and of its precarious subsistence economy—a basic factor in the Brazilian economic problem in later periods—are therefore linked with the slow decline of the great sugar industry, an industry which at its best was perhaps the most profitable colonizing and agricultural business of all time.

12. ECONOMIC CONTRACTION AND TERRITORIAL EXPANSION

The seventeenth century was the period of greatest difficulty in the political life of the colony. In the first half of the century, the development of the sugar economy was interrupted by the Dutch invasions. At the time the losses suffered by Portugal were even greater than those of Brazil, in spite of the fact that the latter was the theater of war. The Dutch administration was concerned with retaining in the colony a part of the revenue collected from sugar, a circumstance which favored more intensive development of urban life. From the point of view of Portuguese trade and revenue, the losses were probably considerable. Simonsen has estimated the value of merchandise lost to Portuguese trade at around £20 million,[1] not to mention the concomitant heavy military expenditures. When military operations came to an end, a stage of falling prices set in

[1] Roberto Simonsen, *História Econômica do Brasil*, 3d ed. (São Paolo, 1957), p. 120.

caused by the loss of the monopoly. In the latter half of the century the profitability of the colony declined considerably both for Portuguese trade and for the treasury, with accompanying difficulties in the administration and defense of the colony.

In the stage of prosperity of the sugar economy, the Portuguese had been concerned with extending their dominions to the north. Interest in protecting the sugar monopoly was probably behind this expansionist trend. At the end of the sixteenth century nearly all the tropical lands in the hemisphere—that is, potential sugar-producing territory—was in the hands of the Spanish and Portuguese, at that time united under a single government. Inroads by the Dutch, French, and British occurred all along the line from the Caribbean to the Brazilian Northeast. It was the responsibility of the Portuguese to defend the part of the line lying south of the mouth of the Amazon. Thus, by defending Spain's possession against her enemies, the Portuguese themselves settled on the mouth of the great river, in a key position for control of the whole immense basin.

Experience had already shown that mere military defense, without effective occupation of the land, was a barren enterprise, either because other nations would not recognize any rights other than those over land effectively occupied or because, lacking permanent land bases, defense operations became much more costly. At the high point of the sugar cycle, Portugal had occupied the entire coast as far as the mouth of the Amazon by expelling the French, Dutch, and British intruders. At least in that part of the Western Hemisphere the risk of a competitive economy arising was eliminated. Occupation was followed by decisions aimed at the creation of permanent settlements. Once, in the early seventeenth century, about three hundred islanders from the Azores had been sent to Maranhão. But when a period of political and economic difficulty began for the Portuguese government those northern colonies were left to their own devices, and the vicissitudes they had to face plainly show how difficult it was for settlement colonies in the Western Hemisphere to survive.

The soil of Maranhão was not so fertile as the Northeast *massapé* (clayey black soil) from the point of view of sugar production. Nevertheless, the greatest difficulty lay not there but in the disorganization of markets for sugar, tobacco, and other tropical products, which prevented the Maranhão colonists from beginning capitalization and development. Their troubles were the same as those facing all the Portuguese colonies in the Western Hemisphere, but were further aggravated by the fact that they were trying to get under way at a time when others were already enjoying something they had previously accumulated. In its initial phase Piratininga (the present-day São Paulo plateau region) had taken advantage of the vigorous contemporary expansion of the sugar economy, and its inhabitants went into the business of selling Indian slaves at a time when imports of Africans were only just commencing. This activity made it possible for the southern colony to survive. The Maranhão colonists tried to do this too, but they had to face the isolation caused by the occupation of Pernambuco by the Dutch followed by the decline of the sugar economy.

During the latter part of the seventeenth and the early eighteenth centuries, the colonists in the so-called state of Maranhão[2] struggled energetically to survive. Created for political purposes but abandoned by the Portuguese government, the small colony underwent such a setback that after fifty years,

---

[2] In view of the obstacles caused to navigation by the prevailing winds, between the north coast of Brazil and the other "captaincies," when the former was occupied the Portuguese government felt it advisable to set up a separate colony directly controlled out of Lisbon. This colony, founded in 1621, was called the state of Maranhão, as opposed to the state of Brazil, and it comprised the region between Ceará and Amazonas.

according to a chronicler, "to get his bread from the earth, a man must have a farm; to eat meat, he must have his own huntsman; to be able to eat fish, he needs a fisherman; and to dress in clean clothes, he has to have a washerwoman . . ." [3] Lack of any activity capable of producing something marketable compelled each family to become completely self-sufficient, something possible only for those who managed to hold onto a number of Indian slaves. Thus Indian hunting became a prerequisite for survival.

The struggle by the northern colonists to get native manpower and the tenacious reaction against this practice by the Jesuit fathers, who had developed much more rational techniques for integrating the Indians into the economy of the colony, were decisive factors in the economic exploration of the Amazon basin. In their hunt for Indians, the colonists became better acquainted with the forests and came to realize the potentialities therein. In the first half of the eighteenth century, the region of present-day Pará became an exporting center for forest products: cocoa, vanilla, cinnamon, cloves, and aromatic resins. Harvesting of these products was, however, dependent on intensive utilization of Indian manpower. Working scattered through the forests, the Indians were hardly inclined to submit to the prevailing forms of slave labor organization. It was up to the Jesuit fathers to find a proper solution to the problem. By leaving the Indians in their own communities, Jesuit missionaries tried to obtain their voluntary coöperation. In view of the small value of the objects received by the Indians in payment, extensive exploitation of the forests became profitable with the linking of the Indian villages dispersed throughout the immense region. This superficial penetration had the advantage that it could be expanded indefi-

[3] Observation made by Pe. Antônio Vieira, in 1680. Quoted by Simonsen, *op. cit.,* p. 310.

nitely. It was not dependent upon any system of coercion. Once the interest of the Indians was aroused, penetration proceeded in a more subtle manner: once the need for a new article was created, a bond of dependence became established from which the Indians could no longer extricate themselves. This explains how the Jesuits, with such limited means at their disposal, were able to penetrate so deeply into the Amazon basin. Thus the very poverty of the state of Maranhão, by compelling the colonists to struggle tenaciously for Indian manpower—and the corresponding Jesuit reaction, first as mere protectors of the Indians, later in a search for more rational forms of coexistence, and finally in the form of servile exploitation of such manpower—was to become a decisive factor in the enormous territorial expansion carried out during the first half of the eighteenth century.

At the same time that the northern colonists were struggling to survive, through intensive Indian hunting and gaining increasing knowledge of forest exploration, great difficulties were also facing the colonists in the former São Vicente settlement in the south in their endeavor to maintain even their precarious standards of living. The impoverishment of the sugar region, by curtailing the market for native slaves, also had repercussions on the southern region, in which marketable articles were likewise lacking. Hides and leather, long since exported by the southern ports too, grew in relative importance, and commerce growing out of stock breeding became of increasing interest to the Portuguese rulers. By that time the River Plate region was also developing as a great cattle-breeding center, and its leather was a serious threat to one of the few products of the Portuguese colony whose market had not been disorganized by the Caribbean development. The Portuguese inroads through the River Plate estuary, where in 1680 they founded the colony of Sacramento, may therefore be viewed as one more episode in Brazilian territorial expansion related to the vicissitudes of the declining stage of the sugar economy. The colony of Sacramento, which remained in Portuguese hands with a few interruptions for almost a century, made it possible for Portugal greatly to strengthen its position in the leather trade. The colony was, moreover, an entrepôt for smuggling into one of the main ports of entry into Spanish America, at a period when Spain had lost most of its fleet but persisted in maintaining the monopoly of trade with her colonies.

As subsistence sectors grew in relative importance—in the north, south, and Northeast hinterland—it became increasingly difficult for the Portuguese government to transfer to Portugal what small fiscal dues could be levied. Because such levies had to be paid in Portuguese currency, their transfer caused increasing scarcity of currency within the colony, whose difficulties at the time were already increasing. In Portugal, troubles were even more serious. The fall in the value of sugar exports, on the one hand, was bound to create difficulties for the treasury authorities, while at the same time making it necessary to readjust the entire system in line with a much lower level of imports. The repeated currency devaluations (the value of the pound sterling rose from 1,000 réis to 3,500 réis between 1640 and 1700), reflect the extent of unbalance in the Portuguese economy. In the colony such devaluations, although to some extent lightening the burden of the sugar-exporting regions, acted to the detriment of the poorer areas with little or nothing to export and whose demand for imports was extremely inelastic because this demand was limited to such essentials as salt. Rising prices of imported manufactures reached such a point that in the poorest regions, such as Piratininga (São Paulo), a suit of clothing of imported material or a shotgun might be worth more than a residence.[4] These factors favored a sharper reversion to forms of sub-

[4] Simonsen, *op. cit.*, p. 221.

sistence economy, with atrophy in the division of labor, reduction in productivity, dissolution of the system into increasingly smaller productive units, extinction of the more complex forms of social intercourse, and substitution of general law by local custom.

PART III

The Slavery Economy
of Mining (Eighteenth Century)

13. COLONIZING AND INTERCONNECTING THE SOUTHERN REGIONS

What could Portugal expect of its huge South American colony, growing poorer day by day while maintenance costs increased simultaneously? Everything seemed to point to the fact that tropical agriculture there could not be expected to provide another miracle similar to that of sugar. Vigorous competition for the tropical products market had begun, with the main producers—the French and English colonies—being supported by the markets of their respective home countries. To an observer at the end of the sixteenth century the fate of the colony would have seemed uncertain. It was clearly understood in Portugal that the only solution was to discover precious metals. Hence there was a reversion to the original concept, according to which possession of lands on the American continent was economically justifiable only if they could produce such metals. The Portuguese rulers were soon to become aware of the enormous asset to mineral prospecting inherent in the knowledge of the hinterland possessed by the men of the Piratininga plateau. The fact was that they had failed to discover gold in their roamings through the backlands only because they lacked technical knowledge. The technical assistance they received from the mother country proved decisive.

The exhaustion and poverty both in the mother country and in the colony may account for the extraordinary rate of development of the gold economy during the first few decades of the eighteenth century. There were mass migrations from Piratininga; in the Northeast great resources were mobilized, mainly in the form of slave manpower, while in Portugal a spontaneous migratory flow toward Brazil occurred for the first time. The colony was to undergo a complete change of face.

Hitherto the existence of the colony had been tied in with a business setup consisting of a few large sugar mills; emigration had little attraction for the rank and file with few possessions. Transfer from Portugal to Brazil made sense only to those with means available for financing a relatively large undertaking. Furthermore, emigration needed subsidizing, and did not fit in with any economic purpose. In the sugar region the only regular immigrants were the craftsmen and skilled workmen who came to work directly in the mills. In São Vicente immigration was at the outset financed by the grantee himself, and was aimed at economic purposes which, as it turned out, were doomed to failure. Elsewhere, chiefly in the north and extreme south, immigration had been financed by the Portuguese government with the objective of establishing settlements for political purposes. It will readily be understood that this immigration did not achieve any large proportion. Data on population are uncertain and scarce, but clearly indicate that population of European origin grew slowly during the seventeenth century.

The mining economy opened up a European migratory cycle entirely new to the colony. Because of its characteristics the Brazilian mining economy afforded prospects to persons of limited means, inasmuch as no large mines were being worked —as was true in the silver areas in Peru and Mexico—but only the alluvial metal was being taken from the stream beds. There are no precise data on the volume of the migratory flow from the Atlantic islands and Portuguese mainland territory bound for Brazil in the eighteenth century. It is, however, known that alarm was aroused in Portugal and that strong measures were even taken to stem the migratory trend. If due account is taken of the stagnant economic conditions prevailing in Portugal, chiefly in the first half of the eighteenth century when the country's few manufacturing activities were disorganized, emigration must have attained great proportions to give rise to so strong a reaction. In fact, all indications are that colonial population from European stock increased tenfold in the course of the mining century.[1] It may be surmised that this population transfer was to a great extent financed by the immigrants themselves, who were small proprietors liquidating their possessions, possibly enticed by the hope of amassing a fortune quickly in the new El Dorado.

Even though the other basis of the mining economy was slave labor, it differed widely from the sugar economy because of its general organization. At no time did the slaves comprise a majority of the population. Further, because of the organization of labor, the slave was afforded greater initiative and

---

[1] Judging by the information available, the population of Brazil amounted to perhaps 100,000 in 1600, a maximum of 300,000 in 1700, and about 3,250,000 in 1800. The population of European origin was probably about 30,000 in 1600, and could hardly have been as much as 100,000 by 1700. Ignoring any European migratory contribution during the seventeenth century, it may be deduced that the natural rate of growth was at most sufficient to triple the population in the course of a century. If we assume this rate of growth prevailed for the following century, then the population of European origin (ignoring the migratory flow) would have amounted to about 300,000 by the end of the eighteenth century. As available data indicate that at that time the population of European origin actually amounted to somewhat more than a million, it may be deduced that Portuguese immigration into Brazil during the mining century was not less than 300,000 and may have been as high as half a million. In view of this, it may be presumed that Portugal made a larger population contribution to Brazil than did Spain to the whole of her colonies in the Americas.

permitted to circulate within a more complex social environment. Many a slave even managed to work for his own account, under commitment to pay his owner periodically a specified amount, which arrangement of course opened up for him the possibility of purchasing his own freedom. The existence of this possibility in itself was likely to act as a highly favorable factor in the mental development of the slave.

In the environment for the freemen—born either in the home country or in the colony—differences were still great between the mining economy and sugar production. In the latter, no freeman below the level of the small circle of large landowners could ever hope to attain a true status in society. And when the sugar economy became stagnant, the possibilities of a social climb for the freeman were curtailed still further. Consequently, a class of freemen with no positive social role began to grow and at times became a serious problem. The chances for an enterprising man in the mining economy were much greater. If he had resources available, he could organize a *lavra* (mining operation) of large proportions with a hundred or more slaves. Nevertheless, fixed assets per slave or per production unit were much lower than those for a large sugar mill. If his initial assets were small, he could manage to restrict his business to the minimum proportions permissible in line with the availability of manpower, with only a single slave if necessary. In short, if his means were such as to permit no more than his own sustenance for a limited period, he could operate as a *faiscador* (a kind of wildcat prospector). If blessed by fortune, he could very soon rise to the status of an entrepreneur.

The very nature of the mining enterprise did not stimulate as much attachment to the land as prevailed in the sugar regions. Fixed assets involved were small, since life on a lavra was always beset by uncertainty. The organization was such as to permit a change of location at short notice. On the other hand, the high profitability of the business was conducive to a concentrating of all available resources in the mining activity. The combination of these two factors—uncertainty and corresponding mobility of the enterprise, and high profitability and resultant specialization—was to become inherent in the organization of the entire mining economy. Profitability being greater in the initial stages of mining in each region, excessive concentration of resources in mining activities always led to serious food supply difficulties. Rising prices of foods as well as of beasts of burden in the neighboring regions were responsible for the form of distribution of the economic benefits resulting from mining activities.

Cattle breeding, having found in the south exceptionally favorable environmental conditions for expansion in spite of low profitability, was still lingering on, thanks to leather exports. With the advent of the mining economy, cattle breeding was to undergo a literal revolution. Southern cattle, the price of which had always remained at extremely low levels by comparison with those prevailing in the sugar regions, rapidly increased in value and occasionally brought exceptionally high prices. Even the Northeastern cattle region, whose market had been shrinking because of the decline of the sugar economy, tended to look southward in search of flourishing markets in the mining region. Such a displacement of Northeastern cattle was bound to cause a rise in the prices paid by the mills, whereby strong official reactions as well as attempts at interdiction were aroused.

Another characteristic of the mining economy with far-reaching effects on the neighboring regions was rooted in its transportation system. Located at great distances from the coast, widely dispersed through hilly country, the mining population was dependent for everything on a complex transportation system. The mule convoy was the lowest unit of the entire system. The almost complete absence of local supplies of food, the great inland distances to be covered by all imported goods, the need for traveling over extensive routes through mountainous areas in order to reach working sites—all contributed to making the transportation system of basic importance in the operation of the economy. Thus a great market for beasts of burden was created.

If the supply of cattle for beef and mules for transportation is viewed as a whole, it may be said that the mining economy of the eighteenth century afforded a market of greater proportions than that provided by the sugar economy even at the height of its prosperity. Thus the benefits from the mining economy were distributed throughout the southern cattle-breeding region to an extent substantially larger than in the Northeast hinterland. The region which is today known as the state of Rio Grande do Sul, where mule breeding developed on a large scale, thus became integrated into the entire Brazilian economy. Each year thousands of mules came up from Rio Grande do Sul, becoming the main source of income for the region. These animals were concentrated in the São Paulo region and sold in great market fairs to buyers from several regions. Thus the mining economy indirectly permitted a kind of articulation among the various southern regions of Brazil.

In contrast to what happened in the Northeast, where an economic void was the point of departure for the formation of a cattle-breeding economy as an offshoot of the sugar economy, in southern Brazil cattle breeding was in existence before mining. In fact, the upsurge of mining occurred when the Piratininga subsistence economy had already gone through a century and a half of poverty. Furthermore, in Rio Grande do Sul and even in the present-day state of Mato Grosso some rudimentary forms of a cattle-breeding economy based on leather exports were already in existence. These distant regions existed independently of one another and most probably would have tended to develop in subsistence systems without links of economic solidarity among them. The mining economy opened up a new cycle of development for them all. On the one hand, it substantially increased the profitability of the cattle-breeding economy, inducing broader utilization of land and herds. On the other hand, it had made the various regions interdependent through forms of specialization, some taking up breeding, others fattening and distribution, and still others becoming the main consumption markets. It is an error to suppose that cattle breeding was what bound those regions together. The linking factor was actually the demand for cattle radiating from the dynamic center set up by the mining economy.

14. THE FLOW OF INCOME

The geographical basis for the mining economy was spread over a vast zone lying between the Mantiqueira Mountains (in the present-day state of Minas Gerais) and the Guiabá region (in the present states of Mato Grosso and Goiás). In some areas the curve of production rose and fell sharply, causing sudden flows of population back and forth; in others the curve was less marked, permitting more regular population growth as well as the permanent settling of important centers of population. The average income of such an economy—that is, its average productivity—is somewhat difficult to define. At certain times it might reach extremely high levels in a particular subregion; the higher these levels, the greater would be the subsequent fall. The easily worked alluvial deposits were the first to become exhausted. Hence the "richer" regions were often those with the shortest useful life.

Gold exports grew throughout the first half of the eighteenth century, reaching a high point around 1760, when they amounted to £2.5 million. Yet they were already declining rapidly by the third quarter of the century, and by 1780 amounted to less than £1 million. The 1750's witnessed the greatest prosperity of the mining economy, with exports then standing at about £ 2 million. Surmising that four-fifths of the value of the gold exported would correspond to income created within the mining region itself, and that such income would be translated into imports to an equal value, and, further, that the import coefficient would be 0.5—the total yearly income of the mining economy could not have been more than £ 3.6 million at the period of greatest prosperity. Because the free population in the mining region at that time cannot have been less than 300,000, it is to be inferred that the average per capita income was substantially lower than that of the sugar economy at a corresponding stage.

Even though the average income in the mining economy had been lower than that in the region of the sugar plantations, the markets for the former presented much greater potentialities. Dimensions in absolute terms were greater, inasmuch as imports amounted to a smaller proportion of total expenditures. On the other hand—and this is the main facet of the question—income was much less concentrated because the free sector of the population was far larger. The market structure was necessarily different, with common consumption goods constituting a much more meaningful part whereas the opposite was true for luxury articles. Moreover, the population —although scattered over vast areas—was for the most part concentrated in urban and semiurban groups throughout those areas. Finally, the great distance between the mining region and the seaports contributed to a relative increase in prices of imported articles. This series of circumstances made the mining region much more suitable for the development of activities connected with the internal market than the sugar region had hitherto been. Notwithstanding, the endogenous development of the mining region—that is, that based on a market within the region itself—was nearly nonexistent. It is easy to understand how mining activities had absorbed all available resources in the initial stages. It is, however, not so easy to explain why even low-grade manufacturing activities did not develop at all, once urban centers were established, when they could be expanded in a subsequent phase of import difficulties. Many an explanation for this fact has been sought in Portuguese policies, inasmuch as one of Portugal's main goals was to raise barriers to the colony's manufacturing development. However, the decree of 1785, prohibiting any manufacturing activity, did not seem to provoke any major reaction, and it was more or less obvious that manufacturing development had been practically nil throughout the previous periods of prosperity and decline of the mining economy. The main cause was perhaps to be sought in the technical inability of immigrants to start manufacturing activities on any major scale.

The incipient manufacturing development of Portugal at the end of the seventeenth century had resulted from an active policy entailing imports of skilled manpower. The Methuen Treaty of 1703 with England destroyed this budding industry and had far-reaching consequences for both Portugal and Brazil. If immigrants with some manufacturing experience had arrived in Brazil, there would have been many opportunities for new enterprises at the proper time, with the development of organizational and technical capabilities the colony was never to know. A clear illustration may be found in the iron-working sector. The demand for iron was considerable in a region where shod animals existed in the tens of thousands; but in spite of abundant iron ore and charcoal, the development of steelmaking was possible only occasionally because of the technical skills of a few African slaves. A comparison, for example, between the above state of affairs and the situation of the United States, which began exporting iron to England at about the same period, shows that what was lacking in Brazil was early introduction of a technique unknown to the immigrants.

In the second half of the eighteenth century, the prime condition for manufacturing development in Brazil lay in the manufacturing development of Portugal itself. The flow of gold from Brazil may actually be held responsible for much of the relative backwardness of Portugal in that century within the context of the economic development process of Europe. In fact, although gold created favorable conditions for the colony's endogenous development, it is nonetheless true that it hampered the utilization of available possibilities by stunting the development of manufactures in Portugal itself. If Portugal had accumulated some manufacturing techniques, these would have been transferred to Brazil, legislative dispositions to the contrary notwithstanding, as occurred in the United States.

The Methuen Treaty stands as an important landmark in the economic development of Portugal and Brazil. This document was signed at the close of a period of great economic difficulties for Portugal, coinciding with the decline in sugar exports from Brazil. As this decline was protracted, persistently curtailing importing capacity, the viewpoint began to prevail in Portugal that there was a need for producing internally those things that sugar could formerly provide through abundant imports. Thus a period of direct and indirect incentives for the installation of manufactures began for Brazil. In a period of two decades beginning in 1684, Portugal had even managed nearly to abolish textile imports. Such a policy was entirely in accordance with the spirit of the times: six years earlier England had forbidden all trade with France so as to preclude the entry of French manufactures. Notwithstanding this policy, a vigorous reaction was to be expected within Portugal herself, mainly from the powerful wine producers and exporters, the country's dominant group. The English endeavored to ally themselves with that group so as to overthrow the Portuguese protectionist policy. The Treaty of 1703 did, as a matter of fact, grant Portuguese wines a reduction of one-third of the rate of duty paid by French wines in the English market. In return, Portugal agreed to raise the embargo on imports of English textiles.

If Portugal in the first half of the eighteenth century had

faced the same difficulties she had had in the previous fifty years, the Methuen Treaty would have had but limited effects on her history. Wine exports being small in value, the deficit on the country's commercial balance with England would have tended to worsen, causing greater devaluation of the currency and sundry other difficulties. In such conditions it is probable that some reaction would take place, aimed at restoring the protectionist policy. It is more or less obvious that Portugal could not pay with wine exports for the textiles she imported, and that the Methuen Treaty therefore had no real basis for survival. It so happened, however, that Brazilian gold began to flow into Portugal precisely at the time the treaty became effective. At the outset limited quantities of bullion came in, but some ten years later it was arriving in substantial amounts. Thus, almost impromptu the required conditions for enforcing the treaty were created, so as to make it operate as a mechanism for reducing the effect of gold as a multiplier over and above the level of economic activity in Portugal. On the one hand, the growing demand for manufactures coming from the colony would automatically be transferred to England, with no effect whatsoever on the Portuguese economy beyond income generated by some brokerage and taxes. On the other, the increase in public outlays—current expenditures or non-reproductive investments—was soon filtered through imports, with a restricted multiplying effect on other internal productive activities.

It is difficult to estimate to what extent the Portuguese economy, within the framework of a protectionist policy, could have reacted positively to the general expansion of demand created by the mining cycle in Brazil. Taking into account the fact that at that time there were vast population transfers toward Brazil and conspicuous nonreproductive investments—such as building of monuments, construction work, and so on, chiefly after the Lisbon earthquake in 1755—there would be some likelihood of attempts at manufacturing development being faced with a relative manpower scarcity. Notwithstanding this fact, all indications are that if the country depended on a manufacturing nucleus, the profits of the latter would have been such that capital accumulation within the sector would be rapid. Hence, at the beginning of the industrial revolution in the second half of the eighteenth century, Portugal could have been in a position to defend its own manufacturing production and therefore to assimilate the new production techniques that were being developed. To the nonexistence of a manufacturing nucleus, at a stage when production techniques were being revamped in the last quarter of the century, must be ascribed the fact that Portugal became an agricultural dependency of England. Without the counterweight of a manufacturing sector, the great landowners and wine exporters continued to carry too much weight in the country's economic policy, as was to become manifest in the second half of the century, when the Portuguese statesman, the Marquis of Pombal launched forth upon a vast drive to change the course of events.

On the European economy as a whole, Brazilian gold had a positive effect in that the expansion of demand thereby created was concentrated in the very country best equipped to derive maximum profit from the situation. In fact, England— thanks to structural transformations in her agriculture and the progress of her political institutions—was the only country in Europe to follow up systematically, throughout the century before the industrial revolution, an enlightened policy of incentives to manufacturing. "From the Revolution till the revolt of the colonies," says Cunningham, "the regulation of commerce was considered not so much with reference to other elements of national power, or even in its bearing on revenue, but chiefly with a view to the promotion of industry." [1] At a

---

[1] W. Cunningham, *The Growth of Modern Industry and Commerce. Modern Times, Part I* (Cambridge, 1921), p. 458. England's isolation

time dominated by the most strict mercantilism, in which it was particularly difficult to develop trade in manufactures, England found in the Portuguese-Brazilian economy a fast-expanding and nearly unilateral market. Her exports were paid for in gold, which gave the English economy exceptional flexibility in its operations on the European market. She thus found herself for the first time in a position to balance indirectly her trade in construction materials and other raw materials from northern Europe with manufactured products. The English economy thus acquired greater flexibility and a tendency to concentrate on investments in the manufacturing sector as the most indicated for rapid technological evolution. Further, by receiving most of the gold then being produced in the world, English banking houses reinforced their position even more

---

and relative backwardness within the framework of manufacturing development in Europe at the end of the Middle Ages early gave her a clear notion that without protection and an active policy of importing know-how, manufacturing expansion would be impracticable. In this respect a well-known authority states: "The earliest instance of the prohibition of exports is found in the action of the Oxford parliament of 1258. The barons then 'decreed that the wool of the country should be worked up in England, and should not be sold to foreigners, and that every one should use woolen cloth made within the country.' And on the consolidation of woolen manufactures in the fifteenth century: 'The growth of woolen manufactures during the second half of the century was stimulated by a consistent "protective policy," vigorously carried out.' This began with the accession of Edward IV, who throughout his reign relied upon the industrial and mercantile classes. In 1463 the importation of woolen cloth was prohibited, together with a number of other manufactured articles: and the prohibition, which in that act had been only temporary, was specially renewed and made permanent in an act of the following year. Moreover, the scale of export duties was arranged, if not then, soon afterwards, in such a way as to encourage the export of cloth rather than of wool." W. J. Ashley, *An Introduction to English Economic History and Theory, Part II* (London, 1893), pp. 194 and 226.

and Europe's financial center transferred from Amsterdam to London. According to English sources, imports of Brazilian bullion in London were at one time as high as £50,000 a week, permitting a substantial accumulation of gold reserves without which Britain could hardly have carried on the Napoleonic Wars.[2]

15. ECONOMIC REGRESSION AND EXPANSION OF THE SUBSISTENCE AREA

Since no permanent forms of economic activity were created in the mining regions, with the exception of some subsistence agriculture, it was only natural that with the drop in gold production rapid and general decline should set in. As production was reduced, the major mining concerns underwent a process of capital loss and liquidation. There was no possibility of replacing slave manpower, and with the passing of time many a mining entrepreneur became reduced to a mere prospector. Decline thus occurred through a slow shrinkage of the

[2] "The extent to which Portugal took off our manufactures, and thus encouraged industry in this country, appeared to be measured by the vast amount of Brazilian bullion which was annually imported from Portugal. This was estimated at £50,000 per week. . . . We cannot wonder that, according to the ideas of the time, Methuen's achievement was rated very highly: he had opened up a large foreign demand for our goods, and had thus stimulated the employment of labour at home; while much of the returns from Portugal came to us in the form which was most necessary for restoring the currency, and most convenient for carrying on the great European war." Cunningham, *op. cit.*, pp. 460–461.

capital invested in the mining sector. The delusion that a new discovery might occur at any time induced the entrepreneur to stand by and watch the gradual destruction of his assets rather than promote the transfer of some net balance to another economic activity. The entire system was therefore undergoing a general process of atrophy and loss of vitality, and eventually broke down into a mere form of subsistence economy.

Had the mining economy evolved into a more complex system, reactions would certainly have been different. Three-quarters of a century later in Australia, unemployment caused by the collapse of gold production was the point of departure for a protectionist policy which made possible the early industrialization of that country.[1] The need for absorbing the enormous manpower surplus which was being created as gold production diminished—a problem rendered the more serious in that the wool and agricultural sectors had already intro-

---

[1] The course taken by the Australian gold economy is illustrative of the flexibility of a system which had access to a more advanced technology. With the discovery of gold, the population of Australia practically tripled in a decade, rising from 438,000 in 1851 to 1,168,000 in 1861. Under such conditions it is easy to imagine the drainage of labor from the pre-existing wool economy and the pressure upon food supplies. These two sectors endeavored, however, to protect themselves by adopting more advanced techniques, and succeeded in accelerating their development during the period of the great expansion of gold production. The wool producers were even benefited by the reduction in return freight brought about by the great migratory movement. As one Australian author observes: "As the diggings attracted labour, squatters and farmers were forced to overhaul their productive technique and adopt labour-saving devices. Squatters fenced their runs: boundary riders replaced shepherds; farmers used better ploughs and more scientific means of cultivation. . . . In ten years (1850–60), the number of sheep in Australia increased from 16 to 20 million and the value of wool exported rose from £1,995,000 to £4,025,300. The area under crop doubled itself in eight years, 1850–58." G. V. Portus, *Australia, An Economic Interpretation* (Sydney, 1933), p. 25.

duced labor-saving devices in order to survive—contributed in the state of Victoria to a clear recognition that only through industrialization could the region's structural problem be solved. If the country had remained under the exclusive influence of wool-exporting groups, the prevalence of liberal ideas would have precluded any industrialization policy at the time.

In Brazil, the existing slave-labor regime avoided the arising of major social friction brought about by the collapse of gold production. Losses were greater for those who had invested heavily in slaves and now saw their profitability decreasing day by day. The system was subject to slow capital losses, but was nevertheless to preserve its structure at all times. In contrast to what was happening in the sugar economy—which sustained its profitability to a certain point by maintaining relatively high levels of production—profitability in mining tended to fall off to nothing, and the liquidation of productive enterprises was complete. Many of the former entrepreneurs became mere faiscadores, and eventually reverted to a mere subsistence activity. A few decades were enough for the entire mining economy to collapse, with the decline of urban nuclei and the dispersal of most of their inhabitants throughout a zone of subsistence economy—a vast region with difficult means of communication, in which small groups were isolated from each other. This relatively large population was to find space for expansion along the lines of a subsistence economy, and ultimately became one of Brazil's major population groups. In this instance, as in the Northeastern cattle-breeding economy, population expansion had its aftermath in a process of atrophy of the monetary economy. Hence, in a region whose settlement took place under a system of high productivity and extremely scarce manpower, a regression occurred involving a disconnected mass of population working on the lowest of productivity levels at subsistence farming. In no other part of the Western Hemisphere was there an instance of so rapid and so complete a process of involution from an economic system chiefly composed of population of European stock.

PART IV

The Economy of
Transition to Paid
Labor (*Nineteenth Century*)

16. MARANHÃO AND THE FALSE EUPHORIA AT THE END OF THE COLONIAL EPOCH

The last quarter of the eighteenth century was another period of trouble for the colony. Exports, which by 1760 had amounted to nearly £5 million, in the last quarter of the century averaged slightly more than £3 million a year. Sugar was facing new difficulties, with the total value of sales falling to levels lower than those attained at any time in the previous centuries.[1] Gold exports during this period averaged a little

---

[1] Data relative to the sugar output and prices have been carefully compiled by Roberto Simonsen, *História Econômica do Brasil*, 3d ed. (São Paolo, 1957), table facing p. 114. It is, however, possible that these data do not precisely reflect the situation of the sugar economy during the eighteenth century, and may show it under a more favorable aspect than it really had. Simonsen uses the quotations for crude sugar in London without bearing in mind that the law of 1739, whereby the British market was reserved for sugar from British crown colonies, had the effect of raising prices in England by comparison with international quotations. "The effect and significance of the 1739 act lay in its power to raise the price of sugar in the British market . . ." The producers in the British Antilles, taking advantage of the monopoly prices available to them in the British market—rapidly expanding in the eighteenth century—lost interest in exports, and this made it possible for Brazilian sugar to win back certain markets. See F. W. Pitman, *The Development of the British West Indies* (Oxford, 1937), pp. 170, 185–187.

more than half a million pounds sterling a year. Meanwhile, the population had climbed to more than three million. Per capita income at the turn of the century was probably not more than 50 United States dollars a year, in terms of present-day buying power, assuming a free population of about 2 million. This was perhaps the lowest level of income in Brazil throughout the entire colonial period.[2]

Taken as a whole, the Brazilian economy might be viewed as a series of systems some of which were mutually connected whereas others remained nearly isolated. Connections centered in two main nuclei: the sugar and the gold economies. Connected with the sugar nucleus, although in an increasingly loose manner, was the cattle-breeding economy of the Northeast, whereas to the mining nucleus was linked the southern cattle-breeding hinterland, spreading from São Paulo to Rio Grande do Sul. These two systems were in turn loosely connected through the São Francisco River, whose riparian cattle breeding had the benefit of being midway between the Northeast and the south-central regions, thus being able to choose the market affording greater advantages at any particular time. In the north were the two autonomous centers of Maranhão and Pará. The latter lived exclusively on the forest-extractive economy organized by the Jesuit fathers and based on exploitation of Indian manpower. The Jesuit system seems to have been highly productive—although only scanty information is

---

[2] Assuming for a favorable year at the end of the eighteenth century an export value of £4 million, and optimistically supposing that the value of exports amounted to but a quarter of total income, it may be deduced that the latter was about £16 million or about $100 million a year. For a free population of two million, per capita income would therefore be about fifty dollars a year. This datum is a mere suggestion, as even the very concept of income can be applied only with considerable reservations to an economy in which a large part of the product does not enter the monetary sector.

available about the Order, which did not pay taxes or publish statistics—but it entered into decline with the persecution it suffered under the Marquis of Pombal. Although an autonomous system in itself, Maranhão was linked with the sugar region through the cattle-breeding periphery. Thus Pará alone existed as a completely isolated nucleus. The three main economic centers—the sugar strip, the mining region, and Maranhão—were interconnected, although in a fluid and indefinite manner, through the extensive cattle-breeding hinterland.

Of the three main systems, the only one to attain some effective prosperity in the last quarter of the eighteenth century was Maranhão. This region had enjoyed the initial advantage of careful attention from the Portuguese government headed by Pombal, then engaged in a life-or-death struggle against the Jesuit Order. The colonists of Maranhão were traditional enemies of the padres on the issue of Indian slavery. Pombal helped the settlers by establishing a highly capitalized trading company responsible for financing the development of the region, traditionally one of the poorest in Brazil.[3] As important as the financial aid, however, was the change in the world market for tropical products brought about by the United States Revolutionary War, soon to be followed by the industrial revolution in England. From the outset, the company's directors were well aware that cotton was the tropical product with the fastest-growing demand and that rice produced in the English colonies and consumed chiefly in southern Europe was under no restriction from any colonial agreement. The company's assets were thus concentrated on production of those

---

[3] Though aiding the colonists, Pombal did not support their intentions of enslaving the Indians. Actually, this statesman was responsible for eliminating once and for all the overt and disguised forms of native slavery in Brazilian lands. Financial assistance provided made it possible to import African labor on a large scale and this completely changed the ethnic picture of the region.

two products. When the fruits of this policy began to ripen, it so happened that the great rice-producing center was temporarily excluded from the world markets by the United States Revolutionary War. Maranhão production therefore found itself in a highly favorable position of adequate development and capitalization. The small colony, whose port had received only one or two ships a year, and whose inhabitants were dependent on the labor of a few Indian or Negro slaves in order to survive, went through a period of exceptional prosperity at the close of the colonial era and began to harbor as many as 150 vessels a year while exports rose to about £1 million annually.

With the exception of the Maranhão nucleus, the colonial economy underwent a period of serious depression in the last decades of the eighteenth century. In the gold region, the depression was particularly serious and was to last for the next fifty years. This decline was also indirectly to affect the southern cattle-breeding region, which had to cope with a prolonged period of internal difficulties. Nevertheless, in the early nineteenth century, a series of events bestowed on the colony a disguised form of prosperity, the more deluding in that the transfer of the Portuguese government to Brazil and the opening of the Brazilian ports in 1808 had produced a general atmosphere of optimism.

The last quarter of the eighteenth century and the first two decades of the nineteenth were marked by a series of political events which had great repercussions in all world markets for tropical products. The first of those events was the United States Revolutionary War, whose indirect reflections in Maranhão we have already mentioned. The second was the French Revolution and the subsequent troubles in the Antilles colonies producing tropical products. Finally, there were the Napoleonic Wars, the blockade and counterblockade of Europe, and the dissolution of the vast Spanish Empire in the Americas.

In 1789 the great French sugar colony of Haiti collapsed.

In this small territory were concentrated almost half a million slaves, who rebelled and destroyed a large part of the wealth accumulated on the island, producing a change in the sugar market. Hence, a new stage of prosperity opened up for the Brazilian sugar-producing region. In fact, the value of Brazil's sugar exports grew almost ten times during the Napoleonic Wars. There was intensive industrial activity in England during those war years, and the demand for cotton increased considerably. Following the lead of Maranhão, the Northeast invested resources in the production of cotton. The troubles arising in the Spanish colonies were also to have their effect on the market for tropical products and leather. Thus nearly all the colony's products were benefited by temporary price rises. The total value of exports almost doubled between the last decades of the eighteenth century and the closing of the colonial period, reaching nearly £4 million a year. Nevertheless, this prosperity was of a precarious kind, based on anomalous conditions in the world market for tropical products. Once that stage passed, Brazil was to face serious difficulties, in the early decades of her existence as an independent nation, in defending her status in markets to which her products traditionally went.

17. COLONIAL LIABILITIES

The repercussions in Brazil of political events in Europe at the end of the eighteenth century and beginning of the nineteenth, on the one hand speeded up the country's political evolution, but they also helped prolong the phase of economic difficulties which began with the collapse of gold. When Portugal was occupied by French troops, Lisbon was eliminated as an entrepôt for trade with the colony, and direct contact with markets still accessible became essential. The "opening of the ports" in 1808 was the result of pressure of circumstances.[1] It brought in its wake the treaties of 1810, granting England the position of a privileged power with extraterritorial rights and preferential tariffs at extremely low levels. For the entire first half of the nineteenth century these treaties seriously hampered the autonomy of the Brazilian government in the economic sector. The final separation from Portugal in 1822 and the 1827 agreement, whereby England consolidated her position, were two other landmarks of this period of important political events. Finally, reference must be made to the elimination of the personal power of Emperor Dom Pedro I, in 1831, and the resulting definitive ascension to power of the dominant colonial class composed of the heads of the exporting agricultural sectors.

Broadly viewed, these events may be said to lead to the

[1] The "opening of the ports," although in practice it was to prove almost exclusively to the benefit of the British, had been decreed without consultation with the latter, because Viscount Strangford—British representative who was to be the mentor of the economic policies of the Portuguese government from the time it was established in Rio de Janeiro—was not aboard that part of the fleet which called at Baía. It appears that the Prince Regent was reluctant to accept the arguments of José da Silva Lisboa (later Viscount of Cairú) in favor of the opening of the ports, showing how little notion Portuguese ruling circles had of what was really going on. The British—who believed less in Adam Smith than did José da Silva Lisboa—were also not satisfied, as may be deduced from the words of their representative in Rio, a Mr. Hill, to Prince Regent Dom João, regarding the measure taken: "It could not fail to produce a good effect in England but that had it authorized the admittance of British vessels and British manufactures upon terms more advantageous than those granted to the ships and merchandise of other foreign nations, it would necessarily have afforded greater satisfaction." Letter from Hill to Canning, dated March 30, 1808, as quoted by Alan K. Manchester, *British Pre-eminence in Brazil: Its Rise and Decline* (Chapel Hill, 1933), p. 71.

more or less evident conclusion that the privileges granted England were a natural consequence of the way in which independence was achieved, without any major wear and tear on resources. The former colony had, however, to take upon itself the responsibility for a part of the liabilities Portugal had formerly assumed in order to be able to survive as a colonial power. If independence had resulted from a protracted struggle, Brazilian territorial unity would hardly have been preserved, inasmuch as none of the regions in the country had sufficient hegemony over the others to enforce such unity. Regional interests would have been bound to appear in the form of a much more concrete reality than national unity, which came into being only when the Portuguese government was transferred to Rio de Janeiro. The strong and fruitless fight Bolívar had to wage in order to preserve the unity of New Granada may be cited as an instance of how difficult it is to enforce an idea which does not have its counterpart in the reality of prevailing interests.

It would, however, be wrong to take it for granted that the privileges bestowed on England were mainly responsible for Brazil's failure to acquire the traits of a modern nation in the first half of the nineteenth century, in line with the example set by the United States. The fundamental difference between the viewpoints of the Viscount of Cairú*—certainly the most enlightened representative of the intelligentsia of the colonial agricultural class—and of the Viscount of Strangford is that in the latter some mercantilist biases still persisted whereas the Brazilian more clearly reflected ideas which were to prevail in England in later years. Since there was no conspicuous merchant class in the colony (major trade being a monopoly of the

---

* Viscount of Cairú (1756–1835) was a Brazilian lawyer and economist, one of the main figures influencing the opening of the ports in 1808.—Translators.

home country), the result was that the only articulate class was that of the great agricultural landlords. Whatever might be the procedure for gaining independence, this class was destined to win power, as indeed happened mainly after 1831. Spokesmen for major agriculture clearly saw that Portugal was a costly entrepôt, and the dominant opinion at the time was that the colony urgently needed freedom of trade. The disappearance of the Portuguese entrepôt immediately resulted in lower prices for imported merchandise, greater abundance of supplies, larger credit facilities, and many obvious advantages for the large farmer class.

As a kind of huge plantation for tropical products, Brazil was closely integrated with European economies, on which the colony was dependent. The country was not an autonomous system, but rather a mere appendage of other major systems. If integration were to be complete—as had happened in the British West Indies—the identity of interests of the ruling classes in both the main and subsidiary economies must also be complete. Such an ideological communion could not exist between Brazil and Portugal, for the latter was only an entrepôt with conflicting interests vis-à-vis the colony.

During the first half of the nineteenth century, conflicts between the ruling group of Brazilian plantation owners and the British, which helped to create among the former a clear recognition of the need for thorough political independence, did not originate in discrepancies in economic ideology. They resulted mainly from the lack of consistency of the British in the application of the liberal ideology. The Treaty of Commerce of 1810, although bestowing resounding praises on the new liberal system, was in reality a privilege-creating instrument. On the other hand, the British did not show any interest in opening markets for Brazilian products, which competed with those of their own Caribbean dependencies. If implemented on a purely unilateral basis, the liberal ideology was bound to create serious difficulties for the Brazilian economy, precisely at a state when the large-farmer class began to rule the country. In this troublesome period, England endeavored to enforce the prohibition of importing African slaves. Between difficulties in selling their products and fears of a sharp rise in costs produced by the barring of African slave imports, the Brazilian large farmers decided on a strong defense of their own interests, provoking and challenging British ire. The British government—taking its stand on stolid moral reasons and pressed by West Indies interests, which saw in the very persistence of slavery in Brazil the main reason for the decline of the sugar market—resorted in vain to every possible means of interrupting the transatlantic slave trade.

Therefore, the tension that prevailed throughout the first half of the nineteenth century between the British government and the Brazilian ruling classes[2] did not conceal any major conflict of interests. Hence there are no grounds for thinking that, if the Brazilian government had enjoyed full liberty of action, the country's economic development would have been more rapid. It must, however, be recognized that the customs privileges granted England, and later enforcement of a general 15 per cent ad valorem customs tariff at a stage of stagnating foreign trade, created serious difficulties for the Brazilian government. The taxing of imports is the usual means whereby countries with a primarily exporting economy collect their basic revenues. The only alternative for Brazil was to tax exports, which in a slave-holding economy meant cutting off profits to the great landlords.[3] Caught, therefore, between the need for taking a cut in profits at a troublesome time and the

[2] The conflict was not with the British local commercial interests, because they continued to prosper in the shade of the privileges they enjoyed, nor was it precisely with the Brazilian government, which gave out repeated exhortations to end the traffic which was "illegal."

[3] A tax of 8 per cent ad valorem on exports was introduced at the stage of greatest fiscal difficulties.

impossibility of increasing duties on imports, the Brazilian ruling classes were faced with a difficult choice.

The central government, afflicted with an extraordinary scarcity of financial resources, saw its authority challenged throughout the entire country at a period when economic difficulties were causing a general atmosphere of dissatisfaction in almost every part of Brazil. The northern provinces—Baía, Pernambuco, and Maranhão—went through a stage of serious economic trouble. Sugar prices were falling steadily in the first half of the century, while cotton prices dropped even lower. In Baía and Pernambuco, and especially in Maranhão, per capita income seems to have declined sharply during the entire period. In the south, economic difficulties were piling up as an aftermath of the decline in the gold economy, which was the chief market for cattle bred in the south. The numerous armed uprisings in the north and the protracted civil war in the south reflected this process of impoverishment and troubles.[4]

In the midst of this series of problems coffee began to emerge as a new source of wealth for Brazil. By the 1830's it was gaining ground as the principal Brazilian export product and showed steady progress. Owing to this new source of wealth, a solid stabilizing nucleus of capital formed around Rio de Janeiro, which became the focal point of resistance against the disintegrating forces at work in both the north and south.

Due account must be taken that there was almost no fiscal setup in the country to understand the importance of customs duties as a source of revenue and means of sustenance for the government. Restricted to this sole source of revenue, the cen-

---

[4] In the 1830's and 1840's, Brazil passed through an almost uninterrupted period of rebellions and civil war. The states of Pará, Maranhão, Ceará, Pernambuco, Baía, Minas Gerais, São Paulo, Mato Grosso, and Rio Grande do Sul underwent internal convulsions. In Pará, Ceará, and Pernambuco the period of convulsions lasted for years, and in Rio Grande do Sul the civil war continued for decades.

tral government found itself in serious financial difficulties during the phase of consolidating independence. The elimination of the Portuguese entrepôt did permit an increase in revenues; but, once that readjustment had been made, the government had almost no further means of increasing the collection of revenue until the conclusion of a treaty with England in 1844. The country's experience during the 1820's—the first decade of independent existence—is illustrative, and explains most of the difficulties in the ensuing two decades. During that decade the central government did not succeed in collecting enough revenue through the fiscal system to cover even half its expenditures, which had been increased by the war with the so-called Eastern Strip (Uruguay).[5] The deficit was financed chiefly by issuing paper currency, whose volume more than doubled in the 1820's.[6]

Because of the small monetary economy, its high import coefficient, and the impossibility of increasing customs duties, the effects of issuing paper currency were concentrated on the exchange rate—the value of the pound sterling in terms of milréis doubled between 1822 and 1830.

Financing the government budget by issuing paper currency was reflected in the rise in prices of imported articles—caused by the external devaluation of the currency—which particularly affected the urban population. The great-landlord class,

---

[5] The Portuguese government, taking advantage of the state of confusion prevailing in the Spanish colonies, had occupied the Eastern Strip of Uruguay in 1815, which came to be the Cisplatina province of Brazil. Aided by Argentina, the Uruguayans rebelled in 1825 and succeeded, under the auspices of Great Britain, in having their independence recognized by the two neighboring powers.

[6] Between 1824 and 1829 the government of Brazil obtained some external loans, although under extremely burdensome conditions, to an effective total of £4.8 million. These funds were, however, completely absorbed in the direct expenditure on independence, including a part of the £2 million indemnification paid to Portugal.

which was largely self-supplied by its own estates and whose monetary expenditures were cushioned by the slave-labor system, was relatively little affected by the consequences of the issuing of paper money. These consequences were felt mainly by the urban population of small tradesmen, public employees, clerks, and military men. In fact, the subsequent inflation caused an impoverishment of those classes, which accounts for the predominantly urban character of the uprisings of the time and the increased hatred of the Portuguese, who, being predominantly merchants, were considered responsible for the difficulties that harassed the population.[7]

[7] There were countless rebellions of army garrisons for which no plausible explanation can be found other than, as the historians called it, "increased indiscipline." "In Pará," says João Ribeiro, "the mutinous troops arrested the generals and imprisoned or murdered the governors, with the factious assistance of the whole of the unruly elements, and it was only after four years that it proved possible to reëstablish the order and prestige of authority." In Pernambuco, the "troops sacked the city; the tumult lasted for many years . . . In Maranhão the anarchists did their best to liquidate the cream of society." *História do Brasil,* 16th edition, pp. 377–378. Grievances against the Portuguese were another form of the same outbreaks, the most notorious instance being that of the "Praieira" (beachcomber) rebellion of Pernambuco (1847–1848): "The *praieiros* demanded nationalization of the retail trade, and even the deportation of Portuguese linked by family ties with the people of Brazil. To the cries of *'mata marinheiro!'* ["death to the sailors!"] many Portuguese were assassinated during the days of greatest tumult." *Ibid.,* p. 389.

18. COMPARISON WITH
THE DEVELOPMENT OF
THE UNITED STATES

The difficulties indirectly created as a result of, or aggravated by, the restrictions imposed on the Brazilian government by the commercial treaties of 1810 and 1827 with England are no justification for the present criticism of those treaties, which argues that they prevented Brazil's industrialization at the time by taking the protectionist machinery out of the hands of the government. Close study of events at the time shows that the Brazilian economy passed through a stage of sharp unbalance, caused mainly by the relative decline in export prices and by the action of the government—whose responsibilities had grown with political independence—aimed at increasing its share of the national expenditures. The exclusion of the Portuguese entrepôt and the greater facilities for transportation and marketing as a result of the establishment of many English firms in Brazil caused a relative decrease in import prices and a rapid expansion of the demand for imported items. Consequently strong pressure was exerted on the balance of payments and was reflected in the exchange rate. On the other hand, as has already been indicated, the financing of the budgetary deficit of the central government considerably increased the pressure on the exchange rate. In the absence of a substantial flow of foreign capital or of adequate expansion of exports, this pressure resulted in the external depreciation of the currency, which in turn led to a sharp rise in the prices of imported articles. If a general 50 per cent ad valorem tariff had been adopted from the outset, the protectionist effect would not have been so great as that resulting from the devaluation of the currency.[1]

A detailed analysis of the facts shows that it would not have been within Brazil's power, assuming complete freedom of action, to adopt a policy identical with that of the United States in the first half of the nineteenth century.[2] The question has often been asked: Why did the United States become an industrial nation in the nineteenth century, keeping abreast of the European countries, whereas Brazil evolved in such a manner that it became a vast underdeveloped region in the twentieth century? Putting aside the superstitious fatalism implicit in the theories of inferiority of climate and race which have for some time prevailed, the issue has acquired a more precise meaning from the economic point of view.

The development of the United States through the first half of the nineteenth century is inseparable from that of the European economy itself, being to a much lesser extent the result of internal protectionist policies adopted by the United States. Protectionism was part of the general economic policy well into the nineteenth century, when the bases of the country's

---

[1] Assuming an increase of 100 per cent in the price of imported merchandise is accompanied by an increase of 33 per cent in the general price level, the resultant effect is at least identical with the introduction of a 50 per cent *ad valorem* customs duty.

[2] This point of view, a current one among authorities on the Brazilian economy, is espoused, for instance, by Roberto Simonsen: "Brazil had, at that time, to implement a policy similar to that which the U. S. adopted during the period of its economic formation. As producers of colonial articles, despite being faced by a world shut off on account of 'colonial polices' [allusion by Simonsen to one of the aberrations in the Portuguese version of the 1810 trade treaty in which the English word "policy" was translated as "policia," meaning "police" in Portuguese], our country became a champion of economic liberalism on the American continent." *História Econômica do Brasil,* 3d ed. (São Paolo, 1957), p. 406.

economy had already been consolidated. In line with the first American tariff of 1789, cotton textiles were taxed at only 5 per cent ad valorem and the average for all other merchandise amounted to 8.5 per cent.[3] Several further readjustments allowed the tariff on cotton textiles to rise to 17.5 per cent in 1808, at which time the American textile industry was already consolidated also.

To understand the development of the United States in the period immediately following the gaining of independence, due account must be taken of the peculiarities of the former colony, as outlined in Chapters 5 and 6. At the time of her independence, the population of the United States was about the same size as that of Brazil. Social differences, however, ran deep; whereas in Brazil the ruling class was made up of large farmers and slave owners, in the United States a class of small farmers and a group of great merchants dominated the country. This difference is plainly evident in the disparity between the two interpreters of the ideals of the ruling classes in the respective countries: Alexander Hamilton and the Viscount of Cairú. Both were disciples of Adam Smith. But Hamilton became the champion of a process of industrialization which was not well understood by the American small-farmer class, and advocated and promoted a bold and positive governmental policy of direct incentives to industry and not merely passive measures of a protectionist nature,[4] whereas Cairú superstitiously believed in the "invisible hand" and repeated: *laissez faire, laissez passer, laissez vendre.*

The restrictive measures on manufacturing which England

[3] Ugo Rabbeno, *The American Commercial Policy* (London, 1895), p. 117.

[4] "He [Alexander Hamilton] attached much greater importance to bounties and premiums to be granted directly to the various branches of industries, and insisted on the adoption of them either exclusively or conjointly with the customs duties." *Ibid.,* p. 137.

imposed on her colonies in the mercantilist era were applied in a very special form in the United States, because the system of farming for export did not yield results in the northern colonies. Relations of such colonies with the mother country evolved in a unique manner as mentioned in Chapters 5 and 6. The general outlines of British policy were: to stimulate in the northern colonies those industries not competing with the home country, so as to reduce imports from other sources; to avoid competition by the colonies' manufactures with British industries in other colonial markets. Restrictive measures began to be enforced when the northern colonies started competing with the mother country in exports of manufactures.[5] There was some concern with hampering the production of steel in the colony, but as a compensation iron production was encouraged so as to reduce England's dependency on the Baltic countries. One of the most reputed scholars in this field has said: "In studying those times, the presumption becomes better defined with every new detail of fact revealed, that upon the whole the industrial development of the colonies was about where it would have been had their economic policies been governed by their own people." [6] Further, the colonies themselves, facing many a difficulty in importing needed manufactures, soon became aware of the need for stimulating internal production. As early as 1655, Massachusetts had passed a law obliging every family to produce all the cloth it needed. Many colonies forbade the export of certain raw materials, such as

[5] "The first of those was an act passed in 1699, upon the complaint of English manufacturers and merchants, to the effect that the colonists were exporting wool and woolens to foreign markets in competition with those of Great Britain . . . In 1732, Parliament prohibited the exportation from one colony to another, or from the colonies to England or Europe, of hats manufactured in America." Victor S. Clark, *History of Manufactures in the United States, 1609–1860* (Washington, 1916), pp. 22–23.

[6] *Ibid.,* p. 30.

leather, so that these could be processed and finished locally. Then too, there was the extraordinary progress of shipbuilding, which was destined to play a fundamental role in the development of the colonies at the time of the Napoleonic Wars. Even before independence, three-quarters of all North American trade was carried in the country's own ships.[7]

The Revolutionary War, by interrupting for several years the supply of British manufactures, created powerful incentives to internal production, which already had a solid basis for expansion. Soon after the war a period of serious political difficulties began in Europe which were to create extraordinary incentives for the development of the United States economy. For a number of years the United States was the only neutral power with a large merchant fleet. Faced with difficulties in obtaining European supplies, the British West Indies and French Antilles turned to the North American market for their food. Between 1789 and 1810 the United States merchant marine grew from 202,000 tons to 1,425,000 tons, and all the ships were built in the country itself.[8]

The technical experience accumulated since the colonial era, the lucidity of some of the nation's leaders in apprehending the true sense of the economic development which was accompanying the industrial revolution, and the great accumulation of capital during the Napoleonic Wars—all these factors are, however, not sufficient to account for the transformation of the country in the first half of the nineteenth century. For a long

---

[7] "According to one estimate 30% of the 7,700 vessels flying the British flag in 1775 were American built, and 75% of American commerce were carried in her own bottoms." F. A. Shannon, *America's Economic Growth* (New York, 1951), p. 91.

[8] "From 1795 to 1801 the average net earnings of our merchant marine were supposed to exceed $32,000,000 a year, which alone would pay for more imported goods per capita than the colonists had used prior to the revolution." Clark, *op. cit.*, p. 237.

time in the future, the North American economy was to depend
on exports of primary materials for its own development. In
fact, it was as an exporter of a raw material—cotton—that the
United States had, almost from its beginning, taken its stand
in the vanguard of the industrial revolution. In the last quarter
of the eighteenth century and the first half of the nineteenth,
the industrial revolution was basically a far-reaching transformation of the textile industry. This phenomenon is easily explained because of the fact that textiles are the main processed
merchandise of pre-capitalistic societies. The market for textiles had already been developed, whereas that for other manufactures existed only in embryo. The two basic features of the
first stage of the industrial revolution were mechanization of
manufacturing processes in the textile industry and utilization
of cotton in place of wool in that same industry,[9] inasmuch as
cotton production was easier to expand. Although England introduced processes of mechanization, the next step depended
upon the United States: the supplying of huge quantities of cotton which made it possible in a few decades to change the
structure of textile supply throughout the world. Between 1780
and the mid-nineteenth century, cotton consumption by British mills increased from 2,000 to 250,000 tons. This enormous
expansion in the consumption of cotton textiles did not reflect
an autonomous growth of demand. In this first stage, the expansion was achieved mainly through intensive competition

[9] These two aspects of the industrial revolution are to a certain extent
inseparable, as the introduction of cotton facilitated per se the transformation of working methods. "The cotton industry was especially
well adapted as a field for experiments. With regard to the problem of
mechanical spinning it afforded especially favorable conditions for in-
ventors. For cotton fiber, being more cohesive and less elastic than
wool, is easier to twist and stretch into a continuous thread." Paul Man-
toux, *The Industrial Revolution in the Eighteenth Century* (London,
1928), p. 213.

against local manufactures based on handicrafts and a relative reduction in the consumption of other fibers. The main instrument of this competition was reduction in prices: between the last decade of the eighteenth century and the first half of the nineteenth, the price of British cotton manufactures was cut by two-thirds.[10] This reduction to a great extent reflected the decline in cotton prices, which was made possible by a series of circumstances favoring large-scale production of the material in the United States.[11]

Cotton, which came to represent more than half of the value of United States exports, was the first dynamic element in the development of the United States economy in the first half of the nineteenth century. Abundant fertile areas in Alabama, Mississippi, Louisiana, Arkansas, and Florida were used for cotton cultivation, as they were to be for coffee in Brazil. The new forms of extensive farming always entailed the search for new lands and penetration into the interior of the continent. Mainly as a reflection of the expansion of this system in the South, the North American Midwest was settled by the great migratory influx from Europe to the heart of the continent along the great rivers, linking them with the Southern markets.

As occurred in Brazil when the ports were opened, the

---

[10] Between 1790–1800 and 1840–1850 average prices of British cotton textiles were actually reduced by one-fifth. But, bearing in mind that in the first period there was a price increase caused by the abnormal market conditions, I have estimated the reduction due to the long-term trend at two-thirds. For basic data see: W. W. Rostow, *The Process of Economic Growth* (Oxford, 1953), Appendix II.

[11] W. W. Rostow, studying this problem with reference to the 1812–1830 period, states: "Of the decline in cost of No. 100 yarn, about two thirds was accounted for by the fall in raw material costs. . . . The proportionate contribution to cost reduction of raw materials is greater in the lower grades of yarn than in the more expensive products: 71 per cent, for No. 40 yarn; only 5 per cent, for No. 250." *Ibid.,* pp. 203–204.

United States commercial balance with England most often showed a deficit during the first few decades of the nineteenth century. However, this deficit—rather than burdening the exchange position as it did in Brazil, so as to cause readjustments to increasingly lower levels of currency values—tended to be transformed into medium- and long-term debts invested in bonds of the national and state governments. A flow of capital was created almost automatically which was to be of fundamental importance in the development of the country. Such were the results of the government financial policy as conceived by Hamilton and of the pioneer action of the federal government at the outset and of the state governments later in building an economic infrastructure and providing direct incentives to basic activities.[12]

19. THE LONG-TERM DECLINE
IN INCOME LEVEL
IN THE FIRST HALF
OF THE NINETEENTH CENTURY

A basic requirement for the development of the Brazilian economy in the first half of the nineteenth century was expansion of exports. To attempt to stimulate industrialization at the time without the support of expanding import capacity was to look for the impossible in a country completely lacking in any tech-

---

[12] During the first half of the nineteenth century the state's action was fundamental in United States development. It was only in the second half of the century—when the influence of big business underwent substantial growth—that the ideology of noninterference by the state in the economic sector began to prevail.

nical foundation. The incentives which had been provided for the iron industry at the time of King Dom João VI failed, not because of the lack of protection, but simply because no industry automatically creates a market for itself and the market for iron products was almost nonexistent. The country's small consumption dropped with the decline of mining activities. It had been spread through the various provinces, and required a complex marketing organization. Industrialization had to begin with those products which could already depend upon a market of a certain size—as with textiles, the only manufacture whose market included the slave population. However, the sharp decline in prices of English textiles made it difficult for even the few existing Brazilian textile handicrafts activities to survive. The fall in prices was such that it became nearly impossible to protect any local industry by means of tariffs. There was a need for establishing import quotas. It must be recognized, however, that to bar imports of a product whose price was declining so sharply would have been tantamount to a substantial reduction in the real income of the population at a time when the people faced serious difficulties. Further, the establishment of a modern industry would have faced many obstacles because the British were most reluctant to export machinery.[1]

Quite apart from the consideration that an intelligent indus-

---

[1] "The British government took every precaution to prevent the new machinery, or a practical knowledge of it, from leaving the country, and British agents even shipped back to England such machines as they could acquire in the U. S." Victor S. Clark, *History of Manufactures in the United States, 1609–1860* (Washington, 1916), p. 533. The mechanization of the United States textile industry was mainly carried out with machinery manufactured in the country itself, which was possible thanks to the coöperation of specialized British workmen who immigrated, eluding the control of the British authorities. The possibility of achieving high profits in an economy whose market was expanding rapidly induced them to run the risks involved.

trialization policy would be impracticable in a country ruled by a class of large farmers and slave owners, it must be recognized that the primary condition for the success of such a policy had to be a steady, broad expansion of the exporting sector. The main cause of the great relative backwardness of the Brazilian economy in the first half of the nineteenth century was therefore the damming up of its exports. During that period, average annual growth of the sterling value of Brazilian exports did not exceed 0.8 per cent,[2] whereas population was increasing at an annual rate of about 1.3 per cent.[3] The 0.8 per cent rate of growth does not, however, convey a precise idea of what had occurred in Brazil, inasmuch as the entire expansion in exports recorded for the period was provided by coffee, production of which was concentrated in regions around the city of Rio de Janeiro. Besides coffee, the value of exports for 1850 was probably below that for the early years of the century. Export statistics by main articles (available from 1821 on), provide a clearer view of the matter. Between 1821–1830 and 1841–1850, the sterling value of sugar exports increased by 24 per cent—in other words, at an average annual rate of 1.1 per cent; the value of cotton exports was reduced by 50 per cent; hides and leather underwent a 12 per cent reduction, and tobacco remained unchanged. In fact, tobacco was the only item for which prices remained stable. Sugar exporters had to more than double the quantities shipped for a 24 per cent in-

[2] I estimate 1800 exports to have been about 4 million pounds, based on data published in Roberto Simonsen, *História Econômica do Brasil*, 3d ed. (São Paolo, 1957). For 1849–1850 the value of exports was £5,932,000. *Anuário Estatístico do Brasil*, 1939–1940, p. 1358. The remaining data relating to the foreign trade of Brazil from 1821 are from this same source.

[3] The rate of 1.3 per cent is based on a comparison between the 1850 population of 7 million and that of 1808 (4 million). For estimates of the population of Brazil in the nineteenth century, see *Anuário Estatístico do Brasil*, op. cit., p. 1293.

crease in value; cotton exporters received half the value, though exporting only 10 per cent lower quantities; exports of hides and leather, though doubled in quantity, brought a value 12 per cent lower.

These price declines are not wholly meaningful per se, inasmuch as the real value of exports would have remained unaltered if import prices had also been declining. Only an index of terms of trade—that is, the ratio between import and export prices—could give a clear idea of the effects of price changes on the productivity of the country's economy. Such an index, in indirect form though with reasonable accuracy, can be obtained for the period. The decline in Brazilian export prices between 1821–1830 and 1841–1850, was about 40 per cent. For imports, the price index for British exports may be considered as a fairly good source. This index remained perfectly stable between the two decades.[4] Thus the decline in the index of terms of trade amounted to approximately 40 per cent—in other words, real income from exports grew 40 per cent less than their physical volume. As the average annual value of exports increased from £3,900,000 to £5,470,000—a 40 per cent growth—real income derived from the exporting sector grew in the same proportion, whereas the production effort in this sector approximately doubled.

These data may be taken as a fairly clear indication that real income per capita declined noticeably in the first half of the nineteenth century. To maintain such a level of income, once the relative importance of the exporting sector had been reduced, it would have been necessary for some changes to take place, which obviously did not occur. In fact, only intensive development of the sector unconnected with foreign trade could have made up for the relative decline in exports. Usually,

[4] W. W. Rostow, *The Process of Economic Growth* (Oxford, 1953), Appendix III.

activities unconnected with foreign trade are those industries and services situated in urban zones. There is, however, no indication that the country's urbanization had undergone any speed-up in that period.[5] What probably happened was a relative increase in the subsistence sector in the form already described in Chapter 15. The subsistence economy being of much lower productivity than the exporting sector, an increase in its relative importance in a phase of comparative stagnation of the exporting sector would necessarily have to be reflected in a reduction in per capita income for the population as a whole. The value of exports per inhabitant among the free population, which had been about 2 pounds sterling per year in the mid-nineteenth century, was now a little more than one pound. Even assuming, as an extreme example, that the proportion of export value in the national product had suffered a reduction to one-sixth of that product—for the latter years of the eighteenth century I suggest the hypothesis of one-fourth—the average per capita income of the free population[6] would have been reduced from $50 to $43 in terms of present-day purchasing power. Granting a margin of error in such calculations, it can be assumed that the trend was toward a decline in the first half of the century. It is likewise probable that per capita income at the time had reached a lower point than in the entire colonial era, if the various regions of the country are considered as a whole.

[5] The population of the city of Rio de Janeiro, the most prosperous urban center in the country at that time, was apparently growing at an annual rate of 1.3 per cent, identical with that of the country as a whole. See estimates of the population of the city in *Anuário Estatístico do Brasil, op. cit.,* p. 1294.

[6] I assume the population in 1850 to have been 7 million, including 2 million slaves, which are not taken into consideration in figuring the per capita income.

20. THE GENESIS OF
THE COFFEE ECONOMY

By the mid-nineteenth century it would have been difficult for an observer studying the Brazilian economy to conceive the scope of the transformations which were to occur within its framework during the next fifty years. Three-quarters of a century of stagnation or decay had elapsed. The rapid, migration-based population growth of the first three-quarters of the eighteenth century had been followed by a relatively slow vegetative growth. Phases of progress, such as the one in Maranhão, were predominantly local in their effects, and had no bearing on the country as a whole. The establishment of a rudimentary administrative system, a national bank, and a few other governmental projects—in addition to preserving national unity—were the net results of that protracted period of difficulties. The basic national problem—that of the expansion of Brazil's labor force —had come to a literal dead end. The African source of supply had been stopped without any alternative solution in sight.

To the present-day observer it does seem perfectly clear that in order to overcome the phase of stagnation Brazil then needed to become reintegrated into the expanding lines of international trade. In a country without techniques of her own and in which almost no capital was being created for use in new activities, the only way out for economic development in the nineteenth century was international trade. Development based on the internal market becomes possible only when the economic system attains a certain degree of complexity with relative technological autonomy. I have already discussed the importance of the dynamic drive of the exporting sector to the development of the United States in the first half of the nineteenth century. It would have been impossible also to rely on an influx of foreign capital into a stagnating economy. The few loans contracted abroad in the first half of the century were for nonproductive purposes, and therefore enormously aggravated an already problematic fiscal situation. With the stagnation of exports, and because the government could not increase duties on imports, the servicing of the external debt was bound to cause serious fiscal troubles which in turn helped to reduce public credit. The influx of capital in the nineteenth century was chiefly aimed at indirect investments. To raise funds in the capital markets it was necessary to provide projects either with the most attractive prospects or with guarantees of interest by whoever had the necessary credit available. Possibilities of presenting attractive projects in a stagnating economy were practically nil. Further, what credit could be sought by the government of a country with a decaying economy and whose tax-collecting capabilities were restricted? To be able to depend upon the coöperation of foreign capital, the economy must first of all resume growth by its own efforts.[1]

---

[1] The notion that British capital did not come to Brazil during the first half of the past century on account of the conflict with the British government over the persistence of the African slave trade does not seem to have much basis in fact. Poor relations with the British government continued for a number of years after the suspension of the traffic without preventing the emergence of a substantial flow of capital. When in 1863 the British government, on a trifling excuse, blockaded the port of Rio de Janeiro and seized several Brazilian vessels for the purpose of intimidating and dominating the imperial government, there was a strong movement of protest in England, headed by financial groups with interests in Brazil. An article in the *Daily News* of February 12, 1863, asked: "Who of us . . . can trade safely with Brazil or any other country, who can buy Brazilian or foreign bonds of any kind, who can with common prudence invest his money in the railway shares of small and defenceless states . . . if mines like this are to be sprung under his feet by his own government?" Quoted by Alan K. Manchester, *British Pre-eminence in Brazil: Its Rise and Decline* (Chapel Hill, 1953), p. 283.

Possibilities for traditional Brazilian exports to recuperate their necessary dynamic trend and to afford the country a new stage of development were remote in the mid-nineteenth century. The declining trend in prices of the respective articles has already been mentioned. The sugar market became less promising day by day. Beet sugar—production of which had been developed in continental Europe at the time of the Napoleonic Wars—had become strongly rooted in vested interests within the traditional importing markets. The British market continued to be supplied by the West Indies colonies. In the United States, the fastest expanding import market, production was widely developed in Louisiana, which had been purchased from the French in 1803. There was also a new source of supply in the sugar market, prospects of which might be said to be expanding extraordinarily, almost from day to day. Taking advantage of extremely low freight rates for shipments to the United States, Cuba had opened her ports to all friendly nations while still a Spanish colony and had become the main supplier of the North American market. Cuban exports, which had amounted to only 20,000 tons a year at the end of the eighteenth century, rose to more than 300,000 tons by the mid-nineteenth century,[2] more than trebling Brazilian sales for the same period.

The situation of cotton, second article on the Brazilian export list in the early nineteenth century, was even worse than that of sugar. North American production, integrated within the interests of the British importing market, in addition to benefiting from fast development of internal demand,[3] also

[2] For data on Cuban exports, see Ramiro Guerra y Sánchez, *Azúcar y Población en las Antillas* (Havana, 1944), Appendix II.

[3] The consumption of cotton in the United States increased from an annual average of 32.5 million pounds in 1804–1814, to 239.0 million pounds in 1844–1854; in England the increase was from 89 million in 1811–1819 to 640 million in 1845–1854. See W. W. Rostow, *The Process of Economic Growth* (Oxford, 1953), Appendix I.

enjoyed relatively low freight rates. Organized under the slavery system, with relatively abundant manpower and with abundant availabilities of first-class soil (which were utilized destructively), it held complete sway over the market. Cotton production had been a highly profitable business for some Brazilian regions, especially Maranhão, at a time when the product was selling at relatively high prices. But when large-scale production commenced in the United States and cotton became the main raw material for world trade, prices fell by more than two-thirds and have remained at that level—with some fluctuations—since the 1830's. At such price levels the profitability of the cotton business was extremely low for Brazil and was a mere complement to the subsistence economy in the producing regions. Not until the outbreak of the United States Civil War, temporarily excluding North American cotton from world markets, did the cotton economy in Brazil enter a new phase of prosperity in the nineteenth century.[4]

Tobacco, leather, rice, and cocoa were minor products whose markets did not afford great possibilities of expansion. In the leather market, River Plate production was gaining an increasing share, whereas rice output was losing ground to United States growers who had introduced fundamental changes into methods of cultivation. Tobacco had lost the African market with the interruption of the slave trade, and exports had to be shifted to other regions. Cocoa—consumption of which was only then beginning to gain popularity—could at best be viewed as a hopeful future prospect. Brazil's problem was in finding exportable products in whose production land was a basic factor. In fact, land was the sole produc-

---

[4] The difficulty in competing with United States cotton faced not only Brazil. It is well known that the British government, concerned with excessive dependence on United States sources, appointed more than one commission to study the possibilities of developing cotton production inside the empire, but results were mediocre.

tion factor abundant in Brazil. There was almost no capital, and manpower was basically composed of a reservoir of a little more than two million slaves, most of whom were involved either in the sugar industry or in domestic service.

By the middle of the century, however, the predominance of a relatively new product had already been observed. The new item had production characteristics entirely in line with Brazil's ecological conditions. Coffee, though brought to Brazil in the early eighteenth century and cultivated in many parts of the country for local consumption, acquired commercial importance only at the end of the century when a rise in prices was caused by the disorganization of another great producing center: the then French colony of Haiti. In Brazil's first decade as an independent nation, coffee already accounted for 18 per cent of exports by value, taking third place in the list after sugar and cotton. In the subsequent two decades coffee moved into the lead, and came to comprise more than 40 per cent of the country's exports by value. As already noted, the whole increase in the value of Brazilian exports in the first half of the nineteenth century was attributable solely to coffee.

When coffee became an export article, production was concentrated in the hilly regions around the capital. In those areas close to Rio de Janeiro there was a relatively abundant supply of manpower because of the decline of the mining economy. Furthermore, given the proximity of the port, there were no problems of transportation, inasmuch as the means of access to the port—the mule convoy—was abundant. Hence the first phase of coffee expansion was carried out with the utilization of preëxisting and underutilized resources. Rising prices, since the last decade of the eighteenth century, had caused expanding production in a number of areas of the Western Hemisphere and Asia. That expansion was followed by a period of declining prices which extended through the 1830's and 1840's. The fall in prices did not, however, discourage Brazilian producers, who found in coffee a chance to utilize productive resources nearly idle since the decline of the mining economy. In fact, coffee exports increased more than five times between 1821–1830 and 1841–1850, although average price levels had declined about 40 per cent in that period.

The second and—especially—the third quarters of the nineteenth century were basically periods of early growth for the coffee economy. The coffee enterprise permitted intensive utilization of slave manpower, being similar in this way to the sugar economy. It did, however, entail a much lower degree of capitalization inasmuch as utilization of the land factor was more important. Capital was fixed, the coffee plantation being a permanent form of cultivation, and the monetary needs for replacement were much smaller than in the sugar economy, since the equipment used was simpler and, more often than not, of local manufacture. Organized on the basis of slave manpower, the coffee enterprise enjoyed monetary costs still lower than those of the sugar undertakings. Hence only a sharp rise in manpower prices could interrupt its growth, if abundant land were available. In its first stage, the coffee economy had available to it the underutilized slave manpower reservoir in the former mining region, which accounts for its development in spite of the scarcely favorable price trend. In the third quarter of the century, coffee prices showed a sizable upward trend while sugar prices remained depressed, and strong pressure was created toward transfers of manpower from the north to the south.

The period of early development of the coffee economy was likewise that of the formation of a new managerial class destined to play a substantial part in the country's future development. That class initially comprised men from the region itself. The city of Rio de Janeiro was the main Brazilian consumption market, and the consumption habits of its population had undergone a substantial change at the time of arrival of the Portuguese court. Supplying that market began to be the main economic activity of the nuclei of rural population which had been settled in the south of the province of Minas Gerais as an aftermath of mining expansion. Trade in food and beasts of burden for its transportation was an economic activity of some importance in that part of the country, and led to the formation of a group of local commercial entrepreneurs. Many of these men, who had accumulated some assets in the trading and transportation of food and coffee, turned toward the actual production of coffee and became pioneers in its expansion.

If the formative processes of the ruling classes in the sugar and coffee economies are compared, some fundamental differences will readily be noticed. At the time of the formation of the ruling class in sugar, commercial activities were the monopoly of groups established either in Portugal or in the Low Countries. The production and commercial phases were kept strictly apart, and the men in charge of production lacked any perspective of the sugar economy as a whole. All fundamental decisions were made at the commercial stage. Thus isolated, the members of the sugar-producing class could not develop a clear concept of their own interests. With the passing of time they began to lose their true economic function, and executive tasks came to be mere matters of routine, carried out by overseers and other employees. It can therefore be easily seen how the former entrepreneurs evolved into a class of idle landlords living within a small rural environment whose eventual descendants were to be the easygoing patriarch class to which so much space is dedicated in the essays of twentieth-century sociologists on Northeastern Brazil. Separation from Portugal did not bring about any fundamental changes, because the production phase remained isolated and guided by men of purely ruralistic spirit. As a result, British interests were able completely to dominate the commercial activities of the sugar-producing Northeast. Once the Portuguese groups were weakened, a void arose which was easily filled.

The coffee economy was formed under quite different conditions. Since the beginning, the vanguard was composed of men with business experience. Throughout the early phase of development, production and trading interests were intermingled. The new ruling class was formed through a struggle along a broad front: acquisition of land, manpower recruiting, internal transportation, marketing at the ports, official contacts, involvement in financial and economic policies. The proximity of the country's capital was of course of great advantage to the rulers of the coffee economy. Soon they were to grasp the enormous importance of the government as an instrument of economic action. This trend toward subordination of the political apparatus to the interests of an economic group attained its climax with the achievement of state autonomy at the time of the proclamation of the republic. The central government submitted to interests too heterogeneous to respond with the necessary alacrity and efficiency to the demands of local interests. Decentralization of power permitted even more complete integration of the groups ruling the coffee economy with the political and administrative machinery. But what particularly singles out the coffee men is not merely the fact that they acquired control of the government; it is rather the fact that they utilized that control to attain objectives perfectly well defined within the context of a specific policy. It was this clear concept of their own interests that differentiated them from other dominating groups previously existing or contemporary.

At the end of the third quarter of the nineteenth century, the details of the Brazilian economic problem had undergone a basic change. The product which was to provide for the country's reintegration into the expanding currents of world trade had emerged; and once the early developmental stage was concluded, the coffee economy found itself in a position to self-finance its extraordinary subsequent expansion; cadres were formed within the new ruling class which were to assume the leadership of the great coffee expansion. However, the manpower problem still remained to be solved.

21. THE MANPOWER PROBLEM: POTENTIAL INTERNAL SUPPLY

By the mid-nineteenth century, the working force of the Brazilian economy was basically composed of a mass of slaves amounting at most to perhaps some two million persons. Any planned enterprise had to come to grips with the inelasticity of manpower supply. The first population census taken in Brazil, in 1872, shows there were approximately 1.5 million slaves in the country at that time. Taking into account the fact that the number of slaves at the beginning of the century had been somewhat more than one million, and that in the first half of the nineteenth century probably many more than half a million were imported, it may be deduced that the death rate among them exceeded the birth rate.[1] It is interesting to observe the

---

[1] Complete data on the entry of slaves into Brazil, even during the period of political independence, are not known. Especially irregular are the data relating to entries into the ports in the north. Between 1827 and 1830 there was great intensification of the traffic, as in the latter year "it was supposed" to cease under the agreement with England. Entries into the port of Rio exceeded 47,000 in 1828 and 57,000 in 1829, but fell off to 32,000 in 1830. These imports were evidently abnormally large, inasmuch as they caused substantial unbalance in the market and prices fell by half between 1829 and 1831. Another period of heavy imports was that preceding the total cessation of the traffic, which occurred between 1851 and 1852. As a matter of fact, throughout the five-year period 1845–1849, average yearly imports amounted to 48,000 slaves. It can hardly be supposed that total imports in the first half of the nineteenth century were lower than 750,000 (an annual average of 15,000), but it is also not very likely that they much exceeded one million. Imports into the United States between 1800 and 1860 amounted to about 320,000 slaves, of whom some 270,000 were smuggled in after the abolition of the slave traffic in 1808. The maximum figure for im-

different ways in which the slave inventory evolved in the two main countries involved in slavery in the Western Hemisphere: the United States and Brazil. Each of the two began the nineteenth century with an inventory of nearly one million slaves. Brazilian imports during the century were three times as numerous as those of the United States. Nevertheless, at the outbreak of the Civil War, the United States had a slave working force of about four million whereas Brazil at the same period had roughly 1.5 million. The explanation for this phenomenon lies in the high rate of growth of the North American slave population, a great part of which lived on relatively small estates in regions of the so-called "Old" South. Feeding and working conditions in the Southern states were probably relatively favorable, inasmuch as with the continuing rise in the price of slaves the masters began deriving some income from the natural growth of the slave population.[2] The supply of

---

ports in a single decade (75,000) was attained in the period immediately preceding the Civil War. Data relative to the United States cited by L. C. Gray, *History of Agriculture in the Southern United States to 1860* (Washington, 1933), II, p. 650.

[2] Historians in the Southern United States persistently deny that a slave-breeding industry grew up in the so-called "selling states." Obviously this is a delicate subject, in which it would not always be easy to define the true meaning of the "good intentions" involved. Actually, the efficient slave breeder would always be the one who succeeded in making the slaves' lives happier. In the words of one outstanding United States historian: "On many well managed plantations there were positive, though entirely ethical, measures for encouraging the rate of increase. The partial exemption from labor during pregnancy, additions of extra food, clothing and other comforts after childbirth—these were powerful stimuli in the direction that coincided with the master's self-interest. On some plantations a woman with six or more children was exempted from all labor. On other plantations ten children exempted the mother from field work." *Ibid.*, p. 663. "A planter here and there may have exerted a control of mating in the interest of industrial and commercial eugenics, but it is extremely doubtful that any appreciable

slaves in the new Southern states, where the great cotton expansion was taking place, began to depend basically on the growth of the slave population of the old slavery states. In fact, between 1820 and 1860 the number of slaves transferred from the seller states to the buyer states seems to have reached 742,-000.[3] Home-bred slaves naturally presented a number of advantages, since they were culturally integrated into their working communities—the plantations—had been better fed, were already acquainted with the English language, and so on.

The fact that the Brazilian slave population had a death rate far higher than its birth rate indicates that living conditions were probably extremely precarious. The diet of the slave masses working on sugar plantations was especially deficient. When the demand for slaves to work on coffee plantations in southern Brazil began to grow, internal traffic became intensified to the detriment of regions already operating at reduced profitability. The depressed cotton regions, especially Maranhão, suffered because of severe manpower drainage toward the south. The sugar region, with more capital coverage, was in a position better to protect itself. Moreover, it is probable that the reduction in the supply of Africans and the rising prices of the latter had led to an intensification in the utilization of the slave, thus causing further depletion of the slave population.

With Africa, the sole important source of immigration, cut off, the manpower issue became more serious and called for an urgent solution. To understand the nature of this problem, consideration must be given to certain features of the Brazilian

---

number of masters attempted any direct hastening of slave increase." U. B. Phillips, *American Negro Slavery* (New York, 1918), p. 362. In any event, in no state was legal stability granted to the family of the slaves: the children could be taken away from the parents and the wife from the husband, to be sold in different directions.

[3] Gray, *op. cit.*, p. 650.

economy at the time and the way it was expanding. The growth of European economies in the nineteenth century consisted fundamentally of a technological revolution. As new techniques were adopted, successive sectors of the previously existing economic system disintegrated. Because such disintegration was extremely rapid in the initial phases, the manpower supply grew rapidly enough to supply the expanding mechanized sector and exert strong pressure on wages. On the other hand, the disintegration of the pre-capitalist system intensified the urbanization process, which in turn made medical and social assistance easier, thus entailing an intensification in the growth of the population. As a matter of fact, a substantial increase in the rate of population growth was recorded in England during the last quarter of the eighteenth and first quarter of the nineteenth century despite the fact that, according to the most authoritative scholars, it can hardly be denied that during this same period living conditions for the working classes took a definite turn for the worse.[4]

In Brazil, growth took place merely in extent. It consisted of increasing utilization of the available factor—land—through the incorporation of greater quantities of manpower. Thus, the key factor to the solution of the entire economic problem lay in the manpower supply. The question might therefore be raised: Was there not a potential source of manpower in the ample subsistence sector, in permanent process of expansion? This is a matter which must be made quite clear if the nature of the development of the Brazilian economy in that and subsequent stages is to be understood.

The subsistence sector, running from the north to the far south of Brazil, was characterized by its extreme dispersion. Because it was based on cattle breeding and on farming with

[4] For a recent reappraisal of this last problem, see E. J. Hobshawn, "The British Standard of Living 1790–1850," in *Economic History Review* (August, 1957).

most rudimentary techniques, its economic density was reduced to a minimum. Although land was the most abundant factor involved, ownership of that land was highly concentrated. The system of the *sesmarias* (vacant lands granted in enormous extensions) had contributed to the fact that landownership, previously a royal monopoly, passed into the hands of a few persons having access to royal favor. However, this was not the fundamental aspect of the problem; because land was abundant, there was no direct payment for it involved. Within the subsistence economy each individual or family unit had to produce its own food. The *roça* (a clearing in the woods or cultivated tract) was and still is the basis of the subsistence economy. However, the subsistence farmer does not merely live off the produce of his cultivated tract. He is linked with a major economic group—most often engaged in cattle breeding —whose leader is the landowner and within which he has his roça. For that group he performs assorted tasks, of an economic nature or otherwise, receiving a small remuneration which provides him with coverage of minimum monetary expenses. At the level of the roça, the system is exclusively of a subsistence nature; at the level of the major unit, it is of a mixed character with the importance of the monetary strip varying from region to region and from year to year within each region.

If land is abundantly available, the subsistence system naturally tends to grow and this growth most often implies a reduction in the relative importance of the monetary strip. The capital available for the tenant (*roçeiro* is of a minimum type, and the method he utilizes for occupying new land is of the most primitive kind. Groups working together fell the larger trees and then use fire as the sole means of clearing the terrain. Among felled trunks and stumps not completely consumed by the fire, they plant their crops. For the bare purpose of feeding a family this farming technique is considered adequate. It has commonly been alleged in Brazil that the reason for this primitive farming lies in the habits of the *caboclo,** though actually the caboclo is himself merely a consequence of the subsistence economy. Even if he had much more advanced farming techniques available to him, the man in a subsistence economy would be compelled to abandon them, inasmuch as the product of his labors would have no economic value. Regression of production techniques and forms of work organization would for all practical purposes eventually transform such a farmer into a caboclo.[5]

Although the more important unit in the subsistence economy was in reality the individual farmed tract, from the social point of view the most significant one was that under the leadership of the landlord. What basically interested the large proprietor was to have the greatest possible number of persons living within his holdings, it being up to each one of them to look after his own sustenance. Thus the landlord at a moment's notice could count upon having available such manpower as he might need. Furthermore, in view of the conditions prevailing in those regions, the prestige of each proprietor was dependent upon the number of men he could utilize at a given moment for any particular purpose. Thus the tenant in the subsistence economy, though not tied to the land by any title of property, was actually chained by social links to a group within which the mystique of loyalty to the leader was cultivated for the preservation of that social entity.

* Men working in subsistence agriculture, chiefly Indian half-breed.— Translators.

[5] An acute observer of certain aspects of the Brazilian economy as of the beginning of the present century, Pierre Denis, has the following comment on one of the colonies of Europeans which the Brazilian government established at the cost of high expenditures and subsidies. "As regards farming, they have adopted the customs of the caboclo, that is, the native Brazilian worker. They have let themselves become corrupted, the Director of the colony tells me." *Le Brésil au XXe siècle* (Paris, 1928), p. 223.

Except in some regions of major population concentration and somewhat different characteristics—such as southern Minas Gerais—the subsistence economy was generally so dispersed that manpower recruiting from it would have been an extremely hazardous job, calling for great mobilization of resources. As a matter of fact, such recruiting would be practicable only if the coöperation of the large landowner class could be relied on. Experience showed, however, that such coöperation would be difficult to achieve, because an entire way of living, a social organization, and a political power setup were at stake.

Not only in the subsistence system was available manpower working at the lowest rates of productivity and capable of being considered as a potential manpower reserve. In the urban areas, too, a mass of underemployed population had likewise been concentrated, which could scarcely find any permanent occupation. The main hindrances here were those related to the discipline of farming activities and the living conditions on the large farms. Difficulties of adaptation of such manpower, and—to a lesser degree—of that coming from the primitive subsistence system, gave support to the view that native free manpower was not suitable for large-scale farming. Consequently, even at times when a solution to the manpower problem seemed most uncertain, there was no move toward the idea of widespread internal recruiting financed by the government.[6] Some thought was given to importing Asiatic manpower under a system of semiservitude along the lines of that

---

[6] There prevailed in Brazil an attitude of extreme hostility toward any internal transfers of labor, which is not difficult to account for in view of the political power of the groups whose interests were thereby affected. For instance, when a government-financed plant was approved during the Campos Sales government (1898–1902) for transfer of the population of Ceará to the south, a large-scale campaign was organized to thwart its execution.

in the British and Dutch West Indies. By the third quarter of the nineteenth century, the problem of manpower supply in Brazil had become so serious that even to a man of such vision and experience as Mauá* no better solution occurred than that of the semiservitude of Asiatics.[7]

22. THE MANPOWER PROBLEM: EUROPEAN IMMIGRATION

As an alternative solution to the manpower problem, it was suggested that a flow of European immigration be encouraged. The spectacle of the enormous flow of population leaving Europe for the United States seemed to indicate the course to be taken. Even before independence, "colonies" of European immigrants had begun under government initiative. Yet those settlements—which according to the phrase of Mauá "weighed with an iron hand" upon the country's finances—led an anemic, vegetative life, making no contribution toward a change in the problem of inadequate manpower supply. The fundamental issue was to increase the Brazilian working force available for large-scale agriculture. There was no precedent in the Western Hemisphere for European-originated manpower migration intended for work on large plantations. The obstacles faced by the British in coping with the problem of the manpower deficit on their Caribbean plantations are well

---

* Baron (later Viscount) Mauá (1813–1889), financial and industrial leader under the Brazilian empire, organized the Bank of Brazil.— Translators.

[7] Visconde de Mauá, *Autobiography* (Rio de Janeiro, 1943), pp. 218 and 226.

known. For instance, a great many of the Africans seized on ships dealing with Brazil were reëxported to the West Indies as "free" labor.[2]

In the United States, as we have seen, the basic solution came through a great intensifications in the growth of the slave population, largely because many slaves did not work on great plantations. Even though these two movements—the expansion of the plantations and the European migratory flow—were interconnected, they were actually autonomous phenomena. The expansion of the North American plantations would have taken place even without the European migratory current, although the latter, by expanding the internal demand for cotton and cheapening food supplies, gave an impulse to that expansion. The migratory current, however, could hardly be accounted for—at least on the scale observed during the first half of the century—without expansion of the plantations. Cotton bales are bulky[3] and take up much space aboard ship, whereas the manufactured goods imported by the North Americans were of great economic density—these facts favored a reduction in the return freight rates from Europe to the United States. It was this decline in passage rates—on both cargo and passenger-plus-cargo ships—that permitted such a volume of spontaneous emigration from Europe to the United States. These low rates in themselves would not have been sufficient inducement, however, for a heavy migratory current to be created. The fundamental factor was an expanding market upon

[2] "After emancipation . . . there was a serious shortage of labour which was partially met by various expedients. One of these was the importation of negroes freed from slave ships; 14,113 such freed slaves were for example imported from Sierra Leone between 1840 and 1850. Trinidad and British Guiana at a later date imported Indian indentured labour on a large scale . . ." Sir Alan Pin, *Colonial Agricultural Production* (Oxford, 1946), p. 90.

[3] Besides cotton, even bulkier lumber exports acquired great importance in United States sales to England.

which immigrants relied in order to sell the products of their labor. This expansion was to a great extent a reflection of the development of Southern plantations on the basis of slave labor.

The colonies established in various parts of Brazil by the imperial government were totally lacking in any economic basis; their *raison d'être* was a belief in the innate superiority of European labor, especially of a race different from that of the Europeans who had originally colonized Brazil. Transportation and installation costs were paid by the government, and public works were promoted for the purpose of providing jobs for the colonists. Some of these projects were prolonged to an absurd extent. And in almost every instance in which—after heavy expenditure—the colony was left to its own fate, it tended to wither and revert to a mere subsistence economy. A good illustration is the German colonization in Rio Grande do Sul. In 1824 the imperial government set up the first colony in the region in São Leopoldo, and after the protracted civil war (1835–1845) the provincial government made heavy investments in order to recommence and intensify immigration from that source. But the life of the colonies was extremely precarious because, with no market available for production surpluses, the monetary sector soon atrophied and the colony reverted to a rudimentary economic system of subsistence. European travelers passing through those regions were surprised at the colonists' primitive ways of living, and ascribed the evils afflicting them to the country's inadequate laws and to a number of other similar reasons. The practical result of all this was that a movement of public opinion arose in Europe opposed to emigration to the slave-exploiting empire in the Americas, and as early as 1859 German emigration to Brazil was prohibited.

If the colonies were to make a success of an immigration policy, and by their example attract spontaneous currents of settlement, they would have needed to be engaged from the start in profitable productive activities. Such an objective could be attained only by integrating the colonies into lines of production of an exportable article or by guiding it immediately into the production of articles for which a market was available within the country. Production for export was organized along the lines of great plantations requiring an amount of fixed capital not accessible to colonists in the installation stage. If, despite everything, they decided to plant coffee, the colonists would be compelled to compete with enterprises exploiting slave manpower. Furthermore, it is perfectly understandable that the ruling class of the coffee economy, whose influence on the government was already decisive, did not display any interest in subsidizing immigration which would be of no assistance in the solution of the manpower problem on their plantations but would instead compete with them in the coffee market. On the other hand, the possibility of producing for the internal market depended on expansion of that market, which in turn presupposed the development of an exporting economy. And as the key to a solution to the problem of exports lay in the supply of manpower, this brought the whole matter back to where it had started.

Recognizing that the colonization policy of the imperial government made no contribution toward a solution of the manpower problem in large-scale agriculture, the ruling classes of the coffee economy took a direct interest in the matter. In 1852 one of the great coffee planters, Senator Vergueiro, decided to recruit workers from Europe on his own account. Obtaining from the government a subsidy to cover cost of transportation, he succeeded in transferring eighty families of German peasants to his farm near the town of Limeira, in what is today the state of São Paulo. This initiative aroused some interest, and more than two thousand persons were similarly transferred, mostly from German states and from Switzerland. Senator Vergueiro's idea was merely an adaptation of the system whereby English emigration to the Southern United States had been organized in colonial times: the immigrant sold his future labor. In the British colonies, such financing was done by the entrepreneur. In Brazil, the government covered the major part of the financing: the passages for the families. It is easy to understand how this system could quickly degenerate into a form of temporary servitude, to which there was not even a set time limit as in the British colonies. In reality, the actual cost of immigration was entirely paid by the immigrant, financially the weaker party. The government financed the operation, but the colonist mortgaged his own future and that of his family, whereas the farmer retained for himself all the advantages. The colonist was obligated to sign a contract whereby he was committed not to leave the farmer until his entire debt was paid. It is easy to imagine to what extent the abuses of such a system could grow under the conditions of isolation in which the colonists were living, with the farmer the only source of political power. The reaction in Europe—where everything about a slave-exploiting country aroused immediate concern—was not slow to appear. In 1867 a German observer forwarded to the International Society for Emigration a report showing that "colonists" emigrating to Brazilian coffee plantations were actually subjected to a system of disguised slavery.[4] The approach adopted was clearly at fault, and it was essential for all aspects of the problem to be reappraised.

From the 1860's on, the issue of manpower supply became particularly serious. The improvement in prices made coffee growing an increasingly attractive proposition; furthermore, the sharp rise in cotton prices caused by the Civil War in the United States sparked a great expansion in cotton-growing states in northern Brazil, with the result that slave traffic toward the south was even more restricted. Pressure of events

[4] For a critical appraisal of the Haupt report, see Pierre Denis, *Le Brésil au XXe siècle* (Paris, 1928), pp. 122–125.

obviously called for far-reaching measures. The evolution began with the system of payments to the colonists.[5] The regime initially adopted was that of partnership, within which the colonist's income always remained uncertain because he had to assume half the risk faced by the large landlord. The loss of a crop could bring poverty to the colonist because of his precarious financial situation. In the 1860's a mixed system was introduced whereby the colonist had some guaranty as to the main part of his income. His basic job consisted of tending a number of coffee trees, and for this task he received an annual monetary salary. This salary was supplemented by variable wages paid at harvest time according to the volume of the crop.

The second problem calling for a solution was that of traveling expenses. Because the colonist was responsible for payment of traveling expenses for himself and his family, it was inevitable that fear of a threat to his future freedom would arise. Since the coffee farmers were those most interested in immigration, it was only natural that transportation costs should be paid by them; but if this solution were adopted, only the wealthier farmers would be able to afford to promote the coming of immigrants. On the other hand, since it was not possible to force colonists to stay in a particular place, the farmers would be paying for the transportation of immigrants who might work for somebody else. The solution came in 1870 when the imperial government proceeded to defray the transportation costs of immigrants who were to work on coffee farms. Furthermore, the farmer had to pay immigrants' expenses during the first year of their activity—during the stage of maturing of their work. The farmer had also to make avail-

---

[5] By assimilation with the immigrants who, on the initiative of the imperial government, had come for the purpose of forming settlement colonies, the world colono ("colonist") came to be applied to every immigrant coming in to do farm work, although in nearly every instance these were mere wage-earning hands.

able to the immigrants plots of land on which they could grow basic food for the sustenance of their families. In this manner immigrants had their transportation and installation costs paid and had reasonable expectations of future income. This series of measures made it possible, for the first time in the Western Hemisphere, to secure a heavy migratory flow of European origin for work on the great plantations.

Despite all this, it is probable that such immigration would not have reached the high levels it did except for a series of favorable conditions of supply. During the same period in which the problem was evolving favorably toward a solution in Brazil, the process of political unification of Italy was taking place, with far-reaching economic consequences to the peninsula. The southern region of Italy—the so-called Kingdom of the Two Sicilies—with its lesser degree of development and lower farming productivity, found itself in serious straits because of competition from the more highly developed northern regions. Hence southern Italy's industries—textile production had attained a relatively high degree of development—became disorganized, and a state of chronic depression arose for the southern provinces. Pressure on the land by the rural population surplus fed to the growth of social unrest. The migratory solution, through emigration, therefore seemed a literal safety valve.

Bases were established for the formation of the large migratory current that was to permit expansion of coffee production in what is today the state of São Paulo. The numbers of European immigrants entering that state rose from 13,000 in the 1870's to 184,000 in the following decade, and to 609,000 in the 1890's. Total immigration figures for the last quarter of the century amounted to 803,000, of which 577,000 came from Italy.[6]

---

[6] For data on the number of immigrants and their points of origin, see *Anuário Estatístico do Brasil,* 1937–1939, Appendix.

23. THE MANPOWER PROBLEM: AMAZONIC TRANSHUMANCE

In addition to the large migratory flow of European origin toward the coffee region, another great population transfer occurred in Brazil in the last quarter of the nineteenth century and first decade of the twentieth: a transfer from the Northeast to the Amazon region.

The economy of the Amazon had been declining since the end of the eighteenth century. Once the ingenious system of exploitation of native manpower devised by the Jesuit fathers was abandoned, the region reverted to a state of economic lethargy. In a small part of the state of Pará farming for export was developed closely in line with the evolution of Maranhão, with which the former had been commercially integrated through the operations of the trading company founded at the time of the Marquis of Pombal. Cotton and rice also went through a phase of prosperity in the region during the Napoleonic Wars, though never attaining figures meaningful for the country as a whole. The foundations of the economy of the Amazon basin remained as always the same products extracted from the forests which had enabled Jesuit penetration into that extensive region in the beginning. Of those extractive products, cocoa continued to be the most important. Its method of production, however, did not permit the product to attain major economic significance. Average exports in the 1840's were 2,900 tons a year; in the following decade they rose to 3,500 tons, falling off to 3,300 tons in the 'sixties. The production of other forest articles was always faced by the same difficulty: the almost nonexistent population and the exacting task of organizing production on the basis of scarce local native manpower. For example, this was true of rubber, which had been exported since the 1820's. Such exports averaged 460 tons a year in the 'forties, 1,900 tons in the 'fifties, and 3,700 tons in the 'sixties. At the same time rubber prices were climbing. From £45 per ton in the 'forties, the average export price rose to £118 in the next decade. In the 'sixties it was £125 per ton, and in the 'seventies £182.[1]

Rubber was destined to become—at the end of the nineteenth century and in the early twentieth—the raw material with the fastest-growing demand in the world market. Just as the textile industry had been a feature of the industrial revolution at the end of the eighteenth century, and railroad building a feature of the mid-nineteenth century, the internal-combustion–vehicle industry was to be the main dynamic factor of the industrialized economies from the 1890's to the 1930's. Because rubber was an extractive product, and since most of the rubber trees then existing were concentrated in the Amazon basin, the problem of increasing production to meet growing world demand was an extremely difficult one. There was obviously a need for a long-term solution, because the possibilities of increasing production in the Amazon basin did not seem to be very great. Once it had been shown that one or more of the varieties of rubber-producing trees could be adapted to other regions with similar environmental conditions, rubber production could be developed in places where an already existing supply of manpower and resources was adequate to cover the protracted period of growth.

However, the speed with which the demand fr rubber was increasing in industrialized countries at the end of the nineteenth century called for a short-term solution. The evolution of the world rubber economy thus took place in two stages: in the first, an emergency solution was found to the problem of supply; in the second, production was organized on a rational

[1] *Anuário Estatístico do Brasil,* 1937–1939, Appendix.

basis, providing means of supplying the rapid expansion of world demand.[2] The first stage of the rubber economy was developed entirely in the Amazon region, in the face of great difficulties created by the environment. Prices were to continue their upward trend, reaching an average of £512 per ton for the three-year period 1909–1911—a figure more than ten times higher than the prevailing level for the previous half-century. The conspicuous price rise clearly indicated that the supply of rubber was inadequate and that an alternative solution was bound to emerge. In fact, when Far Eastern rubber was introduced into the market on a regular basis after World War I, prices were permanently reduced to a level somewhat lower than £100 per ton.

Even more markedly than with coffee, expansion of rubber production in the Amazon was a question of manpower supply. Although possibilities of increase were not great, exports of Brazilian rubber rose from an average of 6,000 tons in the 1870's to 11,000 tons a year in the 1880's, 21,000 tons in the 1890's, and 35,000 tons in the first decade of the twentieth century. This increase in production was exclusively due to the influx of manpower, because production methods did not change at all. Available data on migratory flow into the Amazon region during the period are unreliable, and concern almost exclusively embarkations at Northeastern ports. Yet the populations of the states of Pará and Amazonas grew from 329,000 in 1872 to 695,000 inhabitants in 1900. Assuming an annual growth of 1 per cent—in view of the admittedly poor health conditions in the region—the internal flow must have amounted to 260,000 persons, disregarding those who had already settled in the region later to become the territory of Acre. Of this immigrant total, about 200,000 arrived in the 1890's, as may be inferred from a comparison between the

[2] During the 1940's the third stage of the rubber cycle was to commence, with progressive replacement of natural rubber by synthetic.

1890 and 1900 censuses. Surmising a similar influx in the first decade of the twentieth century, the shift in population toward the Amazon basin was not less than half a million persons.

This enormous human migration clearly indicates that at the end of the nineteenth century there was already a substantial manpower reservoir in existence in Brazil. Furthermore, all indications are that if it had been impossible to solve the problem of coffee farming with European immigrants, an alternative solution would have appeared within Brazil itself. Apparently European immigration left the Northeastern population available for the expansion of rubber production.

The population of the Northeast, as already indicated, had been occupied since the first century of colonization in two economic sectors: sugar growing and cattle breeding. The depression of the sugar economy in the second half of the eighteenth century caused the progressive transformation of cattle-breeding activities into a subsistence economy. In such an economy, population tends to grow according to the availability of food, which in turn directly depends on the availability of land. A comparison of the evolution of the subsistence nuclei in various parts of Brazil shows this problem of land availability in its true significance. European settlement colonies in Rio Grande do Sul, Paraná, and Santa Catarina were in particularly favorable situations. The quality and abundance of their land provided them with a more than adequate food supply, even at a low level of agricultural technique. Thus in spite of the primitive ways of their monetary economy, those colonies had the highest rate of population growth, which was a cause of amazement to European visitors at the end of the nineteenth century and early twentieth. The large populations of the settlements and the surplus production of food therein were to become basic factors in the rapid development of the southern region of the country in subsequent periods when the expansion of the internal market, spurred by coffee development, created incentives previously nonexistent.

In the central region, where the mining economy had once flourished, population tended to be scattered over wide areas because of the scarcity of good land. A migratory current toward the state of São Paulo thus formed well before the introduction of coffee farming there.[3] Another trend headed toward Mato Grosso, first occupying the well-irrigated lands of the Triângulo Mineiro (Mining Triangle). The vanguard of such population transfers—except in settlement regions where land-ownership was the main concern of the working man—was always composed of enterprising individuals with some capital, who were soon to get property titles over great extensions of land; furthermore, utilization of that land was shared with many others within a subsistence economy system.

In the Northeast region a population expansion had been under way since the sixteenth century. In some subregions, in the second half of the nineteenth century, symptoms of population pressure on land resources became evident. The development of cotton farming in the first few decades of the nineteenth century had favored a diversification of economic activities, contributing to an intensification of population growth. In the 1860's, when the sharp rise in cotton prices was caused by the Civil War in the United States, cotton production was intensified and some regions, such as Ceará, were to experience for the first time a period of prosperity. Such waves of prosperity contributed, however, to the creation of a structural unbalance within the subsistence economy, to which the population always reverted in subsequent stages. That structural problem had become extremely serious at the time of the protracted drought from 1877 to 1880, when the region's

[3] On the transhumance of the population from the old mining regions, before the great coffee expansion phase, see Pierre Monbeig, *Pionniers et Planteurs de São Paulo* (Paris, 1952), pp. 116–120. This interesting work also contains a fine description of the physical environment of the coffee economy.

cattle disappeared completely and about 200,000 human beings starved to death. Action aimed at aiding the distressed
population had wisely been guided from the start toward the
promoting of emigration to other regions of Brazil, especially
the Amazon basin. The concentration in the seaboard cities
of refugees from the drought facilitated recruitment. On the
other hand, the prevailing conditions of utmost poverty hampered, at least for a time, the reaction of groups ruling over the
economy of the region, who saw in the drainage of manpower
the loss of their main source of wealth. Once the migratory
flow had started, it became easier to keep it under way. Interested in emigration, the government of the Amazon states
organized propaganda services and granted subsidies for costs
of transportation. In this way the great migratory current was
formed, permitting the expansion of rubber production in the
Amazon basin, and affording the world economy a breathing
space in which to prepare for a definitive solution to the
problem.

When the two great population movements in Brazil at the
end of the nineteenth century and in the early twentieth are
compared, some striking contrasts become apparent. The
European immigrant—of a demanding nature and aided by his
own government—arrived on the coffee plantation with all
expenses paid and with housing and sustenance costs paid until
the first crop. At the year's end he would be looking for another farm where greater advantages could be obtained on the
job. He would always have an available plot on which to plant
food crops essential to his family sustenance, which protected
him against unscrupulous merchants insofar as his main expenditures were concerned. The situation of the *nordestino*
(man from the Northeastern states) in the Amazon was quite
different: he started work already heavily in debt, because as
a rule he was compelled to reimburse the whole or a part of his
traveling expenses as well as the costs of working tools and
installation. To feed himself he was dependent on supplies

which were manipulated under a regime of strict monopoly by the same entrepreneur to whom he was indebted and who bought the product of his labor. The great distances and the precarious nature of his financial situation reduced the nordestino to a regime of servitude. Between the long treks through the forest and the solitude of the cabin wherein he lived, he was worn out in an isolation such as perhaps no other economic system has ever imposed on man. The dangers of the forest and the unhealthfulness of the environment also helped shorten his working life.[4]

The plans of the nordestino migrant bound for the Amazon —enticed either by the fanciful propaganda of agents paid by the rubber interests or by the example of the few fortunate ones who came back with some money—were based on the prices the product had attained in its best phases. When these prices declined permanently, poverty spread fast. Without means for returning home and unaware of what was happening to the world rubber economy, the migrant resigned himself to staying. Compelled to eke out his budget through local hunting and fishing activities, he regressed to the most primitive form of subsistence economy—that of the man living in the tropical

[4] The greater contrast between the two migratory movements is, however, to be seen in the results of the subsequent development of the two regions. The coffee economy, throughout fifty years of ups and downs, was to prove sufficiently sound to prolong itself into a process of industrialization. By the mid-twentieth century its population was to enjoy a relatively high standard of living—at least a good deal higher than that of the southern European regions from which that population had emigrated. The rubber economy, on the other hand, was destined to enter into a sudden and lasting state of prostration. The immigrant population was fated to be reduced to a state of extreme poverty in an environment in which it would be impossible to find a way out by adopting another production system of some profitability. A few years later it was found to have permanently declined to living conditions even poorer than those that had existed in the region of origin.

forest—and that economy can readily be gauged by its low reproductive rate. Despite the political consequences which may have been involved,[5] and the fortuitous enrichment of a small group of persons, the great population shift of nordestinos toward the Amazon was nothing more than an enormous waste of human beings at a period when the fundamental problem of the Brazilian economy was how to increase the supply of manpower.

24. THE MANPOWER PROBLEM: ELIMINATION OF SLAVE LABOR

In the second half of the nineteenth century, despite permanent expansion of the subsistence sector, inadequate manpower supply was the core of the problem faced by the Brazilian economy. I have already discussed the ways in which this problem was solved in two regions in fast economic expansion: the São Paulo plateau and the Amazon basin. There is another aspect of the problem, which at the time seemed really to be the most fundamental: the issue of servile labor.

In this, more than in any other issue, it is difficult to separate the strictly economic aspects from those of a broader social

[5] The search for the rubber trees led the Brazilians to penetrate into the territory bordering on Bolivia, whose boundaries with Brazil and Peru had not yet been completely defined in this region. As a result of this invasion, the territory of Acre was created and finally annexed to Brazil subject to an indemnification to Bolivia of 2 million pounds plus an obligation on the part of Brazil to build a railroad providing Bolivia with access to the navigable course of the Madeira River, a tributary of the Amazon.

nature. Since slavery in Brazil was the basis of a long-estab-
lished way of life, and since the slave-based economic system
had great structural stability, the upper classes of the system
considered that the abolition of servile labor would cause
social "hecatomb." Even the more lucid and fundamentally
antislavery minds, such as Mauá, never managed to grasp the
true nature of the problem, and were badly frightened at the
approach of such an unavoidable disaster.[1] The prevailing
thought was that the slave comprised a form of "wealth" and
that the abolition of slavery would bring about the impoverishment of the part of the population responsible for creating
wealth in Brazil. Alarmist calculations were made of the
hundreds of thousands of contos de réis* of private wealth
that would disappear at once through a legal trick. Others
argued that, on the contrary, the abolition of slavery would
liberate many assets, inasmuch as the entrepreneur would not
be forced to tie up substantial parts of his capital in manpower
or in the marketing of slaves.

Abolition of slavery, like agrarian reform, does not imply
per se either destruction or creation of wealth. What it does
amount to is merely a redistribution of property within a
community. The apparent complexity of the problem arises
from the fact that property rights over the working force, when
passing from the slave master to the individual laborer himself,
cease being an *asset* included in bookkeeping entries and become a mere potentiality. From the economic point of view,
the fundamental aspect of the problem lies in the repercussions
of the redistribution of property on the organization of production, as well as on the utilization of available factors and distribution and final utilization of the income created.

[1] See Visconde de Mauá, *Autobiography* (Rio de Janeiro, 1943), pp.
219–220.

* One conto de réis is still today a current expression for one thousand
cruzeiros. At the time, it meant one thousand milréis.—Translators.

Like agrarian reform, the abolition of slavery would entail some changes in the way of organizing production and in the degree of utilization of factors. In fact, only under special conditions would abolition be limited to a formal transformation of slaves into hired workers. On some islands in the British West Indies, on which the land had been completely occupied and the former slaves had no possibility of emigrating, the abolition of slavery acquired that very aspect of a formal change, with the freedman receiving a monetary wage established in accordance with the prevailing subsistence level. This was in turn a reflection of the living conditions of the former slaves.[2] In this extreme instance the redistribution of wealth

---

[2] The instance of the island of Antigua is cited in the specialized English literature as proof of the purely formal nature of the abolition of slavery in places where the land was monopolized by a social class. The assembly of the island released the slaves from the obligations created by the Apprenticeship System, introduced by the British Parliament as a transitory measure toward the abolition of slavery. Under that system, slaves more than six years of age were obliged to work six years for their masters, for seven and a half hours a day, in return for food, clothing, and housing. The slave had the possibility of working at least another two and a half hours a day for wages. The large estate owners of Antigua immediately granted complete freedom, and reached an agreement to set a subsistence wage on an extremely low basis. The result was that the former slaves, instead of working seven and a half hours a day to cover their subsistence costs, as would have been necessary under the apprenticeship system, actually had to work ten hours a day to achieve the same purpose. There being no practical possibility of finding employment off the plantations or of emigrating, the former slaves had to submit. It could correctly be proclaimed in the British Parliament at that time that the millions of pounds of indemnification paid by the government of Great Britain to the Antillian slave owners were a mere present, of no practical benefit to the life of the working populations. In other words, the abolition of slavery brought nothing but benefits to the slavers themselves. For a complete analysis of the case of Antigua, see Law Mathieson, in *British Slavery and Its Abolition, 1823–1838* (London, 1926).

had not been accompanied by any change in the organization of production or distribution of income. The opposite extreme would be that in which the supply of land was altogether elastic, in which event freed slaves would tend to leave the former plantations and to engage in subsistence farming. Then, changes in organization of production would be conspicuous, lowering the degree of utilization of factors and the profitability of the system. However, this extreme could hardly occur, because the entrepreneurs, being deprived of manpower, would tend to offer high wages and thus retain some of the former slaves. The ultimate consequence would therefore be a redistribution of income in favor of manpower.

Neither of these two extremes mentioned was to occur in Brazil. However, the sugar region was more in line with the former state of affairs, whereas the coffee region resembled the latter. In the Northeastern region the more easily farmable land was almost fully occupied at the time of the abolition of slavery. Freed slaves quitting the sugar mills were faced with serious difficulties of survival. There was already a surplus population weighing heavily upon the urban zones, and that surplus had been a serious social problem since the early nineteenth century. In the hinterland the subsistence economy had been expanded to great extremes, and the symptoms of population pressure were already being unmistakably felt in the semiarid *agreste* and *caatinga*.* These two natural barriers imposed limits on the mobility of the mass of newly freed slaves in the sugar region. Displacements were made from farm to farm, and only a small fraction of the slaves drifted out of the region. Under such conditions it was not difficult to attract and settle a substantial part of the former slave working

* *Agreste* and *caatinga* are both variants of the tropical savanna; the former is the transition zone between the humid coastal strip and the semiarid hinterland, whereas the latter is a sagebrush area.—Translators.

force at relatively low wages. Although there are no specific studies on this subject, it can hardly be assumed that material living conditions of former slaves changed perceptibly after abolition. Thus there is little probability that abolition led to a redistribution of income to any significant extent.

In the decade preceding abolition the sugar industry had undergone important technical changes, receiving the benefit of heavy investments of foreign capital under the auspices of the central government.[3] On the other hand, the last decade of the nineteenth century was marked by fundamental changes in the world sugar market as a result of the political independence of Cuba. Massive investments of North American capital were made in the island's sugar industry, which acquired a privileged position in the United States market.[4] In Brazil both the technical innovations and the export difficulties contributed to a reduction in the demand for manpower. Thus the contraction of manpower supply caused by the abolition of slavery was not to have any major consequences on the utilization of resources, and most probably did not produce any perceptible change in income distribution.

In the coffee region the consequences of the abolition were of many kinds. In the provinces which are today the states of Rio de Janeiro and Minas Gerais, and to a small extent in São Paulo, substantial coffee-growing enterprises had been formed

[3] In 1875, Parliament approved a law authorizing the imperial government to guarantee interest on foreign capital invested in the sugar industry to a total of 3 million pounds. In the next ten years fifty sugar mills were installed with modern equipment, almost all of them financed by English capital under the aegis of this law.

[4] The treaty of reciprocity signed between Cuba and the United States, after the island had won its independence, granted Cuban sugar a 20 per cent cut in United States tariffs. This privilege, added to the reduced costs of transportation and the facilities created through the great influx of American capital, made possible the exceptional spurt of Cuban production during the first quarter of the twentieth century.

on the basis of slave labor. The rapid destruction of the fertility of the land occupied in this first coffee expansion, mainly in hilly regions subject to erosion, and the possibility of utilization of more distant land after the introduction of railroads, had already placed such farming in an unfavorable position in the period immediately preceding abolition. All indications were that when abolition was proclaimed there would be a large migratory movement toward the fast-expanding new regions which could pay substantially higher wages. Nevertheless, precisely at that time there began the great European migratory current toward São Paulo. The advantages of the European laborer over the former slave are too obvious to need further emphasis. But, even though there were no strong incentives for the former slaves to transfer en masse to the São Paulo plateau, their position in the old coffee region became much more favorable than that of those in the Northeastern sugar region. The relative abundance of land made it possible for the former slave to take shelter under the subsistence economy. Dispersion was nevertheless much smaller than might have been expected, owing perhaps to social rather than specifically economic reasons.

The favorable job situation existing in the coffee region afforded the freed slaves relatively high wages. In fact, abolition caused an effective redistribution of income in favor of manpower in the coffee region. Nevertheless, that improvement in real remuneration for labor seems to have had negative rather than positive effects on the utilization of factors. A better understanding of this aspect of the matter may be achieved by examining the broader social traits of slavery. The man raised under slavery is altogether unfit to respond to economic incentives. Because he has almost no habits of family life, the idea of accumulating wealth is almost entirely alien to him. Moreover, his rudimentary mental development sets narrow limits upon his necessities. Work being a curse for the slave and leisure an unattainable blessing, raising his pay above the cost of his necessities—which are defined by the slave's subsistence level—promptly induces a strong preference for leisure.

In the old coffee region, where in order to retain the working force it was necessary to pay relatively high wages, there was soon a slackening in working standards. Being able to meet his subsistence expenses on two or three working days a week, the erstwhile slave saw a more attractive proposition in "buying" leisure than in working when he felt he had enough to live on. Hence one of the direct consequences of abolition, in the regions of most rapid development, was a reduction in the degree of utilization of the working force. That problem had broader social repercussions, which are beyond the scope of this work. At most, I shall mention here only that the low mental development of the slave population led to partial segregation after abolition, delaying their assimilation and stunting the economic development of the country. Throughout the first half of the twentieth century the great mass of the descendants of the former slaves were to go on living within a limited system of "necessities" and playing a purely passive role in the economic transformations of Brazil.

Considered from a broad point of view, abolition was a measure of political rather than of economic nature. Slavery was more important as the basis of a regional system of power than as a form of organization of production. Once slave labor was abolished, almost no changes of true significance took place in forms of production organization or even in distribution of income. Nevertheless, one of the basic mainstays of the regional system of power established during the colonial era had been eliminated. It had survived for nearly the entire nineteenth century, acting as a stifling influence on the economic development of the country.

25. INCOME LEVEL AND RATE OF GROWTH IN THE SECOND HALF OF THE NINETEENTH CENTURY

Viewed as a whole, the Brazilian economy attained a relatively high rate of growth in the second half of the nineteenth century. Foreign trade being the dynamic factor of the system, the key to the process of growth in that period lies in the behavior of that trade. There was a 214 per cent increase in the Brazilian export quantum between the average for the 1840's and that for the 1890's. This increase in the physical volume of exports was accompanied by a rise of approximately 46 per cent in the average prices of export products. On the other hand, there was a reduction of about 8 per cent in the price index for imported products, so that the improvement in terms of trade amounted to 58 per cent. A 214 per cent increase in the export quantum together with a 58 per cent improvement in terms of trade means a 396 per cent increase in real income generated by the exporting sector.[1] Thus the most dynamic sector of the

---

[1] The quantum indices and prices of exports have been calculated on the basis of the 1841–1850 decade, covering the following products: coffee, sugar, cocoa, maté, tobacco, cotton, rubber, and hides. For the decade in question these products accounted for 88.2 per cent of the value of exports, a proportion which increased to 95.6 per cent during the 'nineties. The import price index used is that for British imports, which provides a good indication as to the trend in prices of manufactured goods in world trade. It is, however, possible that the prices of Brazilian imports may have fallen even further than is indicated by

economy grew fivefold in the period. How much did the entire income generated within the Brazilian territory during those fifty years actually increase? Available information on this subject does not allow of more than mere conjectures. There are substantial disparities in the figures for the main exported products. Thus although the export quantum rose by 214 per cent, the actual quantities of sugar exported increased by only 33 per cent and those of cotton 43 per cent. Moreover, despite a 46 per cent increase in the price index for exports, prices of cotton rose only 32 per cent and those for sugar declined by 11 per cent. Real income from these two products together increased by only 54 per cent during the period under consideration. Sugar and cotton being the only two significant articles on the export list for the Northeast,[2] it is to be clearly inferred that the development recorded for the second half of the nineteenth century did not involve the whole of Brazil.

In analyzing the behavior of real income during the aforementioned period, the Brazilian economy may be conveniently divided into three main sectors: the first consisting of the sugar and cotton economies and the vast subsistence economy zone linked with them (though by ever-weakening ties), the second comprising the mainly subsistence economy in the south, and the third being centered in the coffee economy.

The first of these systems comprises the strip running from the state of Maranhão to the state of Sergipe. The state of

---

the index in question, owing to the large volume of wheat in Brazil's purchases and to the substantial decline in the price of this product in the last quarter of the nineteenth century.

[2] The situation of hides, which also figure in exports from the Northeast, was no more favorable, inasmuch as exported quantities rose by 48 per cent whereas prices fell by 3 per cent. Cocoa, exports of which evolved very favorably—with increases of 259 per cent and 119 per cent in quantity and price respectively—became the nucleus of an autonomous economic system in the south of the state of Baía, geographically separate from the previously existing Northeast economy.

Baía has been excluded because its economy underwent a far-reaching change during that period, with the advent of cocoa. The population of the eight states in the region,[3] according to the 1872 census, still represented one-third of the entire Brazilian population; if the population of Baía is included, the total amounts to almost half of the national figure.

The 1872 and 1900 census data show that the population of the aforementioned eight states increased at an annual rate of 1.2 per cent. And if the same rate is applied for the entire half century being considered, a total population increase of 80 per cent will be obtained, well above the increase in real income generated by the exporting sector (54 per cent). Bearing in mind the fact that two systems were then in existence in the Northeast—the seaboard system mainly engaged in export activities, and the "Mediterranean" system based on subsistence—the aforementioned data allow certain hypotheses to be formulated. In the first place, we might consider the possibility that the population in the two systems had grown at about the same rate and that per capita income in the subsistence system had remained stable; in that instance, the decline in per capita income in the exporting system would have been substantial. The other hypothesis is that there might have been a transfer of population from the exporting system to the subsistence sector and that per capita income might have remained steady. Then, even though per capita income remained unchanged in the subsistence sector, there would have been a decline in the average income for the region as a whole, inasmuch as productivity was lower in the subsistence sector. To summarize, if the region was not to undergo a reduction in per capita income, it would have been necessary for productivity to be substantially increased in the subsistence sector, a supposition which is obviously untenable inasmuch as at that

[3] Maranhão, Piauí, Ceará, Rio Grande do Norte, Paraíba, Pernambuco, Alagoas, and Sergipe.

time the pressure of population on the available farmland in the region had already become evident. It must therefore be assumed that there was a decline in per capita income within the system, though such a decline is not susceptible of any precise measurement.

The second system was composed of a predominantly subsistence economy indirectly benefiting from the expansion in exports. Finding within Brazil a market capable of absorbing their production surpluses, some sectors of the subsistence economy were able to expand the monetary part of their productive activities. In the region of the state of Paraná, for example, the great expansion in maté production for export brought a twofold benefit to the subsistence economy, largely composed of populations transplanted from Europe in line with national and provincial subsidized immigration plans. Colonists located further inland could divide their time between subsistence farming and harvesting of maté leaves, thus substantially increasing their income, whereas those nearer the seacoast were benefited by the expansion of the urban market, primarily spurred in turn by the development of exports.[4]

In Rio Grande do Sul the dynamic impulse came from the cattle-breeding sector, through its exports to the country's internal market. Those exports—mainly jerked beef, which was to comprise half the state's total sales to the internal and external markets by the end of the nineteenth century[5]—re-

[4] The average annual value of exports of maté increased from £48,-000 in the 1840's to £393,000 in the 1890's. In the first two decades of the twentieth century the rapid expansion of exports of this product continued, at an extremely favorable price level.

[5] For a calculation of exports from Rio Grande do Sul to the other states and to foreign countries during the last two decades of the nineteenth century see J. P. Wileman, *Brazilian Exchange* (Buenos Aires, 1896), p. 106.

integrated Rio Grande cattle breeding into the Brazilian economy. The region of the "colonies" profited by the expansion of the internal market, either directly through sales of high-quality products such as wines and lard, or indirectly through urban expansion in the state, rendered possible by the increased productivity of the cattle-breeding sector.

The contrast between the region whose economy was predominantly a subsistence one in the south and the Northeast sector is clearly shown in population figures. Between the 1872 and 1900 censuses the population of the states of Rio Grande do Sul, Santa Catarina, Paraná, and Mato Grosso increased by 127 per cent—that is, at an annual rate of 3 per cent, whereas that of the eight Northeastern states grew at a rate of only 1.2 per cent. If the 3 per cent rate is applied over the entire half century we are considering, a growth of 332 per cent will be indicated. This figure is of particular interest, showing as it does that even if no increase in per capita income had been recorded for the economy of the southern region, its absolute growth would have been near that of the exporting sector, which amounted to 396 per cent, as mentioned above. For per capita income to remain stationary it would have been necessary—given abundant, fertile land in the region—for the relative importance of the exporting sector within that economy to undergo no change. Since that relative importance increased —as is to be inferred from Paraná's maté exports and shipments of beef products from Rio Grande do Sul—there is every likelihood that average economic productivity, and hence per capita income also, displayed an increase.

The third system—comprising the coffee-producing region —then covered the states of Espírito Santo, Rio de Janeiro, Minas Gerais, and São Paulo.[6] The over-all population of

---

[6] Coffee was introduced into Brazil at the beginning of the eighteenth century, and is now produced in almost the whole of the country with

these four states increased at a rate of 2.2 per cent between 1872 and 1900. This figure, though much higher than that of the Northeast (1.2 per cent) and Baía (1.5 per cent), is below figures for the Amazon basin (2.6 per cent) and the south (3.0 per cent). Closer analysis, however, will show that great population moves occurred within the coffee region. The population of the two states which pioneered coffee production (Rio de Janeiro and Minas Gerais) grew at a somewhat low rate (1.6 per cent a year); on the other hand, the region that was engaged in coffee production in the last quarter of the nineteenth century (Espírito Santo and São Paulo) shows the extraordinarily high rate of 3.6 per cent a year. These data bring out the fact that the development of the coffee region during that stage was carried out on the basis of a transfer of manpower from the regions of lower productivity —and certainly from the subsistence sector in that region— to others of higher productivity. In other words, the procedure was just the opposite of what occurred in the Northeast during the same period. The rapid expansion of the internal market in the coffee region was bound to have favorable effects on the productivity of the subsistence economy, chiefly concentrated in the state of Minas Gerais. Furthermore, the transfer of manpower from the subsistence to the coffee sector meant that the relative importance of the latter was on the increase. Because of the effects of these various factors, it seems probable that real per capita income for the entire region was growing at a rate not lower than that of the exporting sector. Since the quantity of coffee exported increased 341 per cent and prices 91 per cent between the 1840's and the 1890's, real income generated by coffee exports grew at an annual rate of 4.5 per

---

the exception of the extreme south. The states in the north and Northeast long exported small quantities of coffee. At the end of the nineteenth century local consumption already absorbed almost the entire crop of the small producing states.

cent. In view of the growth in population, the rate of annual increase in real per capita income was about 2.3 per cent.

Two regions of some economic importance have been excluded from the foregoing discussion of the three systems: the state of Baía, which in 1872 contained 13 per cent of the total Brazilian population, and the Amazon basin, with 3 per cent of the total population at the same period. Cocoa production for export had begun in Baía in the second half of the nineteenth century, offering that state an alternative for utilization of land and manpower resources which was not available to other Northeastern states. Yet the relative importance of cocoa at the end of the nineteenth century was minor: it comprised only 1.5 per cent of the value of Brazil's exports in the 1890's. But another traditional export from Baía—tobacco—showed relative recuperation in the second half of the nineteenth century. Mainly restricted at first to be used in bartering for slaves in Africa, Brazilian tobacco began to find a growing market in Europe in this period. The quantity exported increased by 361 per cent between the 1840's and the 1890's, and average prices climbed 41 per cent. Average total annual value of cocoa and tobacco exports grew from £151,-000 to £1,057,000 in the same fifty-year period. These data, however, reveal only one facet of the development of Baía during the latter part of the nineteenth century. Assuming, as a rough approximation, that all the tobacco and cocoa exported from Brazil came from Baía, and that all the sugar and cotton came from the eight Northeastern states, per capita exports from the Baía region would not have been higher than those from the Northeast. There is every indication, therefore, that development in Baía was similarly restricted by the far-reaching effects of factors similar to those affecting the Northeast. Improvement in some regions must have taken place simultaneously with impoverishment in others. Sugar production for export had already completely disappeared at the time, and the expansion of subsistence cattle breeding was taking place on increasingly poor lands. This explains why, despite the migratory flow into the cocoa region at the end of the century—made up chiefly of Northeastern immigrants—the population of the state grew at the low rate of 1.5 per cent a year between 1872 and 1900. Nevertheless, the very fact that this rate was above that for the Northeast is an indication that real income in Baía developed more favorably.

Finally, we must consider the Amazon basin, whose exports attained remarkable relative importance at the turn of the century. The participation of rubber in total exports rose from 0.4 per cent in the 1840's to 15.0 per cent in the 1890's. In the last-named decade the value of per capita exports from the region was twice that of those from the coffee region. Even though a large part of that income did not revert to the region, and a substantial part of that reverting was consumed by imports,[7] it is none the less true that for purposes of figuring the national income as a whole it should be ascribed to the Amazon region.

On the basis of the observations made in the previous paragraphs, I shall now endeavor to make a rough estimate of the trend in per capita income for Brazil as a whole during the period under consideration. The Northeastern region seems to have been the only one in which per capita income declined. However, the absolute income of the region had in fact increased, inasmuch as that produced by the exporting sector rose by 54 per cent. I shall assume that the absolute rate of income growth had been half that of the population—in other words, that per capita income declined at an annual rate of 0.6 per cent. In Baía, the forces acting in opposite directions

---

[7] The multiplier for investments made in rubber was probably very low and perhaps even negative, inasmuch as the increase in output led to abandonment of many other activities and a large part of the needs formerly supplied by local production began to be imported. For an explanation of the concept of the multiplier, see note 5, Chapter 31.

possibly counterbalanced one another, and it could be assumed that per capita income remained stable. In the south, where the population was growing at a rate of 3 per cent a year, there was an evident increase in per capita income which could hardly have been less than 1 per cent a year. For the coffee region, I shall assume a rate of 2.3 per cent per capita per year, as already mentioned. And for the Amazon region I shall limit myself to surmising that the absolute growth of income generated within the region attained twice the rate recorded for the coffee region. On the basis of such hypotheses, it is to be concluded that for the fifty-year period in question real income in Brazil multiplied by 5.4,[8] implying an annual rate of growth of 3.5 per cent and a per capita growth rate of 1.5 per cent. This is a high figure by comparison with the rate of development of the world economy in the nineteenth century. In the same period real income in the United States was multiplied by 5.7 but, owing to the faster growth in the country's

---

[8] As a basis for argument, the relative size of the population, according to the 1872 census, has been taken. The absolute income in each region has then been stepped up in line with the population increase in that region, and in line with the rate of increase or decrease indicated in the text, to give the per capita income, as follows.

Region	Percentage of Brazilian population	Rate of growth of the population	Rate of growth of the per capital income
Northeast	35	1.2	− 0.6
Baía	13	1.5	0.0
South	9	3.0	1.0
Center	40	2.2	2.3
Amazonas	3	2.6	6.2
Totals	100	2.0	1.5

It is implicitly assumed that there were no substantial discrepancies between the levels of per capita income in the various regions of Brazil during the base period—that is, the 1841–1850 decade.

population, the per capita rate of growth was somewhat smaller than that indicated for Brazil. The fundamental difference lies in the fact that although the United States in the second half of the nineteenth century had been maintaining a rate of growth since the last quarter of the preceding century, Brazil entered a stage of growth after three-quarters of a century of stagnation and perhaps of regression in her per capita income.

As indicated earlier, it may be assumed that the per capita income of the Brazilian citizen was probably not less than fifty dollars a year (in terms of present-day purchasing power) in the early nineteenth century, though it had probably suffered a decline in the last quarter of the eighteenth century. I have shown also that per capita income can hardly have stood at that same fifty-dollar level as of the mid-nineteenth century. On this basis, and assuming a rate of increase of 1.5 per cent, I conclude that per capita income stood at $106 per year at the end of the century. If this same rate is applied for the first half of the twentieth century, a per capita income of 224 dollars will be obtained for 1950, which is actually very close to existing estimates for that year. Thus there are some indications that the rate of growth of the Brazilian economy was relatively stable throughout the past century.[9] Another interesting observation is that if the Brazilian economy had attained a rate of growth in the first half of the nineteenth century identical with that for the second half, taking the aforementioned fifty-dollar figure as a starting point, a per capita income of 224 dollars a year would have been attained at the turn of the century. And if the same rate had been maintained for the first half of this century, the real per capita income of the

[9] Though not exceptionally high, the rate of 1.5 per cent for the century is probably higher than the average for the economies of Western Europe. In the United States the rate for the century would seem to have been somewhat higher (1.9 per cent) according to estimates by the National Bureau of Economic Research, quoted by Simon Kuznets.

Brazilian population as of 1950 would have been about five hundred dollars—in other words, it would have been comparable to the average for the countries of Western Europe in that same year.

The data presented in the preceding paragraph throw some light on the problem of the present-day relative backwardness of the Brazilian economy. That backwardness has its roots not in the rate of development for the past century, which seems to have been reasonably rapid, but in the reversal which occurred in the previous three-quarters of a century. Since Brazil was unable to integrate herself into the expanding currents of world trade during that period of fast transformation of the economic structures of more progressive countries, sharp disparities were created between the Brazilian economic system and those of Western Europe. I shall have occasion to refer again to those disparities when analyzing the specific problems of underdevelopment with which Brazil's economy is faced at the present time.

26. INCOME FLOW IN THE WAGE-EARNING LABOR ECONOMY

The most pertinent event that occurred in the Brazilian economy in the last quarter of the nineteenth century was undoubtedly the increase in the relative importance of the wage-earning sector. Previous expansion had taken place either through the slavery sector or through the multiplication of subsistence nuclei. In both instances the flow of income, real or virtual, was circumscribed to relatively small units whose external contacts acquired an international character in the former whereas they were of extremely limited scope in the latter. The new expansion was to occur through the sector based on wage-earning labor. The mechanism of this new system, whose relative importance was to grow rapidly, displays substantial differences by comparison with the old economy based on slave labor or limited almost exclusively to subsistence activities. The latter, as we have already seen, is distinguished by a high degree of stability, maintaining its structure unaltered in both times of growth and periods of depression. The dynamics of the new system are quite distinct from the former ones, and must be analyzed in detail if an understanding is to be gained of the structural transformations that were to lead to the formation of an economy orientated toward the internal market in the first half of the twentieth century.

As a whole, the new coffee economy based on wage labor presented some similarities to the old slavery economy: it was comprised of many producing units closely connected with the currents of foreign trade. If, however, we examine still more closely the mechanism of those units, we shall see that the differences are actually considerable. For easier understanding, let us consider the economic process taking place from the time products are sold to the exporter. The total value of the sale is the gross income of the productive unit, such income being destined to cover the depreciation of real assets utilized in the productive process and to pay for all the factors engaged in production. To simplify the analysis, that income can be divided into two main groups: income to wage-earning labor, and income to the landlord class. The behavior of these two groups, from the point of view of income utilization, is patently distinct. Wage earners transform all or nearly all their income into consumption expenses. The landlord class, whose level of consumption is much higher, retains a part of its income in order to expand its capital, the source of that same income.

Let us see how the flow of income generated by exports is propagated. Consumption expenses—purchases of food, clothing, services, and so on—comprise the income of small producers, retail merchants, and the like. These in turn likewise transform a large part of their own income into consumption expenditures. Thus the sum of all those expenditures must necessarily far exceed the monetary income derived from the exporting activity. Let us now surmise that there is an increase in the external impulse. As the mass of wages grows, the demand for consumption goods automatically increases. Production of the latter can in turn be expanded with relative facility, given the existence of sufficient manpower and underutilized land, mainly in regions where subsistence activities predominate. Hence the increase in the external impulse—acting upon a sector of the economy organized on a wage-labor basis— leads to better utilization of factors already existing in the country.[1] Furthermore, the increase in productivity—a secondary effect of the external impulse—produces results outside the producing-exporting unit. The mass of wages and salaries paid in the exporting sector therefore becomes the nucleus of an internal-market economy. When there is a convergence of certain factors—to which we shall refer later—the internal market finds itself in a position to grow even more intensively than the exporting economy, despite the fact that the growth impulse originates in the latter.

As a rule the external impulse for growth first makes itself felt in the form of rising prices for exported products, which are transformed into greater profits. Entrepreneurs naturally tend to reinvest those profits by expanding their plantations. Given relative elasticity of manpower supply and abundance of land, that expansion can proceed without facing any hindrance either from wages or from income from the land. In fact, transfers of manpower within Brazil as well as immigra-

[1] A typical instance of the better utilization of resources due to expansion of internal demand for consumption goods is afforded by the subsistence economy which arose in southern Brazil with immigrants of European origin. See Chapter 25.

tion took place independent of rises in real wages in those sectors or regions which attracted factors. The coffee sector was actually able to keep real wages nearly stable throughout its long stage of expansion. As long as such wages were higher in absolute terms than those paid in the other sectors of the economy, and as long as production was expanding, shifts in manpower occurred. Thus the existence of a relatively amorphous manpower pool, which had been accumulating in the previous centuries, was of fundamental importance for the development of the new economic system based on wage-earning labor. If expansion of the coffee economy had depended exclusively on European immigrant manpower, wages would have become established at much higher levels, as occurred in Australia and even in Argentina. Internally recruited manpower—utilized mainly in forest clearing, building, and auxiliary tasks—exerted a permanent downward pressure on average wage levels.

This stability of average real wages in the exporting sector did not, however, mean that the same was going to be true of the economy as a whole. With the absorption of manpower by the exporting sector, the latter's relative importance within the economy grew. When factors from the subsistence sector were absorbed there was a rise in the average real wages—and even more in the average monetary wages—inasmuch as in that sector the monetary flow was relatively much smaller. Hence the fact that the growth of the exporting sector was extensive did not prevent the rise of average wages for the economy as a whole. In summary it might be said that as the population grew much more rapidly in the monetary sector than in the economy as a whole, the amount of monetary wages—basis of the internal market—increased more rapidly than the aggregate product.

What economic significance was there in the entrepreneur's favorable situation, permitting him to retain all the benefits derived from occasional rises in prices of export articles? Let us assume for a moment that wages rose as export prices increased. The practical consequence would be that the volume of investments would become smaller, just as the expansion of the exporting sector would be restricted. The absorption of the subsistence sector, as a result, would also be slower. Manpower occupied in the exporting sector would progressively become a privileged group, and there would tend to be a growing spread between wages paid in the exporting sector and those in the subsistence sector.

The increases in productivity in the coffee economy were mainly a reflection of occasional price improvements, usually occurring at times of cyclical rises, whereas improvements in physical productivity resulting from the productive process alone were at a minimum.[2] It might therefore be argued that the transfer to the wage earners of a part of the fruits of those occasional rises in economic productivity would consequently impose on the mass of aggregate wages marked cyclical expansions and contractions. But it might also be claimed that because wages showed greater resistance to compression than profits, the economy would be in a better position to defend itself in the cyclical decline and possibly in the long run, in terms of trade, if it could transfer to the wage earners a part of the increase in productivity obtained at the time of rising prices. However, since such a transfer did not take place, the entire pressure of the cyclical decline was concentrated on the mass of profits. We shall see later how the entrepreneurs managed to transfer that pressure to the other sectors of the community.

---

[2] Increases in productivity might also be due to the opening up of better land, greater transportation efficiency, and so on.

27. THE PROPENSITY TO EXTERNAL DISEQUILIBRIUM

The operation of the new economic system, based on wage-earning labor, presented a series of problems which in the old exporting and slavery economy had only just begun to take shape. One of those problems—which was actually common to other economies with similar characteristics—resided in the impossibility of the system's adapting itself to the rules of the gold standard, basis of the entire international economy during the period with which we are now concerned. The fundamental principle of the gold-standard system was rooted in the assumption that each country should have an available metallic reserve—or one of convertible currency, according to the more modern version of the theory—of a size sufficient to cover occasional deficits on its balance of payments. It is easy to understand how a metallic reserve—coined or otherwise—comprised an unproductive investment which was in reality the contribution made by each country to the short-term financing to the extent of its participation in international trade and to that of the relative range of the fluctuations in its balance of payments.[1] A country exporting primary products usually had a high relative degree of participation in international trade—that is, its per capita foreign trade was relatively much greater than its per capita monetary income. Then too, its monetary economy was subject to much sharper oscillations owing to the mere fact of its relying much more on exports.

---

[1] The balance of payments, by definition, is always in a state of equilibrium. The fluctuations referred to in the text are those in the balance on the current account and in the movement of capital not intended specifically to cover that balance.

The problem facing the Brazilian economy was essentially the following: at what prices could the rules of the gold standard be applied to a system specializing in the export of primary products and with a high import coefficient? That problem was of no concern to the European economists who had always theorized on the subject of international trade in terms of economies of more or less similar degrees of development, with not very different production setups and relatively low import coefficients.

Nineteenth-century monetary theory is undoubtedly a useful instrument for explaining European realities. It was based on the principle that if all countries followed the rules of the gold standard—or, to put it another way, if the currencies of the various countries were based on the same merchandise currency—the available gold would tend to be distributed according to the needs of each country and those of international trade. Thus there would be a solidarity between the price systems of the various countries. It was implicit in this theory that if a country imported more than it exported—leading to disequilibrium in its balance of payments—that country would then be compelled to export gold, thus restricting the volume of its currency. This reduction, in line with the quantitative theory, would cause a decline in prices as a counterpart to the rising price of gold whereupon an incentive to export would automatically be created, with concomitant discouragement of imports so that the disequilibrium would thus be corrected.[2]

In the economies in which imports amounted to a small proportion of the national expenditure, an occasional disequilibrium in the balance of payments could be financed by currency

---

[2] The disequilibrium might also be corrected through capital movements. A relative gold shortage would lead to an increase in the interest rate, thus attracting foreign capital. The deficit on the balance of the current account would thus be offset by a balance on the capital account.

of internal circulation without causing a major decline in the degree of liquidity of the system. This much could not, however, be expected of an economy with a high import co-efficient. In the latter, an abrupt disequilibrium in the balance of payments would cause a major reduction in the volume of currency, producing a literal shock wave through the system. That type of difficulty might have occurred in England, whose import coefficient grew considerably in the course of the nine-teenth century, if that country had not become transformed into a major exporter of capital and if London had not been the ruling center of fluctuations in the world economy.

In an economy such as that of Brazil in the nineteenth cen-tury, the import coefficient was particularly high in the mone-tary sector alone, to which nearly all foreign transactions were restricted. Moreover, disequilibriums in the balance of pay-ments were relatively much greater in scope, reflecting as they did the sharp declines in prices of raw materials vis-à-vis the world market. Finally, account should be taken of the inter-relations between foreign trade and public finances, since im-port duties were the main source of revenue for the central government.

How had that problem affected the old exporting and slav-ery economy? When that economy existed in its simplest form it was not—owing to its very nature—afflicted by any form of external disequilibrium. Monetary demand being equal to ex-ports, the former could obviously be transformed wholly into imports without thereby entailing any disequilibrium. It is only when monetary demand tends to outgrow exports that the pos-sibility of disequilibrium begins to arise. This maladjustment is closely connected with the wage-earning labor regime, as can be readily understood.

When export-generated income grows, there is also growth in the aggregate mass of payments to factors. That income, as has been mentioned, tends to be multiplied first in monetary terms and ultimately in real terms, on account of the existence of underutilized factors. The increase in income therefore takes place in two stages: first as a result of the growth in exports, and second as a result of the effects of the internal multiplier. A part of this increase in income must be met out of imports, in line with the relatively stable ratio existing between increase in income and increase in imports.

The most important fact to be considered is, however, that at the moment when a crisis arose in industrial centers, the prices of primary products declined abruptly, immediately reducing the flow of exchange currency toward the country whose economy was a dependent one. Meanwhile, the effect of the previous increases in value and volume of exports continued to spread slowly.[3] There was thus an intermediate stage in which the demand for imports continued to grow, even though the supply of exchange currency had already been drastically reduced. This was the stage at which there would be a need for mobilizing metallic reserves. The latter would, however, have to be of substantial volume to bring into oper-

---

[3] The way in which Brazilian imports were financed contributed to a worsening of the pressure against the balance of payments at times of depression. Brazilian imports largely came from England or were controlled by British business houses with great liquidity on the Brazilian market. These British firms lent money on a medium-term basis to traders (including those of other nationalities) exporting to other countries. Thus it was the import trade that financed the export trade. When there was a collapse in the demand for Brazilian products abroad, liquid funds arising from sales made during previous periods of prosperity piled up in the hands of the importers. These liquid funds exerted pressure upon the balance of payments precisely at the time when the supply of exchange was reduced. It is interesting to observe the different way in which this same problem arose in the United States, where the liquid funds of the British exporters early displayed a tendency to be applied in public debt bonds. See Alan K. Manchester, *British Pre-eminence in Brazil: Its Rise and Decline* (Chapel Hill, 1953), p. 315, and Leland H. Jenks, *Migration of British Capital to 1873* (New York, 1927), pp. 68–70.

ation the mechanism of the gold standard, not only because the proportion of imports in the total expenditure of the community was very high and the fluctuations in importing capacity large, but also because in an economy of this kind the capital account on the balance of payments behaved adversely in times of depression.

If the nature of cyclical phenomena is studied in dependent economies, in contrast to those in industrial economic structures, it can be seen that the former are always doomed to disequilibrium in their balance of payments and to monetary inflation. In an industrial economy the cycle is linked with fluctuations in the volume of investments. Times of crisis are marked by an abrupt contraction in such investments, automatically reducing over-all demand and unleashing a series of reactions whose effect is to reduce that demand still further. It is easy to understand how that reduction in demand is immediately reflected in a contraction of imports and selling of inventories. On a mere report that a crisis is beginning, the importers—knowing that the demand for imported articles will tend to decline—cancel their orders, causing in turn a sharp decline in prices of imported goods, which in this instance are mainly the primary products supplied by dependent economies. Furthermore, the business contraction caused by the crisis reduces the liquid assets of firms, inducing them to resort to any available funds, including those deposited abroad. In this manner a crisis in an industrial country is accompanied by a contraction in imports, falling prices for imported articles, and an inflow of capital. Finally, inasmuch as a large part of the capital exported in the nineteenth century was either for public loans or for investments in the private sector with interest guaranteed, the servicing of capital comprised a relatively rigid entry in the current account of the balance of payments, thus contributing to a strengthening in the internal position of the capital-exporting countries at times of depression.

In dependent economies a crisis takes a completely different form, starting with a fall in the value of exports due to a reduction either in the value per unit of exported products or in both that value and the total volume of exports.[4] Some time must elapse before the contraction in export values produces its full effect on the import demand, so that an initial disequilibrium may be expected in the balance of payments. Moreover, the fall in prices of imported goods (manufactured products) takes place more slowly and less intensely than it does in prices of the exported primary products—that is, a worsening in terms of trade begins. To these two factors are added the effects of rigidity in the servicing of foreign capital and a reduction in the inflow of such capital.[5] Thus, it can readily be imagined what immense metallic reserves the full operation of the gold standard would call for in an economy such as that of

[4] The former of these phenomena occurs in the instance of food products, demand for which displays low income elasticity, or in other words is little influenced by fluctuations in consumer income. The latter is the instance of the industrial raw materials, demand for which shrinks sharply with cutbacks in industrial activity. In either instance, however, prices decline in view of the reduction in prospects of business profit.

[5] The servicing of foreign capital did not reach the point where it was an excessive burden on Brazil's balance of payments during the second half of the past century. In relation to the value of exports, this servicing would seem to have increased from 9.4 per cent in 1861–1864 to 12.1 per cent in 1890–1892. Nevertheless, with the exception of special instances—in periods in which heavy public indebtedness was contracted for noneconomic purposes, such as the Paraguayan War, the consolidation of the public debt—entries of capital were always lower than servicing on the debt. During one exceptionally favorable period in 1886–1889 capital imports attained 14.3 per cent of total exports, whereas servicing on foreign capital amounted to 14.6 per cent. During a less favorable period, 1876–1885, imports of capital declined to 5.3 per cent whereas servicing on foreign capital stood at 12.2 per cent. On this subject see the meticulous study by J. P. Wileman, *Brazilian Exchange* (Buenos Aires, 1896).

Brazil at the peak of the coffee cycle. To the extent the slavery and exporting economy was being superseded by a new system based on wage-earning labor, it became more difficult to put the gold standard into operation.

Analysis of this point is the more interesting in that it sheds much light on the type of obstacle faced by Brazilian statesmen at the time in getting a grasp of the country's economic realities. Because the Brazilian economy was merely a dependency of the industrial centers, it was difficult to avoid interpreting the country's economic problems by analogy with European events. European economic science in Brazil was filtered through the law schools and tended to become transformed into a body of doctrine which was accepted independent of any endeavor to compare it with reality. Where such reality was far removed from the ideal world of doctrine, this was felt to be a symptom of social pathology. Thus such statesmen passed directly from an idealistic interpretation of reality into the policy-making stage, to the exclusion of any critique of the doctrine in the light of reality.

This mental inhibition preventing the acquisition of a critical and scientific point of view seems to be particularly obvious in monetary problems. The reason for this arises from the fact that there had been no serious attempt in Europe during the nineteenth century to draft a monetary theory outside the gold-standard scheme. The Brazilian statesman with some background in economics was a prey to a series of doctrinaire prejudices on monetary matters, which took the form of the gold-standard rules. As for the currency circulating in Brazil, only its "pathological" aspect was seen—or in other words, its inconvertibility. In trying to apply to this inconvertible currency the rules of the gold standard—particularly those stemming from the quantitative theory—the Brazilian statesman was led further and further away from reality. The historian recording economic concepts in Brazil can only be surprised at the monotonous insistence with which everything occurring in the country's economy—inconvertibility of currency, deficits, and issuance of paper money—was labeled aberrant and abnormal. However, that century-old abnormality never became the subject of a systematic study. In fact, no serious effort was ever made to understand that abnormality, which in the ultimate analysis was the very reality of the Brazilian economic environment. All efforts were spent in a task that historic experience has shown to be in vain: that of subjecting the economic system to the monetary rules prevailing in Europe. This strenuous effort at mimicry, arising from an unshakable faith in the principles of a doctrine with no basis in reality, was to continue for the first three decades of the twentieth century.

28. DEFENSE OF THE LEVEL OF EMPLOYMENT AND CONCENTRATION OF INCOME

We have seen how the existence of a manpower reserve within Brazil, reinforced by a strong migratory flow, afforded the coffee economy a long period of expansion without any upward trend in real wages. The rise in average wages reflected the increased productivity that was being obtained through the mere transfer of manpower from the subsistence to the exporting economy. Improvements in productivity achieved within the exporting economy itself could be retained by the entrepreneur to his benefit, inasmuch as no pressure had formed within the system to compel him to transfer them, wholly or in part, to the wage earners. I have also pointed out that those productivity increases in the exporting sector were purely economic in nature, reflecting changes in coffee prices. To obtain an increase in productivity from manpower or from the land, it would have been necessary for the entrepreneur to introduce some improvements in farming processes or to intensify capitalization—that is, to invest a greater amount of capital per unit of land or unit of manpower.

Since there was no pressure from manpower for higher wages, the entrepreneur had no interest in replacing such manpower by capital—that is, in increasing the amount of capital per unit of manpower. As the benefits of increased productivity reverted to the benefit of capital, the more extensive the cultivation—that is, the greater the quantity produced per unit of fixed capital—the more advantageous the situation of the entrepreneur. Since every increase in productivity was transformed into profit, obviously it would always be more interesting to produce the greatest quantity possible per unit of capital and not to pay the least possible quantity of wages per unit of production. The practical consequence of this situation was that the entrepreneur was always interested in investing his new capital in the expansion of his plantations, there being no incentive for any improvement in methods of cultivation.

The same could be said for land. If land were scarce, once it was occupied the entrepreneurs would have an obvious inducement to improve methods of cultivation as well as to intensify capitalization in order to boost income. Moreover, the occupation of inferior soils would be bound to increase the income from the land—that is, would compel the entrepreneur to transfer to the landowner an increasing part of his profits. To defend himself against this pressure by the income from the land, the entrepreneur would be led to intensify cultivation— in other words, to increase the amount of fixed capital per unit of cultivated land. Actually, land existed in still greater abundance than manpower, being either unoccupied or underoccupied within the subsistence economy. The entrepreneur tried to utilize it by applying a minimum of capital per unit of surface area. Whenever land showed signs of exhaustion, there was some justification for the entrepreneur to abandon it and transfer his capital to virgin soils of higher yield. The destruction of soils—which from the social standpoint may seem inexcusable—is perfectly justifiable from the viewpoint of the private entrepreneur, whose goal is to obtain the maximum profit from his capital. Soil conservation becomes a matter of concern to the entrepreneur only when it has an economic basis. Economic incentives induced him to extend his plantations and to increase the quantity of land and manpower per unit of capital.

The economic conditions within which coffee growing developed did not therefore provide any incentive for the entrepreneur to boost physical productivity from either land or manpower utilized by him. This was, in fact, the rational form of growth of an economy in which both land and manpower were either unoccupied or underoccupied whereas capital was scarce. It might, of course, be argued that the conscious destruction of soils would have negative effects in the long run. Nevertheless it must be remembered that the method of extensive cultivation made possible a volume of production per unit of capital (which was a scarce item) far higher than that which could have been obtained by means of intensive farming methods. The situation might well be compared to that of an extractive industry, inasmuch as the exhaustion of a mineral deposit means exhausting resources whose absence may be regretted by future generations. However, if the exhaustible reserve is utilized so as to start a process of development, not only will the present generation be benefited but also those to come, which will be inheriting that mineral deposit in the form of reproductive capital. Up to a certain point the problem of the soil is less serious, inasmuch as there is always the possibility of recuperation. Instances of irrecuperable destruction of soils are indeed rare.

For the above and other reasons the Brazilian exporting sector did not, during the course of its expansion, display any tendency toward increasing its physical productivity. The fruits of increased productivity, retained by the entrepreneur as mentioned above, mainly reflected occasional price rises. Such price rises occurred throughout the course of an economic cycle. Hence the expectation that the entrepreneur might, by accepting lower profits, turn back a part of what he had gained through extraordinary profits during the favorable phase of the cycle. Fluctuations in export prices would thus be expressed in the form of contraction or expansion in the entrepreneur's margin of profit. This did not happen, however, for more or less obvious reasons. We have already mentioned that the cyclical contractions almost inevitably brought about a disequilibrium in the balance of payments, corrected through readjustments in the exchange rate.[1]

The external disequilibrium, as has been shown, arose from a series of factors inherent in the very nature of the economic system. Periods of crisis penetrated deeply into the system from without, and their impact attained great proportions. We have seen how in the first stage—the one immediately following the decline in export prices—the demand for imports was necessarily prolonged for some time under the indirect influence of the previous expansion in external sales and in the form of financing of imports. The result of this and other factors I have indicated was a disequilibrium—the accumulation

---

[1] The legal parity of the milréis (called the cruzeiro from 1942) had at the time of the winning of independence been 67½ pence (corresponding to 1$600 (1 milréis 600 réis) per eighth of an ounce of 22 karat gold. It declined to 43½ pence in 1833 and again to 27 pence in 1846. In the 1850's the average annual rate was 27 pence (higher than 27 pence for six of the ten years of the decade and above 25 in each year). In the 'sixties the annual average reached 27 one year, and was above 25 during five others. In the 'seventies it reached 27 pence one year, and was above 25 during four others. In the 'eighties it did not reach 27 pence in any of the years of the decade, being above 25 pence for two years and under 20 for two others. In the 'nineties it was below 20 pence for nine of the ten years.

of a deficit on the current account of the balance of payments. If the economy were to operate in line with the rules of the gold standard—that is, through selling out of external assets and metallic reserves—the correction of such disequilibrium would come as a consequence of the general contraction, spreading from the exporting sector to all other economic activities. We have already observed how the contractions of the exporting sector—within the logic of the system—tended to be translated mainly into a reduction in the profit margin. The contraction in aggregate income resulting from the crisis was therefore basically shown in a reduction of payments to non-salaried classes. Since imported articles represented a substantial part of the consumption expenses of those high-income classes, an abrupt contraction in the profits of the exporting sector undoubtedly tended to reduce the demand for imported goods. Moreover, the reduction in profits affected the volume of investments and caused a series of secondary effects tending to reduce demand for imports.

Correction of the disequilibrium through the exchange rate was an operation of quite a different nature, whose consequences were likewise different. With a reduction in prices of exported products—coffee, in this instance—came a trend toward a sharp decline in the external buying power of the local currency.[2] That decline occurred even before the disequilib-

---

[2] The role of the price of coffee as a determinant of the exchange rate was duly noted by Wileman at a time when the more enlightened observers in Brazil were concerned merely with the issues of paper currency and the deficits of the central government. Wileman observed that between 1861–1864 and 1865–1869 the average price of coffee fell from 5$729 to 4$952 (gold) per bag and the average exchange rate declined from 27 6/8 to 21.31; in the 1870–1875 period coffee increased to 6$339 per bag and the exchange rate recovered to a figure of 24.3; in the 1876–1885 period the price declined to 3$247 per bag and the exchange rate dropped to 22¼. Finally, in 1886–1889, it again increased to 5$432 a bag and the exchange rate rose to 24¼. J. P. Wileman, *Brazilian Exchange* (Buenos Aires, 1896), pp. 234-248.

rium had materialized, inasmuch as the mere forecast of an impending disequilibrium was enough to start a race against the external value of the currency. All imported items thus underwent a sharp price rise with an automatic reduction in the demand for them in Brazil. Hence, without the need for selling out of reserves, which were actually nonexistent, the economy managed to correct the external disequilibrium. On the one hand, the buying power of consumers of imported articles was curtailed by the rising prices of the latter; on the other, a sort of tax was imposed on the export of capital by making those wishing to send funds abroad pay more for this privilege.

Reduction in the external value of the currency was also tantamount to a premium for all those selling foreign currencies—that is, the exporters. For example, let us suppose that immediately before a crisis a coffee exporter was selling coffee at $25 a bag and exchanging those dollars for 200 cruzeiros—that is, at an exchange rate of eight cruzeiros per dollar. Once the crisis was under way, there was a reduction of 40 per cent in the selling price per bag to $15. If the economy were operating in a system of exchange stability, that ten-dollar loss would be reflected in a corresponding reduction in profit to the entrepreneur, for the reasons already stated. But, because the readjustment was made through the exchange rate, the results were different. Let us assume that at the beginning of the crisis the value of the dollar has climbed from eight to twelve cruzeiros. Then the $15 per bag that the entrepreneur was charging would be exchanged not for 120 but for 180 cruzeiros. The entrepreneur's losses, which amounted to 40 per cent in foreign currency, were thus only 10 per cent in the local currency.

In the ultimate analysis, the process of correcting the external disequilibrium implied an income transfer from those who paid for imports to those who sold exports. Since imports were paid for by the community as a whole, the exporters were actually promoting the socialization of the losses which economic mechanisms tended to concentrate on their profits. It is true

that a part of that income transfer took place within the entrepreneur class itself, in its double role of exporter and consumer
of imported articles. Notwithstanding this, the bulk of the
income transfer was spread between the great mass of consumers of imported articles and the exporter-entrepreneurs.
The composition of Brazilian imports at the end of the nineteenth century and in the early twentieth century, with 50 per
cent consisting of foodstuffs and textiles, is indicative of the
size of such transfer. During the depression the imports which
contracted less because of the low income-elasticity of the demand for them were those of essential products utilized by the
great mass of the consumers. Those consumer goods exclusively imported for the nonsalaried classes displayed high income-elasticity because of their very nonessential nature.

In summary, it might be said that the increases in economic
productivity achieved in the cyclical rise were retained by the
entrepreneurs on account of the prevailing conditions of abundance of land and manpower. There was thus a tendency toward concentration of income in times of prosperity. Since
profits grew at a higher rate than wages—or, since the former
grew whereas the latter remained stable—it is evident that the
proportion of profit in the entire income from the territory
tended to rise. In the stage of cyclical decline there was a strong
fall in the economic productivity of the exporting sector. Despite this, the mechanism whereby the economy corrected the
external disequilibrium—the readjustment of the exchange
rate—made it possible to transfer losses to the great mass of
consumers. The process of concentrating wealth was therefore
a feature of prosperity, and was not matched by a compensating counterpart in the stages of contraction of income.

The basic reason for this form of operation lay in the struggle for survival of an economic organism with scanty means
of defense. From the standpoint of an industrial center, the
economic crisis took the form of a more or less regular halt in
a steady forward march. This halt made it possible to readjust

some parts of the system which tended to lose coördination in a period of growth. The sharp decline in profitability meant elimination of the less efficient and financially weaker entrepreneurs. It also demanded increasing efficiency on the part of those in a strong financial position, and permitted the concentration of financial power required in a higher stage of development of the capitalistic economy.

In the dependent economy, exporting primary products, a crisis appeared as a cataclysm imposed from without. The contortions that economy was compelled to perform in order to defend itself against the overwhelming pressure from abroad bore no resemblance to the actions and reactions which took place within the industrial economies in the periods of depression and recovery following such a crisis. If the decline in export prices were transformed, as might be expected in line with the logic of the system, into diminishing profits for the entrepreneurs, it is obvious that—dependent on the extent of such losses—many entrepreneurs would have to stop either producing coffee or buying it from small local producers. Since it was not practicable to make such a short-term reduction in costs through lowering wages (the level of which had not risen in the cyclical rise), the only solution remaining for the entrepreneur or for the less financially powerful was to curtail production. A large part of the economic activity would thus tend to be paralyzed, and in view of the characteristics of such activity that paralysis would cause the greatest of all losses.

By its very nature a coffee plantation means long-term investment with large fixed assets. Land used for coffee can be utilized only in a subsidiary manner for other crops. There is no possibility of reducing the planted area for the next productive period, as with cereals. Abandonment of the coffee plantation would mean heavy loss to the entrepreneur because of the size of his fixed capital. Furthermore, since there was no alternate possibility of utilization of the manpower involved, the total loss would be considerable. The population quitting the coffee plantations had to return to the harsh subsistence economy. The decline in monetary income would obviously have a series of secondary effects on the internal market economy, spreading the results of the depression. And this high price would be paid in return for little or nothing. There would probably be a greater concentration of estates, with the financially powerful landowners absorbing the weaker ones. There is, however, no reason for supposing that incentives might be created for increasing productivity. Because of the nature of the economic activity, the only way to obtain short-term physical productivity increases would be by cuts in payrolls, far from being a solution from the standpoint of the community as a whole.

This explains why the economy tried by every available means to defend its level of employment during periods of depression. Whatever the reduction in international coffee prices might be, from the standpoint of the community as a whole there would always be greater advantages in maintaining the level of exports. In this way the level of employment within the country was defended and the secondary effects of the crisis were controlled. Nevertheless, in order to achieve that objective it was necessary that the impact of the crisis not be concentrated on the profits of the entrepreneurs, or many of the latter would be forced to cease operations because of the financial impossibility of sustaining any further reductions in their income.

29. REPUBLICAN DECENTRALIZATION AND FORMATION OF NEW PRESSURE GROUPS

A closer look at the process described in the foregoing chapter leads to the conclusion that income transfers took a number of forms. On the one hand, there were transfers between the subsistence and exporting sectors to the benefit of the latter, inasmuch as prices paid for imports by the subsistence sector underwent an increase over those paid for subsistence products by the exporting sector. On the other hand, there were huge income transfers within the exporting sector itself, because wage earners on coffee plantations, even though producing much of their own food, received the principal part of their wages in cash and consumed a series of common-usage articles which were either imported or semimanufactured in Brazil from imported raw materials. The nuclei more seriously affected, however, were the urban populations. Living on wages and salaries and consuming a number of imported articles, including food, such populations saw their real income especially hard hit by increases in the exchange rate.

The regressive effect on income distribution by depreciation of exchange was intensified, moreover, by the handling of public finances. Import duties, the basis of the central government's revenues, were collected in accordance with a fixed exchange rate.[1] When the currency was depreciated, the ad

---

[1] Inasmuch as the ad valorem tax was paid in national currency at a fixed rate of exchange (27 pence per milréis), it remained stable when the currency was depreciated whereas the value of imported merchandise in national currency increased. Thus government revenue from import duties remained stationary at a time when the cost of imports

valorem amount of such duties diminished, producing two regressive effects: first, the real reduction in levies was greater for products paying the highest duties—that is, for those articles whose consumption was limited to the higher income classes; second, the relative reduction in public revenues compelled the government to issue paper money for financing the deficit, and currency issues had the effect of a highly regressive tax inasmuch as they particularly affected the urban salaried classes.

The reduction in the gold value of government revenues was more serious, because the government had important commitments to be paid in gold. When the milréis was depreciated, the government was compelled to allocate a much greater part of its revenue in local currency to the servicing of the external debt. Consequently, in order to maintain the most essential public services, the government had to issue paper currency. There is no indication that—except during the Paraguayan War (1864–1870)—issues of paper currency had been intended for the expansion of activities in the public sector.[2] On the other hand, to defend the exchange rate the gov-

---

in national currency increased and the cost of exchange even more so. In 1886 the Belisário reform set the value of the milréis for purposes of collection of duties at 24 pence. When the exchange rate rose above that level in the next two years, the value of duties increased more than that of imports whereas the cost of exchange was reduced—all of which contributed to the creating of an exceptionally favorable situation for the public finances in those years. Murtinho gave a radical solution to the problem in 1900 by introducing the gold tariff.

[2] A comparison between the 'eighties and the 'nineties in this respect is highly illustrative. In the former decade the circulating medium remained stationary whereas in the latter it more than tripled. A comparison between the total expenditure of the central government and the value of exports shows, however, that the ratio between the former and the latter declined from 0.72 to 0.49. This reduction partly reflects the transfer of income to the exporting class as a result of exchange

ernment contracted successive burdensome loans abroad, servicing of which entailed incomprehensible fiscal overloading. The increase in the relative importance of servicing the public debt within the framework of government outlays made it more and more difficult for the government to meet those outlays out of current revenues at times of depression. A close connection was therefore established among foreign loans, budgetary deficits, and currency issues, largely resorted to for covering deficits, and disequilibriums on the current account of the balance of payments through fluctuations in the exchange rate.

The *modus operandi* of the fiscal system deserves special attention. Though on the one hand it contributed to a reduction in the impact of external fluctuations, it also intensified the process of regressive income transfers at times of depression. The fact that the fiscal burden lightened when the currency was depreciated—that is, at times when prices of export articles were declining in the international market—undoubtedly acted as a compensating factor for the external deflationary pressure. Nevertheless, the reduction in the fiscal burden was made chiefly to the benefit of high-income social groups. Moreover, the financing of deficits by issuing paper money generated inflationary pressure with immediate effects more strongly felt in urban zones. Hence the external depression (reduction in export prices) became transformed internally into an inflationary process.

In the last decade of the nineteenth century, such internal disequilibriums were intensified as a result of the monetary policy adopted by the provisional government installed after the proclamation of the republic. The monetary policy of the

---

depreciation, but is also a sign that there was probably a considerable reduction in the fiscal burden. Another sign of this reduction is to be seen in the fact that ordinary revenue covered only 80 per cent of the expenditures during the latter decade, as compared with 88 per cent in the former.

imperial government in the 1880's, pervaded by the mirage of convertibility, had led to large increases in the external debt and at the same time had kept the entire economic system in a state of permanent scarcity of money. Between 1880 and 1889 the amount of paper currency in circulation declined from 216,000,000 to 197,000,000 milréis, whereas the value of foreign trade (imports plus exports) grew from 411,000,000 to 477,000,000 milréis. Since it was at this time that slavery was superseded by the wage system and about 200,000 immigrants entered Brazil, it is easy to understand the great scarcity of means of payment then prevailing. The country's monetary system had proved to be utterly inadequate for an economy based on wage labor. Such a system was based on a mass of paper currency issued by the treasury to cover government deficits and to a lesser extent (about 20 per cent) on notes issued by the banks, which also had on some occasions used this privilege. This system had no elasticity whatsoever, and its earlier expansion had resulted from emergency measures taken at moments of crisis or at the mere whim of the rulers. While the regime of slave labor was in force, the flow of monetary income was small and few hindrances resulted from this primitive kind of monetary system. However, after the 1875 crisis it became evident that Brazil needed a minimum of automatic monetary mechanisms. Reform was to wait until in 1888 Parliament approved an ill-defined measure which the imperial government had resisted to the end.

The inability of the imperial government to equip Brazil with an adequate monetary system, as well as its ineptitude in paving the way firmly and positively for the solution of the manpower problem, strongly reflects the growing diversity of interests in the various regions of the country. In earlier periods there had been no such divergency. In both the north and the south the forms of social organization were analogous, and the ruling classes could speak in the same terms and were united on fundamental issues—such as, for instance, the struggle to maintain the slave traffic. In the last few decades of the nineteenth century, however, the divergencies deepened. Social organization in the south underwent rapid transformations under the influence of wage-earning labor both on the coffee plantations and in the urban centers, and small farm agriculture in the so-called "region of colonies" in the southernmost provinces.

The need for administrative action and reforms in public services, education, health, vocational training, banking, and other fields in the south became increasingly apparent. However, the imperial government, in whose administration and policies great influence was wielded by men connected with the former slave-owning interests, showed little sensitvity toward these new problems. The proclamation of the republic in 1889 consequently took the form of a movement in favor of regional autonomy. The new state governments were to play a fundamental role in the field of economic and financial policy making during the first few decades of the republic. The monetary reform of 1888 (previously shelved by the imperial government), in the form in which it was later enforced by the provisional government, granted several regional banks the right to issue currency, thus giving rise to a sudden, enormous expansion in credit throughout the whole of Brazil. The transition from a protracted period of exceedingly difficult credit to one of great facility gave rise to feverish economic activity such as the country had never seen before. The sudden expansion in monetary income exerted considerable pressure upon the balance of payments. The average exchange rate fell from 26 pence in 1890 to 13.15/16 pence in 1893, continuing to decline during the following years until the end of the decade, when it reached 8.7/32 pence.

The tremendous exchange depreciation in the last decade of the nineteenth century, caused mainly by unlimited credit expansion under the first provisional government, generated strong pressure upon the wage-earning classes, especially in the urban centers. That pressure contributed to the social and political unrest of the time accompanied by military uprisings and revolutionary movements, to which the country had grown unaccustomed throughout the previous fifty years. From 1898 the policy of Murtinho was to reflect a new balance of political and economic forces.[3] The reduction in the servicing of the public debt by means of a consolidation loan (1898), the introduction of the gold clause in the collection of import duties (1900), as well as a series of deflationary measures and a substantial increase in the value of exports—up from £26 million in 1896–1899 to £37 million in 1900–1903—made it possible to regain external equilibrium.[4] After 1900, interests directly connected with the external depreciation of the currency (exporting groups) had to face the organized resistance of other groups. Among these were the urban middle classes, civilian and military government personnel, business employees, urban and rural wage-earning workers, farm producers linked with the internal market, as well as foreign firms with concessions for public utilities, not all of which had guar-

[3] Joaquim Murtinho, minister of finance in the Campos Sales government (1898–1902), was the first to adopt in Brazil a series of coördinated economic and financial measures for the specific purpose of reducing pressure against the balance of payments and reëstablishing the government's credit abroad. Murtinho had been influenced by Wileman's book, quoted previously, unquestionably the first objective, systematic analysis—based on a careful critique of statistical sources—of the causes underlying the tendency to external disequilibrium on the part of the Brazilian economy.

[4] The great increase in the value of Brazil's exports between the last decade of the nineteenth century and the first decade of the twentieth —the main factor in the substantial improvement in the position of the balance of payments—had as its basic cause the considerable expansion in rubber exports. The proportion of Brazilian exports represented by rubber increased from 10 per cent in 1890 to 39 per cent in 1910.

antees of interest on their investments. The newly formed industrial groups, more interested in boosting productive capacity than in obtaining additional protection, also resented losses caused by exchange depreciation.

Although republican decentralization gave the government greater political and administrative flexibility in the economic field, to the benefit of the great agricultural exporting groups, the political rise of new social groups whose income was not derived from rural estates—facilitated by the republican government itself—had the effect of substantially reducing the control over the central government previously exercised by those agricultural exporting groups. A period of tension thus began between the two levels of government action—state and federal—and was to continue for the first three decades of the twentieth century.

PART V

*The Economy of Transition
to an Industrial
System (Twentieth Century)*

30. CRISIS IN
THE COFFEE ECONOMY

In the 1890's a situation arose which was exceptionally favorable to the expansion of coffee growing in Brazil. On the one hand, non-Brazilian sources of supply faced a period of difficulty, with Asian production being substantially impaired by diseases which practically destroyed the coffee plantations on the island of Ceylon. Moreover, with republican decentralization the problem of immigration was taken over by the states and was tackled in a far broader fashion by the government of the state of São Paulo—that is, by the coffee farmer class. Finally, the stimulating effects of the great credit inflation of that period brought twofold benefit to the coffee-grower class, providing it with the necessary credit for financing the opening of new land and raising coffee prices in local currency through the exchange depreciation. Brazilian coffee production, which had risen from 3.7 million 60-kilo bags in 1880–1881 to 5.5 million in 1890–1891, attained 16.3 million in 1901–1902.[1]

The elasticity of manpower supply and abundance of land in the coffee-producing countries were a clear indication that in the long run coffee prices would tend to fall under the per-

---

[1] Pierre Denis, *Le Brésil au XXᵉ siècle* (Paris, 1928), p. 176, gives data for Brazilian and world production during the 1870–1905 period.

sistent action of investments in railroads, ports, and maritime transportation, all of which were in a state of growth during the last quarter of the nineteenth century. The problem can be better understood if it is observed from a broader viewpoint. Entrepreneurs in raw materials had to make their choice of investments from among a limited number of articles demanded by the international market. In Brazil, the article presenting greater relative advantages was coffee. So long as coffee prices did not fall to the point of eliminating those advantages, capital available within Brazil continued to flow into coffee plantations. Thus it was inevitable that the supply of coffee should tend to grow, not so much in terms of a growth in demand but because of the availability of underoccupied manpower and land and the relative advantage afforded by that export product.

It so happened, however, that the great expansion in coffee growing at the end of the eighteenth century took place almost entirely within the frontiers of a single country. The exceptional conditions for coffee in Brazil gave entrepreneurs there the chance of controlling three-quarters of the world's coffee. This circumstance permitted the manipulation of the world market which was to lead to a very special trend in the evolution of coffee prices. When the first overproduction crisis occurred in the early twentieth century, Brazilian entrepreneurs soon realized they were in a privileged position for erecting defenses against a fall in prices. All they needed was financial resources for keeping a part of the output off the market—that is, for artificially restricting supply. Inventories thus built up would be mobilized when the market showed greater strength —when income stood at high levels in importing countries—or would serve to compensate for shortages in years of poor crops.

From the time of the 1893 crisis, which was especially protracted in the United States, coffee prices began to fall in the world market. The average export value per bag in 1896 was £2.91, as opposed to £4.09 in 1893. In 1897 a new depression occurred in the world market, with prices declining in the next two years to £1.48 in 1899. Whereas the effects of the 1893 crisis could be cushioned by the external depreciation of the currency, extreme pressure upon the mass of urban consumers (which had already come into existence by 1897) made it impracticable to resort to further depreciation. I have already shown that this pressure had led to growing social unrest and finally to the adoption of a policy aimed at a recuperation of the exchange rate.

Precisely at this time, when it became impracticable to resort to the exchange mechanism to protect the profitability of the coffee sector, the problem of overproduction began to arise. Coffee inventories, accumulating from year to year, weighed heavily on prices, causing a permanent loss of income both to producers and to the country as a whole. The idea of withdrawing from the market a part of these inventories soon developed in the minds of the ruling classes of the coffee-producing states, whose political and financial power had considerably increased as a result of republican decentralization. In the Taubaté Agreement of February, 1906, the bases were established for what was to become known as the price-boosting policy. Essentially, that policy consisted of the following measures. To reëstablish the balance between supply and demand, the government was to intervene in the market and purchase the surpluses. Such buying would be financed by means of foreign loans. The servicing of such loans would be covered by a new tax to be levied in gold on every bag of coffee exported. In order to reach a long-term solution to the problem, the governments of the coffee-growing states were to discourage the expansion of plantations.

The heated discussions aroused by the price-boosting policy were a clear indication of the transformations occurring at that time in the political and social structure of the country. Republican decentralization had strengthened the power of the coffee growers at the regional level. We have already seen that such decentralization—which reached extremes in the enforcement of the banking reform—was involved in the excessive expansion of the coffee plantations between 1891 and 1897. In that same period, however, the groups exerting pressure upon the federal government became more numerous and complex. The increasingly important urban middle classes—within which the civil and military services were conspicuous—were directly affected by the exchange depreciation. The powerful international financial group centering in the house of Rothschild closely observed the economic and financial policy of the Brazilian government, particularly after the consolidation loan of 1898.[2] Finally, importers and industrialists, whose interests conflicted for a number of reasons with those of the coffee planters, found in the republican regime an opportunity of increasing their political power.

The first price-boosting scheme was put into operation by the coffee-producing states—under the leadership of São Paulo —without federal government support. In view of the unwillingness of the latter, the state governments—to which republican decentralization had granted the constitutional power of levying taxes on exports—appealed directly to international credit sources. This decision gave them a victory over their competitors. The federal government was finally compelled to take upon itself the major responsibility for carrying out the task. The financial success of the experiment consolidated the

---

[2] The attitude of Lord Rothschild, who published a letter in violent terms against the "valorization," reflects the fear that another Brazilian government bankruptcy might affect the servicing of the foreign debt, due to be recommenced in 1911. Though not desirous of participating in a risky affair, Rothschild at the same time did not view kindly the prospect that other international financial groups would take advantage of the situation, searching as they were for an opportunity of breaking into a well-defended stronghold of the long-standing financial house to which the Brazilian government had been linked ever since its second foreign loan in 1825.

victory and strengthened the political power of the coffee planters, and for more than a quarter of a century—until 1930—they succeeded in imposing their economic policy on the federal government.

The defense plan prepared by the coffee planters was well conceived, but did leave one aspect of the problem unresolved. With prices holding steady, profits obviously remained high. It was likewise obvious that the coffee business would continue to be attractive to capital formed within it. In other words, investments in this sector would be maintained at a high level, exerting growing pressure upon supply. Thus the artificial reduction in supply engendered the expansion of that same supply and created a more serious problem for the future. That danger was clearly perceived at the time, but was not easily circumvented. The apparent solution lay in avoiding continuous growth in productive capacity or in preventing more intensive growth as a result of price stability at high levels. Preventive measures were, however, fruitless. It would have been necessary for the entrepreneurs to count upon other equally profitable opportunities for investment of the resources which were uninterruptedly accumulating in the form of profits. Price protecting gave coffee a privileged position among primary products in international trade, and its relative advantage tended to increase. Moreover, the high profits made it necessary for the entrepreneur to continue investing. Hence it was inevitable that such investments should tend to find their way back again into coffee planting. The defense mechanism of the coffee economy might, in the ultimate analysis, be viewed as a process of postponing the solution to a problem which tended to become more and more serious.

The complicated defense mechanism of the coffee economy operated with some efficiency until the third decade of the twentieth century, but the world crisis of 1929 found it in an extremely vulnerable position. Thanks to artificial incentives, coffee production had grown considerably in the late 1920's.

Between 1925 and 1929 that growth amounted to almost one hundred per cent, reflecting the enormous amount of planting during the immediately preceding period.[3] Although production was thus increasing, exports remained nearly stable. Between 1927 and 1929, exports provided an outlet for only two-thirds of the quantity produced.[4] The withholding of supplies made it possible to maintain high prices on the international market. These prices resulted in a high rate of profit for producers, who continued to invest in new plantations. On the other hand, demand continued to evolve along traditional lines. Although declining slightly in times of depression, it also expanded little at periods of great prosperity. In fact, despite the great rise in real income which took place in the industrial countries in the 'twenties, such prosperity in no way changed the pattern of the demand for coffee, which grew slowly but steadily with the increase in population and urbanization. In the United States, the principal importer, where per capita real income increased by about 35 per cent in that decade, annual coffee consumption remained at about twelve pounds per inhabitant, although retail prices were stable.[5]

[3] Exportable production of coffee increased from 15,761,000 to 28,-942,000 six-kilo bags, according to data published by the Brazilian Coffee Institute. Statistical data relating to the evolution of the coffee problem from 1925 are given in *O Desenvolvimento Econômico do Brasil* (National Bank for Economic Development—United Nations Economic Committee for Latin America, hereinafter cited as NBED-ECLA), Part II, Chapter 2, Statistical Annex.

[4] Average 1927–1929 production was 20.9 million bags, and exports amounted to 14.1 million. The greatest unbalance occurred in the year of the crisis, when production reached 28,941,000 bags and exports 14,281,000.

[5] The prices paid in 1929 by the United States consumer were no higher than those in 1920 and a little below those of 1925. For details on this problem see *Capacity of the United States to Absorb Latin American Products* (United Nations Economic Committee for Latin America, hereinafter cited as ECLA, 1951).

Accordingly the situation was clearly a structural unbalance between supply and demand. There could be no expectation of a perceptible increase in demand because of the increase in available income in the importing countries. Nor could there be any thought of an increase in consumption in those countries as a result of lower prices. The only way to avoid enormous losses to both coffee growers and the exporting country was to avoid—by withdrawing a part of the production from the market—an increase in supply to above the level called for by demand, so as to maintain a more or less stable short-term per capita consumption level. It seemed perfectly obvious that the accumulating inventories were not likely to be used within the foreseeable future. Even if the world economy managed to avoid a new depression, after the great expansion of the 'twenties, there was no prospect of any outlet for such inventories as long as productive capacity continued to increase. Thus the situation was absolutely untenable.

With the broader perspective from which we can now observe this historic phenomenon, we can ask where the basic error lay in that entire policy, which was unquestionably implemented with exceptional boldness. The error, if we may call it such, lay in failing to bear in mind the inherent characteristics of an economic activity of typically colonial nature, such as coffee growing in Brazil. A balance between supply and demand for colonial products was attained for demand when the market reached a point of saturation, and for supply when all available productive factors (manpower and land) were engaged in production. In such circumstances it was inevitable that colonial products should tend, in the long run, to decline in price.

Maintaining coffee prices consistently at a high level required creating conditions under which the unbalance between supply and demand grew more and more marked. To avoid such a tendency it would have been necessary for the price-defense policy to be supplemented by another series of measures aimed at definitely discouraging investments in coffee plantations. Such a policy of discouragement was impracticable unless other alternatives were open to the coffee-producing entrepreneurs—that is, unless there were opportunities of investing elsewhere at a comparable rate the profits obtained in coffee. Such an opportunity was nonexistent, by definition, because no other colonial product could be the object of a defense policy of the type applied in the instance of coffee. Actually, there was a need for taking a step forward so as to create the aforementioned opportunity artificially. For this purpose it would have been necessary to create incentives for other exports, through a policy of subsidies, and this would have been practicable only if financial resources could be shifted away from the coffee sector. Prices paid to the coffee growers had to be kept at a level capable of discouraging new investments, and the resulting difference between prices paid to the producers and export prices, once other costs had been covered, could have been utilized to create incentives, in the form of long-term loans or direct subsidies, for other exporting activities.

Even if surplus production had been avoided as described above, nothing could prevent the policy of defense of prices from encouraging coffee growing in other countries with land and manpower available under conditions similar to those in Brazil but less advantageous. For Brazilian producers to retain their status as holders of a semimonopoly, it was essential to keep prices at low levels. When producers took advantage of that semimonopolistic situation to protect prices, they themselves were destroying the very basis upon which their privilege was founded. Thus, however well designed the price defense policy, in the long run it was bound to produce negative results, which undoubtedly would have been less widespread if the policy had adhered to broader principles. There is no doubt, however, that as it was adopted it actually precipitated and intensified the crisis in the Brazilian coffee economy.

Let us take another look at the general problem before dwelling on the solution. The 1920's were a period of exceptional prosperity for the industrial countries. Between 1920 and 1929 the gross national product in the United States grew from $103.6 billion to $152.7 billion (at constant prices), amounting to an increase of more than 35 per cent in per capita real income. Meanwhile coffee consumption had remained stable at about 12 pounds per capita per year, and the price paid by the North American consumer remained, with small variations, at about 47 cents a pound. Possibilities of market expansion were therefore practically nil. Prices were being maintained at the cost of a large-scale withholding of stocks. The value of accumulated inventories between 1927 and 1929 reached the enormous figure of 4.2 billion milréis, equivalent to 24 billion cruzeiros at 1950 price levels. In 1929 alone the value of such inventories reached 10 per cent of Brazil's gross national product for the year.[6]

Obviously, this situation had enormous potential ability for disrupting the economy. Financing for those inventories had largely been obtained from foreign banks. The intention had been to preclude external disequilibrium in this manner. Let us see what actually happened. Foreign loans served as a basis for the expansion of money supply intended for buying coffee withdrawn from the market. The sudden large increase in

---

[6] Data on the territorial product and the nominal and real investments for the 1925–1939 period, referred to in this and subsequent chapters, have been drawn up by the author on the basis of the value and physical volume of agricultural and industrial production, on the value and quantum of imports, the terms of trade, and the expenditures of the federal government, using as a deflator for the latter the cost-of-living index for the city of Rio de Janeiro. For the basic data, see *Anuário Estatístico do Brasil,* 1937–1939, and for the indexes of agricultural and industrial output, quantum of imports, and terms of trade, see *Estudio Econômico de América Latina* (ECLA, 1949), Chapter VII.

monetary income obtained by groups which derived their profits from exports evidently could not fail to cause inflationary pressure.[7] Such pressure is particularly heavy in an underdeveloped economy, being immediately reflected in a rapid increase in imports because of the low elasticity of internal supply.[8]

Thus it may be inferred that the policy of accumulating coffee stocks was bound to create inflationary pressure. It so happened, however, that the largest investments in inventories took place in 1927–1929, a period also marked by a substantial flow of foreign private capital into Brazil. The coincidence between the inflow of private capital and the arrival of loans for financing coffee gave rise to an extremely favorable exchange situation and induced the Brazilian government to embark upon a policy of convertibility.[9]

Once the crisis broke, in the last quarter of 1929, it was merely a matter of months before the entire metallic reserve

[7] The increase in the value of exports leads to larger growth in monetary income, in line with the size of the multiplier. Because the supply is inelastic, a series of adjustments to the price level has to be made between the expansion in the monetary income and the increase in the real income.

[8] Between 1920–1922 and 1929, although the quantum of exports increased by merely 10 per cent, that of the imports grew by about 100 per cent. For the basic data, see *Estudio Econômico de América Latina, op. cit.*

[9] In 1926 the Washington Luis government set the parity of the milréis at 0.200 grams of fine gold, corresponding to 5.115/128 pence, and set up a stabilization fund which was to issue paper money against a 100 per cent gold reserve. As in the instance of the conversion fund, set up in 1906 under the Afonso Pena government, the notes issued previously were not convertible; thus two systems of circulating media came into existence in Brazil: one convertible, the other nonconvertible. In 1929, nonconvertible notes in circulation amounted to 2,543,-000 contos, and convertible ones to 848,000 contos.

accumulated by foreign loans was swallowed up by foreign capital fleeing Brazil. Hence the adventure into convertibility of the latter 'twenties—which in the ultimate analysis was a by-product of the coffee defense policy—served only to facilitate the flight of capital. If it had not been for the possibility of conversion existing at the time, the decline in the milréis would have been much sharper, automatically imposing a tax on the export of capital. That levy did of course come into existence in the long run, but it came too late—after all the reserves had evaporated.[10]

31. DEFENSE MECHANISMS
IN THE 1929 CRISIS

When the world crisis burst upon the scene, coffee production, then at high levels, had to go on increasing because growers had continued to expand plantations until that time. In fact, the maximum production was to be attained in 1933—that is, at the lowest point of the depression—as a reflection of the extensive planting of 1927–28. On the other hand, it was quite impossible to obtain credit abroad to finance withholding of new inventories, inasmuch as the international market was deep in the grip of the depression and government credit had evaporated with the disappearance of metallic reserves. The basic aspects of the problem might be stated as follows. Which would be more suitable: to harvest the coffee, or to let it rot on the trees by abandoning a part of the plantations, like factories

[10] The government's gold reserves totaled 31,100,000 pounds in September, 1929; by December, 1930, they had completely disappeared.

that close down during times of depression? If a decision were taken to harvest the coffee, what would be done with it? By a tour de force in the international market, would inventories be stockpiled or would they be destroyed? In the event stockpiling or destruction were decided on, how would such an operation be financed? In other words, who would bear the burden if coffee had to be harvested?

At first sight, the most rational solution would seem to have been that of abandoning the coffee plantations. But the problem was less one of knowing what to do with the surplus coffee than of deciding who was to pay for the losses. Whether the coffee was to be harvested or not, a loss was certain. To abandon coffee plantations without paying indemnification to growers would have meant leaving them to bear the brunt of the heaviest losses. As already described, the economy had developed a series of mechanisms whereby the coffee ruling class had managed to transfer to the community as a whole the bulk of the burden of the cyclical price fall. It was therefore to be expected that the line of least resistance would be adopted.

First, let us see how the classic defense mechanism operated through the exchange rate. The great stockpiling of 1929, the fast selling of Brazil's metallic reserves, and the uncertain prospects of financing the large crops forecast for the near future—all hastened the decline in international coffee prices which occurred simultaneously with that of every other primary product at the end of 1929. That slump reached catastrophic proportions; between September, 1929 and September, 1931, prices fell from 22.5 cents to 8 cents a pound. In view of the characteristics of coffee demand, which does not decline during depressions in countries with a high income level, such a drastic price reduction would have been inconceivable except for the unusual circumstances of supply. The average price paid by the North American consumer between 1929 and 1931 fell only from 47.9 cents to 32.8 cents a pound.[1] The effects of two separate crises—in demand and in supply—were therefore superimposed. The situation was favorable to coffee middlemen, who realized the weakness of the suppliers' position and were able to transfer to Brazilian growers the whole of their losses caused by the general crisis.

The sudden fall in the international price of coffee and the bankruptcy of the convertibility system caused an external devaluation in the Brazilian currency. This devaluation naturally brought great alleviation to the coffee sector of the economy. International coffee prices had declined 60 per cent. The level of the exchange rate was such as to entail a depreciation of 40 per cent.[2] The bulk of the losses could therefore be transferred to the community as a whole through a rise in import prices. There was, however, another side of the problem to be considered. Despite the large decline in prices, the international market could still not absorb the entire production, on account of the inelasticity of the demand in terms of price. Actually, apart from the concern with price defense measures, there was a possibility of forcing the market. This was, in fact, accomplished, and a 25 per cent increase in the physical volume of exports was achieved between 1929 and 1931. Even so, a considerable part of the production remained with no chance whatsoever of finding a market. There was an evident need for supplementary measures.

The depreciation of the currency, although cushioning the

[1] See *Capacity of the United States to Absorb Latin American Products* (ECLA, 1951).

[2] The average value per bag of coffee exported dropped from £4.71 in 1929 to £1.80 in 1932–1934, a decline of 62 per cent. In Brazilian currency the decline was from 192 to 145 milréis—that is, 25 per cent. In the next three-year period the price in pounds fell to 1.29 and that in milréis rose to 159. In these calculations the gold value of the pound before devaluation is still being used.

impact of the fall in international prices on the Brazilian entrepreneur, induced him to continue harvesting and maintaining pressure on the market. This situation led to a new price decline and renewed depreciation of the currency, contributing to further intensification of the crisis. As the degree of depreciation of the currency was much smaller than the fall in prices—inasmuch as the former was influenced by other factors—a point would clearly be reached where the loss to the growers would be large enough to induce them to abandon their plantations. Only then would a balance be reached between supply and demand. An analysis of this readjustment process proves that exchange mechanisms could not be deemed an effective instrument for the defense of the coffee economy under the exceptionally serious conditions created by the crisis in question.

It was indispensable to avoid pressure by unsalable inventories upon the market, entailing a still further decline in price. This was the only way of avoiding a balance at the cost of sheer abandonment of crops—that is, with losses affecting the coffee sector almost alone. But how were stockpiles to be financed? This would obviously have to be done with resources obtained within Brazil, either by retaining a part of the payment for coffee exports or by merely expanding credit facilities. To the extent credit expansion was utilized, there was again a "socialization of losses." This credit expansion in turn was to intensify external disequilibrium, contributing toward a greater depreciation of currency, which indirectly benefited the exporting sector.

But it was not enough to withdraw a part of the coffee production from the market. Quite obviously, such surplus production had no possibility of being sold within a reasonable period. Production forecasts for the next ten years far exceeded the predictable absorption capacity of the buying markets. Destruction of surplus crops was therefore imperative as a logical consequence of the policy of harvesting more coffee than could be sold. At first sight it may seem absurd to foredoom farm crops to destruction. Nevertheless, similar situations occur daily in a market economy. Prices would have to decline much more to induce coffee growers to avoid harvesting, particularly if the effects of the price fall were to some extent nullified by currency depreciation. Since the aim was to avoid the continuance of the downward trend of prices, it is not difficult to understand that a part of the harvested coffee had to be withdrawn from the market and destroyed. Thus a balance between supply and demand was obtained at a higher level of prices.

Coffee prices, being fundamentally dependent on the pattern of supply, thus continued through the 'thirties without showing any results of the recuperation which started in 1934 in the industrialized countries. After dropping to their lowest point in 1933, international coffee prices remained unaltered until 1937, after which they declined still further in the last years of the decade. This great stability of coffee prices, which remained at such a depressed level throughout the 'thirties, is highly significant. It is a matter of common knowledge that the economic recuperation between 1933 and 1937 brought about a general increase in the prices of primary products. The price of sugar, for instance, rose 140 per cent between 1933 and 1937, and that of copper rose a little more than 100 per cent in the same period; yet coffee prices in 1937 were the same as in 1934 and lower than in 1932.

Coffee prices are fundamentally conditioned by factors prevailing on the side of supply, those on the side of demand being of secondary importance in the short run. We have already seen that the great rise in per capita real income during the 'twenties in the United States left coffee consumption in that country unaltered, despite the fact that prices paid by the consumer remained stable. During the depression years, the prices paid by the consumer actually fell by about 40 per cent without any marked change in consumption, which in 1933 was at exactly the same level as in 1929. It might be argued that the price effect would have annulled the income effect—that is, that the increase in consumption caused by the decline in price was annulled by the drop in consumption brought about by the contraction in income. However, this does not seem to have been the reason, inasmuch as in the 1934–1937 period of increase in income, prices paid by the consumer maintained their downward trend, with a figure of 24.4 cents a pound being recorded in 1937 as compared with 25.5 in 1933. There were thus two positive effects from the point of view of increased consumption: rise in real income per capita, and fall in prices. However, consumption remained almost unaltered, being 13.1 pounds per capita per year in 1937 as compared with 13.9 in 1931 and 12.5 in 1933.[3]

Let us consider in greater detail the consequences of the policy of withholding and destroying a part of the coffee output for the express purpose of protecting the coffee sector. By guaranteed minimum buying prices, remunerative to the great majority of coffee growers, the level of employment in the export economy—and, indirectly, in those producing sectors connected with the internal market—was maintained. By avoiding a substantial contraction in money income in the export sector, there was a proportionate reduction in the effects of the unemployment multiplier on the other sectors of the economy. As coffee production rose during the depression, with the largest crop of all time being harvested in 1933, it is obvious that the aggregate income of agricultural producers

---

[3] See *Capacity of the United States to Absorb Latin American Products, op. cit.* The demand for coffee, as the experience of the 'fifties showed, displays a certain elasticity in terms of prices when the latter exceed certain very high levels. In the United States market this level may be considered to be about one dollar per pound retail. If we bear in mind the increase in prices for the 'thirties, the level in question would not be less than 50 cents. Since prices were hovering around 25 cents, it may be deduced that they could exert no effect on demand.

declined less than the prices paid to those growers.[4] Hence, by permitting increased quantities of coffee to be harvested, the government was unconsciously avoiding contraction of the money income to the same extent as that of the average price received by the grower for his production. It can easily be seen what a tremendous decline in farmers' income would have occurred if, for example, one-third of that production had been abandoned on the trees, which was approximately the amount of coffee actually bought up and destroyed between 1931 and 1939.

Let us consider, by means of a simple numerical example, how this contraction in the income of the export sector operates and what influence it has on the level of aggregate income. Let us assume that the unemployment multiplier[5] in the export sector is 3. This means that a reduction of 1 in the income generated by exports will cause an over-all reduction of 3 in the income of the community as a whole. The causes underlying this multiplying mechanism are more or less obvious, and reflect the interdependence of the various parts of an economy. When exporters and producers connected with the export sector receive less money for their sales abroad, they in turn

[4] Average exportable production during the 1925–1929 period was 21.3 million bags, rising to 27.7 in 1930–1934 and to 22.8 million in 1935–1939. In the same period, the export value in Brazilian currency fell from 26.8 thousand contos to 20.3 thousand, and in the third five-year period stood at 22.1 thousand. The data relating to export production are from the National Coffee Institute, and those for exports are from the Ministry of Finance, Economic and Financial Statistics Service.

[5] The multiplier is the factor by which it would be necessary to multiply the increase or reduction in investments (or exports) to ascertain the effects on the aggregate income due to this modification at the investment (or export) level. In this instance I endeavored to measure the effect, over the period of one year, of a reduction in the income directly generated by exports. If the direct reduction is 10 and the total drop in income is 30, the multiplier is 3.

reduce their own purchases. The internal producers affected by this reduction also curtail theirs, and so on.

Let us assume that the income of a country with a dependent economy is generated in two main sectors: one, accounting for 40 per cent, entirely independent of foreign trade—that is, the subsistence sector—and the other, directly composed of export activities and indirectly influenced by those activities. Assuming the unemployment multiplier at a given moment to be 3, we may say that export activities will generate 20 per cent of the aggregate income directly and 40 per cent indirectly. Let us now consider the various situations indicated in the following tabulation.

	Export sector	Sector influenced by export sector	Independent sector	Total income
(a)	20.0	40	40	100.0
(b)	10.0	20	40	70.0
(c)	12.0	24	40	76.0
(d)	7.5	15	40	62.5

Starting with situation (a), we shall then consider various hypothetical situations of income contraction in the export sector and their effects on the aggregate income. In (b) we assume the level of production in the export sector is maintained—that is, unemployment is avoided—although prices paid to the producer in this sector are cut by one-half. The final effect on income is a shrinkage of 30 per cent, 10 per cent by direct effect and 20 per cent by indirect effect of the contraction of prices in the export sector. In (c) we also consider a reduction of 50 per cent in price, but with a concomitant expansion of 20 per cent in the quantity produced, in the export sector. The ultimate effect here is a 24 per cent decline in aggregate income. Example (d) is different from the former ones. In this instance we assume that in order to protect prices a reduction of 50 per cent in the quantity produced has been permitted. In view of this reduction in production, the price fall would be only 25 per cent. Notwithstanding, the final effect would be a contraction of 37.5 per cent in aggregate income, the largest of any of the four hypotheses.

Example (c) approximately reflects the Brazilian situation during the depression years, when prices paid to the coffee grower were cut by one-half, although the quantity produced was allowed to increase. The reduction in monetary income in Brazil between 1929 and the rock-bottom point of the depression was between 25 and 30 per cent, hence relatively small compared with that in other countries. In the United States, for instance, the fall exceeded 50 per cent, despite the fact that wholesale price indexes in that country declined far less than those of coffee prices in international trade. The difference lies in the fact that in the United States price declines entailed an enormous amount of unemployment, whereas in Brazil employment levels were maintained despite the fact that production had to be destroyed. The important thing to bear in mind is that the value of the production destroyed was far lower than the amount of real income which was being created. Brazil was in fact constructing the famous pyramids which Keynes was to envisage some years later.

Thus the policy of protection of the coffee sector during the years of the great depression was actually an authentic program of boosting the national income. Brazil was actually engaged in an anticyclical policy of much broader scope than any even suggested in any of the industrialized countries. Let us see how this occurred. In 1929, net investment in the Brazilian economy amounted to approximately 2.3 million contos (2,300 million milréis) at the buying power of the time. With the crisis those investments contracted sharply, and in 1931 they had declined to 300,000 contos (300 million milréis), always in monetary terms. Despite this decline, in 1931 coffee stockpiles had been accumulated to a value of one million contos (1,000 million milréis). Such an accumulation of stockpiles from the point of view of generation of income had the same effect as net investments. Thus the amount of net investments had not actually been reduced from 2.3 to 0.3 but to 1.3, which figure in fact represented more than 7 per cent of the net product—a high rate for a period of depression.

This explains why the national income of Brazil began to grow once more in 1933, whereas in the United States the first signs of recovery appeared only in 1934. As a matter of fact, in no year during the crisis was there actually a negative net investment figure, as occurred in the United States and generally in every other country. By 1933 Brazil's net investment figure reached 1 million contos, to which should be added 1.1 million in stockpiled coffee. The figure thus stood at 2.1 million, approaching the volume of net investments in 1929. The 2.3 million in 1929 represented 9 per cent of the net product for that year, whereas the 2.1 million in 1933 amounted to 10 per cent of the net product for the latter. Thus the impulse the economy needed in order to grow had already been regained.

It is therefore quite clear that the recovery of the Brazilian economy which took place from 1933 onward was not caused by any external factor but by the pump-priming policy unconsciously adopted in Brazil as a by-product of the protection of the coffee interests. Let us view the matter from another angle. The accumulation of coffee stockpiles before the crisis had its counterpart in debts contracted abroad. Hence there was no net investment, because what was invested in Brazil through the accumulation of stockpiles was disinvested abroad in the contracting of debts. It was as though the stockpiled coffee had been purchased by foreign firms which were postponing in their own interest the shipment of the merchandise abroad. The accumulation of coffee financed from abroad was therefore similar to an exporting process.

This was not true of coffee stockpiles financed internally, once the basis for such financing was credit expansion. Purchase of coffee for stockpiling entailed generation of income, which was added to the income produced by the expenditures of the consumers and investors. When in 1931 a million contos were injected into the economy for buying up and destroying coffee, purchasing power was being created that would partly counterbalance the reduction in expenditures by investors, which had been cut by some 2 million contos. Thus a sharper decline in demand was avoided in those sectors indirectly dependent upon income created by exports.

The actual difference between net investments and the accumulation of unsalable coffee stockpiles resided in the fact that the former gave rise to productive capacity whereas the latter did not. However, this aspect of the problem is of secondary importance at times of depression, when existing productive capacity is generally underutilized. That is why at such times it is far more important to create effective demand leading to the utilization of idle productive capacity than further to boost that productive capacity.

32. THE SHIFT IN THE DYNAMIC CENTER

We have noted how the policy of defense for the coffee sector contributed to the maintenance of effective demand and level of employment in the other sectors of the economy. Let us now see what this implied in terms of pressure on the structure of the economic system as a whole. Financing of coffee stockpiles with external funds did, as we have seen, avoid disequilibrium of the balance of payments. As a matter of fact, the expansion in imports induced by investments in coffee stockpiles could hardly exceed the value of those stocks, inasmuch as they had 100 per cent exchange coverage.

Let us assume that every milréis invested in coffee stocks became multiplied by 3—in line with the defense apparatus already described—thus creating a final income of 3 milréis. It would then be necessary for imports induced by the increase in aggregate income to exceed one-third of that increase for external disequilibrium to be created. For a series of easily discernible reasons, disequilibrium of this kind does not occur unless other factors are involved, inasmuch as the propagation of income within the economy largely reflects that economy's possibilities of itself meeting the needs resulting from increased demand. In the extreme hypothesis of there being no such possibilities—that is, if the whole of the increase in demand had to be met from imports—then the multiplier would be equal to 1 and the aggregate income would increase merely to the extent exports grew. In that instance there would be no possibility of disequilibrium, inasmuch as induced imports would be exactly equal to the increase in exports.

The situation would be entirely different if the accumulation of stockpiles were to be financed through expansion of credit. Let us assume that means of payment were created in a value of one million contos (one thousand million milréis) for the financing of stockpiles and that, through the multiplier, this gave rise to an ultimate flow of income amounting to 3 million contos (3,000 million milréis). Let us also suppose the import coefficient to be 0.33—that is, for each milréis of aggregate income increase the population as a whole (consumers and investors) needed imported goods in a value of 33 centavos. How could such imports be covered? Obviously they could not be covered. The foreign exchange produced by exports was insufficient during the depression years to cover even imports induced by the income created directly and indirectly by those very exports. The reason for this was that, owing to the decline in prices, the rigid components of the balance of payments now imposed a far heavier burden; then too, the withdrawal of capital made the exchange situation even worse.

Thus the policy of boosting income, implicit in the defense of the coffee interests, was also responsible for an external disequilibrium which tended to increase. This disequilibrium was corrected of course by a sharp decline in the external buying power of the currency. The decline was in turn reflected in an increase in prices of imported goods, automatically compressing the import coefficient. The coefficient of 0.33, taken as an example in the preceding paragraph, reflects a specific situation of equilibrium in which internal and external prices were maintained at certain levels. If the external buying power of the currency were to decline sharply, the level of external prices would then have to increase in relation to that of internal ones. Under such circumstances the respective coefficient would automatically tend to be reduced. That is why equilibrium was achieved, albeit at a level of exchange depreciation much higher than it would have been if there had been no creation of income for buying coffee bound for destruction. A study of the evolution of the external and internal buying power of the Brazilian currency in the years after the crisis shows that between 1929 and 1931 the buying power of the milréis dropped about 50 per cent more abroad than within Brazil. This state of affairs to some extent reflects the efforts made by the economy to correct the external disequilibrium produced by maintaining a high level of income inside Brazil. What happened to that income which should have been expended abroad on imports but was pent up within the country? Clearly, it was going to exert pressure on internal producers. As so often happens, the only result of correcting external disequilibrium was to transform it into an internal disequilibrium. A large part of the demand for imported commodities shrank in the face of the relative rise in prices—so much so that if this had not been true, the currency would have continued to depreciate until the demand for imports balanced the supply of exchange for that purpose.

During the depression years, while monetary and real income declined, the relative prices of imported goods increased. These two factors jointly reduced the demand for imports. We have already seen that between 1929 and the bottom point of the depression monetary income in Brazil declined 25 to 30 per cent. During that same period the price index for imported products rose 33 per cent. It will therefore be realized why the reduction in the import quantum was more than 60 per cent. The value of imports therefore fell from 14 to 8 per cent of the aggregate income, and a part of the demand formerly covered by imports was met out of domestic supply.

The increasing importance of internal demand as a growing dynamic factor in this stage of the depression can readily be grasped. Since internal demand remained steadier than demand abroad, the sector which was producing for the domestic market now afforded better investment opportunities than the exporting sector. Thus an almost unprecedented situation arose in the Brazilian economy—namely, preponderance of the sector linked with the domestic market in the process of capital formation. The precarious position of the coffee economy, operating on a policy of destroying one-third of what was produced at a low level of profitability, frightened away from that sector such capital as was still being generated therein. Not only was net profit affected; even maintenance and replacement were practically eliminated. The productive capacity of the coffee plantations was reduced by about one-half for a period of fifteen years following the crisis. Replacement investments being restricted, a part of the capital which had been tied up in coffee plantations was disinvested. Admittedly, a substantial part of that capital was absorbed by other export farming sectors, particularly cotton. The world price for cotton had been maintained during the depression, to the benefit of United States producers and exporters. The Brazilian producers did not fail to take advantage of that opportunity, inasmuch as in 1934 the value of cotton production (prices paid to producers) amounted to about 50 per cent of the value of coffee production, whereas in 1929 it had been only about 10 per cent.

Nevertheless, the main dynamic factor in the post-crisis years was undoubtedly the domestic market. Industrial production, entirely channeled into the domestic market, underwent a decline of less than 10 per cent during the depression and by 1933 had regained 1929 levels.[1] Similarly, farm production for the domestic market rapidly overcame the effects of the crisis. It is obvious that since the level of demand remained high and since a greater part of that demand occurred inside Brazil—in view of the curtailment of imports—activities connected with the domestic market were able to maintain their rate of profitability in most instances and, in some, even to increase it. This increase in profit rates proceeded side by side with the decline in profits in the sector connected with the external market, which accounts for the urge to divert capital from the latter to the former. Activities connected with the domestic market not only grew under the spur of greater profit but also received further impulse by attracting capital generated or disinvested in the export sector.

It is true that the sector connected with the domestic market could not increase productive capacity—especially in the industrial field—without importing equipment, which had be-

[1] Some sectors of industrial production had passed through a stage of relative depression during the 'twenties when imports were favored by the exchange situation. This was the typical situation of the textile industry, whose output of cotton piece goods in 1929 was lower than the high points attained during World War I. The recovery of that industry was a rapid one during the years following the crisis. From a figure of 448 million meters, production of cotton piece goods rose to 639 million in 1933 and 915 million in 1936. See *Anuário Estatístico do Brasil,* 1937–1939, p. 1329.

come more expensive as a result of the depreciation in the external value of the currency. However, the most important factor in the first phase of expansion of production was doubtlessly more intensive utilization of production capacity already available in Brazil. For example, the output of the textile industry rose substantially in the post-crisis years without any increase in productive capacity. This more intensive utilization of installed capacity made it possible to secure a higher rate of profit on invested capital and to create within the industry itself the resources needed for subsequent expansion. Another factor which should be considered is that there was a possibility of buying second-hand equipment abroad at very low prices. Some of the largest industries established in Brazil during the depression years were based on equipment from plants which had closed in the countries hardest hit by the industrial crisis.

The growth in demand for capital goods—reflecting expansion in production for the domestic market—and the substantial increase in import prices for those goods owing to exchange depreciation gave rise to conditions favoring the installation of capital goods industries in Brazil. Industries of this kind are faced with serious difficulties—for obvious reasons—in endeavoring to become established in a dependent economy. The demand for capital goods in such economies coincides with expansion of exports—the main factor in income growth—and hence with an affluent exchange situation. Furthermore, the capital goods industries are those in which the underdeveloped countries, owing to the size of the markets, are in a position of greater relative disadvantage. That relative disadvantage, added to the facilities for importing which prevail at times when the demand for capital goods is on the increase, results in a lack of incentive for such industries in countries with a dependent economy. However, the conditions in Brazil during the 'thirties disrupted that vicious circle. The demand for capital goods grew precisely at a stage when import possibilities were almost nil.

Actually, the output of capital goods in Brazil (judged by

the production of iron, steel, and cement) suffered little as a result of the crisis and began growing again by 1931. In 1932, the rock-bottom year of the depression in Brazil, production had increased by 60 per cent over 1929 figures, and at the same time imports of capital goods had declined to a little more than one-fifth their former figure. There is much significance in the fact that net investment in 1935 (at constant prices) exceeded 1929 levels whereas imports of capital goods were still only 50 per cent of the figure for the former year. The level of the aggregate income had been regained, despite the 50 per cent cut in capital goods imports. It is therefore evident that the economy had not only leavened incentives from within to annul the depressive effects from without and continue growing but that it had also managed to produce a part of the goods necessary for the maintenance and expansion of its productive capacity.

All these factors contributed to basic changes in the Brazilian economy. It should first of all be borne in mind that importing capacity did not recuperate during the 'thirties. Even in 1937 it was still substantially below the 1929 figure. In reality, the import quantum for 1937—although higher than for any other in the decade—was still 23 per cent lower than for 1929. The real income created by exports had diminished. The export quantum had, it is true, shown an increase; on the other hand, as the purchasing power per export unit had declined one-half by reference to the value per import unit, obviously the income produced by exports was much lower.[2] The

---

[2] The evolution of foreign trade during the 'thirties may be clearly deduced from the following data for 1937, the most favorable year of the decade:

Year	Export quantum	Export prices	Import prices	Terms of trade	Importing capacity	Import quantum
1929	100	100	100	100	100	100
1937	130.2	101	196	52	67	76.9

SOURCE: *Estudio Econômico de América Latina* (ECLA, 1949).

farm production value of current prices had increased from 7,500 to 7,800 million cruzeiros, even though production for export had declined from 5,500 to 4,500 million. The role of exports as a farm income producing factor had thus declined from 70 to 57 per cent. Hence, if the economy had merely reacted passively to external stimuli, it would not only have been faced with an even deeper depression but would also have failed to recover within the entire decade.

Recovery was, however, rapid and comparatively vigorous. Industrial output grew by about 50 per cent between 1929 and 1937, and primary production for the domestic market increased by more than 40 per cent in the same period. Thus, notwithstanding the depression imposed on Brazil from without, the aggregate income rose by 20 per cent between the years in question, implying a per capita increase of 7 per cent. Such an increase is by no means negligible if it is borne in mind that in the United States in the same period the per capita income declined substantially. Those countries with an economic structure similar to that of Brazil, but which adopted a far more orthodox policy in the crisis years and were therefore dependent on external influences for recovery, were still in a state of economic depression in 1937.

The significance of this phenomenon is far greater than might be assumed at first sight. We have already mentioned the far-reaching relationship existing between the intensity of the external impulse and the growth of an economy specializing in exports of raw materials. Permitting better utilization of the resources of the soil and preëxisting manpower supply, the external impulse creates the increase in productivity which is the starting point for the capital accumulation process. The mass of wages and other payments to factors created in the export sector represents the embryo of the domestic market. When the external impulse grows, indirect expansion of internal demand tends to integrate into the monetary economy those manpower and soil resources which had been underemployed in the subsistence sector. But when the external impulse declines, on the other hand, the resultant contraction in monetary income tends to create underemployment or underutilization of capacity in the sector connected with the domestic market.

How, then, could the Brazilian economy manage during the 'thirties to counteract the more or less automatic effect of these mechanisms? How were the depressive effects of persistent contraction in external demand offset? In other words, how can we account for the fact that domestic demand did not enter into a state of collapse when external demand shrank? These results, of great significance for the immediate future of the Brazilian economy, are a reflection of the catastrophic dimensions of the coffee crisis and of the scale on which the interests of the coffee economy were protected consciously or otherwise.[3]

The continuing expansion in coffee production after the crisis, in addition to the fact that the growers became accustomed to the protective plans implemented by the government, largely accounts for the maintenance of monetary income in the export sector. The coffee producer cared little whether stockpiling was financed by foreign loans or credit expansion. The decision to continue financing stockpiling without external funds, whatever the effects on the balance of payments might

---

[3] The revolutionary movement of 1930—culmination of a series of abortive military risings beginning in 1922—was based on the city populations and especially the military and civilian administrative circles and industrial groups, and was a reaction against the excessive predominance of the coffee groups—and their allies in international finance involved in the valorization policy—in the federal government. However, in view of the armed reaction in 1932, the provisional government after 1933 took a series of measures aimed at providing financial assistance to the coffee producers, including a reduction of fifty per cent in the bank debts of the latter.

be, had consequences which could hardly have been imagined at the time. Thus monetary demand was maintained at a relatively high level in the export sector. This—combined with the sudden rise in the cost of imports (owing to exchange depreciation), the existence of idle capacity in some of the industries serving the domestic market, and the fact that Brazil already had a small nucleus of capital goods industries—accounts for the rapid growth in industrial production. That growing production came to be the main dynamic factor involved in the process of income generation.

The above-mentioned sudden changes in the economic structure could not fail to produce long-standing forms of disequilibrium, the most significant of which was perhaps that affecting the balance of payments. The crisis found the Brazilian economy more or less adapted to a certain import coefficient. During the 'twenties the ratio between the aggregate product and the value of imports apparently did not change to any great extent. But, as already mentioned, since the monetary income remained fairly high whereas importing capacity shrank sharply, it was necessary for relative prices of imported goods to increase sharply if the equilibrium between demand and supply of exchange to pay for imports was to be reëstablished. Thus a new level of price ratios between domestically produced goods and imported goods came into existence.

Based on this new level of price ratios, industries developed which were intended to substitute for imports. Actually, the very price ratio served as a basis for the industrial entrepreneurs in deciding to invest in one branch or another. Nevertheless, the recovery of the exporting sector was bound sooner or later to bring alterations in the exchange situation, which would undoubtedly undergo some changes once relative levels of export prices improved and more foreign exchange became available. As can readily be imagined, a sudden improvement in the buying power of the Brazilian currency abroad could only entail an immediate increase in the demand for imported goods and a corresponding reduction in the demand for domestically produced goods, thus tending to reduce income by leading to unemployment. The reduction in income would in turn produce a shrinkage in the demand for imported goods, reëstablishing the equilibrium at a lower level of utilization of productive capacity. What was more likely, however, was that the disequilibrium would be corrected through the exchange rate and not through the income level. Thus the improvement in the exchange situation, in causing a sudden increase in imports, would exert new pressure on the balance of payments, and the trend of the exchange rate would be inverted. This would be an extremely unstable situation in which clearly the relative growth of the sector serving the domestic market would make operation of an exchange system with a fluctuating rate impracticable. Consequently, since the operation of the gold standard was impracticable, a degree of exchange stability had to be ensured by other means.

In the typical raw material exporting economy, competition between domestic producers and importers was practically nonexistent. Fluctuations in the exchange rate compressed demand in one sector or another but did not lead to structural changes in supply. But when the two sectors began to compete with one another, fluctuations in the exchange rate began to have too serious an influence for them to be abandoned to the contingencies of the moment. Thus one of the most effective adjusting mechanisms of the economy—at the same time one of the most effective instruments for upholding the time-honored economic structure rooted in the colonial era—ceased to exist.

The consequences of the disappearance of this mechanism were far-reaching, and were largely responsible for the structural modifications which continued to be felt. In managing to overcome the deep crisis of the 'thirties, the Brazilian economy endangered basic sectors of its structure. The resultant maladjustments were to become clearly evident in the period of tension engendered by the war economy of the first half of the next decade.

33. EXTERNAL DISEQUILIBRIUM AND ITS SPREAD

In the preceding chapter, reference was made to the fact that the lowering of the import coefficient had been achieved during the 'thirties at the cost of a far-reaching readjustment in relative prices. The rise in the exchange rate cut the buying power of the Brazilian currency abroad by almost one-half. Although there were fluctuations in that buying power during the decade, the 1938-1939 situation was nearly identical with that at the most crucial time of the crisis. That situation had permitted a substantial relative cheapening of merchandise produced domestically, and it was on the basis of that new level of relative prices that the industrial development of the 'thirties took place.

We have also noted that the formation of a single market for internal producers and importers—as a natural consequence of the relative expansion of the sector associated with the domestic market—transformed the exchange rate into an instrument of enormous importance to the entire economic system. Any change in that rate, in one direction or the other, was bound to induce a change in the level of relative prices of imported products and those produced in Brazil, which were competing against one another within a small market. It was quite obvious that the efficiency of the economic system was going to be affected by the disturbances due to exchange fluctuations.

The possibility of substantial losses caused by the sudden cheapening of competitive imported goods would discourage investment in the sector linked with the domestic market. For no other reason the more highly developed economies had subjected themselves to the delicately adjusted and expensive apparatus of the gold standard, which integrated all the price systems of the various nations into a single unit.

We have noted, however, that for a typical raw material exporting economy the gold-standard system was impracticable. Once that system had been superseded, however, it became impracticable to subsist within the lack of discipline of the previously prevailing price system.[1]

The minor external valorization of the Brazilian currency between 1934 and 1937 entailed serious obstacles for a number of industrial sectors connected with the domestic market. That improvement in the exchange situation was, however, only temporary, and in the last few years of the decade there was a further depreciation in the value of the Brazilian currency abroad, which brought the level of relative prices back to almost the same point at which it had stood after the crisis.[2] At the beginning of the next decade the exchange policy was to be subjected to a definitive testing. Successive accumu-

---

[1] The 1953 exchange reform was a return to the floating exchange system, the only one within which the Brazilian economy has operated until now without creating serious balance of payments problems. The new system also displayed a high degree of flexibility, inasmuch as it set up five water-tight compartments providing that many types of parity levels for the foreign purchasing power of the currency.

[2] The analysis of prices for 1929-1937 period has been made on a basis of the cost of living indexes for the city of Rio de Janeiro and the above-mentioned import and export price levels.

lations of positive balances on the balance of payments were exerting pressure toward a lowering of the exchange rate. Inasmuch as the supply of international exchange was far greater than the demand, it was unavoidable that the quotation for that exchange should decline.

What consequences was this increase in the buying power of the Brazilian currency abroad bound to have? First, it was going to mean lower prices in cruzeiros for exported goods. For instance, exporters, instead of receiving 20 cruzeiros per dollar's worth of coffee exported, might receive only 10. And, since the international price of coffee was set by agreements, valorization of the currency implied, in the ultimate analysis, increasing losses to the coffee sector. The counterpart of that valorization was a cheapening of imported goods, which in turn had direct consequences on the manufacturing sector. Despite the fact that the external supply of manufactured articles was subject to compression, the domestic producer was seriously concerned with the possibility of sudden imports at a price level far lower than that prevailing in the market. This meant that the interests of both the exporters and the producers connected with the domestic market joined forces to oppose revalorization of the currency abroad. It can thus be understood why the Brazilian government froze the exchange rate, thus tacitly preventing any recovery in the purchasing power of the cruzeiro abroad.

A somewhat paradoxical situation arose as a result of this policy. At the same time that the world market became increasingly transformed into a sellers' market—in other words, one in which the number of buyers increased and the supply of goods decreased—Brazil set the external value of its currency at a level of relative prices reflecting the situation during the previous decade, when it had been necessary to lower the external value of the currency so as to recover the equilibrium of the balance of payments. This situation was enormously to favor activities associated with the foreign market. But because it was not always the traditional export lines that were being benefited—the structure of external demand having changed —there were substantial displacements of factors within the economy, to the benefit of the production of those commodities which found an available market abroad. This situation unquestionably contributed to an intensification of the effects of the serious internal disequilibrium which occurred in the economy during the period in question.

The policy enforced during the war years was essentially the same as that adopted immediately after the crisis. It had— as was only natural—entirely different consequences, since the situations were radically different in the two periods. With the fixing of the exchange rate, the level of monetary income was sustained in a manner comparable to what had been done through the buying up of unsalable coffee in the previous decade. In the latter period, no buyers had been available for the coffee; in the new stage, such buyers did exist, but they were buying on credit—or in other words, paying for their purchases with a currency which was in part a mere promise to pay in the future. The consequences on the domestic plane were the same: a flow of buying power was created within the economy without a counterpart in the form of supply of goods and services. The difference between the two situations lay in the effect upon the economic system of this flow of buying power without a real counterpart. At the beginning of the 'thirties this new purchasing power automatically took the place of the one that was shrinking—that is, the one generated by the external demand in the process of weakening. A reduction in the degree of utilization of productive capacity connected with the internal sector was thus avoided. The situation now prevailing was a completely different one. The economy started from a situation wherein productive capacity associated with the domestic market was being intensively utilized. The index of export prices grew by 75 per cent between 1937 and 1942, so that the external stimulus was very considerable. But because the export quantum during the same period was reduced by merely 25 per cent, even if the exchange rate had fallen from 20 to 15 cruzeiros per dollar, monetary income created by external stimuli would not have been curtailed. By freezing the exchange rate, the government was in effect boosting the monetary income of the export sector at a time when the supply of imported products had fallen by more than 40 per cent.[3]

The contrast between the two situations is apparent from the following data. Between 1929 and 1933 the combined effect of the stabilization of the export quantum and the lowering of the prices of exported products induced a reduction in the monetary income provided by exports, to the extent of approximately 35 per cent, notwithstanding the devaluation of the currency. Between 1937 and 1942, these same factors caused an increase of about 45 per cent in the monetary income generated by the export sector. Now, as the reduction in the import quantum during this second period was 43 per cent, it can easily be seen how unbalance was introduced into the economy through the external sector.[4] Since there was no

---

[3] The evolution of foreign trade during the war years may be observed from the following figures.

Year	Export quantum	Export prices	Import prices	Terms of trade	Importing capacity	Importing quantum
1937	100	100	100	100	100	100
1942	84.2	175	156	112	94	56.6
1945	110.8	216	182	118	131	90.3

SOURCE: *Estudio Econômico de Américo Latina* (ECLA, 1949).

[4] The resemblance of the policy to that of the previous decade even involved the purchasing of coffee for stockpiling. Between 1941 and 1943 about 2 billion cruzeiros (at current prices) of coffee stocks were accumulated. Evidently the effects of this policy could but be com-

possibility of avoiding a contraction in the supply of imported goods, the whole increase in monetary income plus a part of the income formerly spent on imports was pent up in the domestic market. Furthermore, if the pressure resulting from war expenditures and the decline in productivity caused by all kinds of wartime difficulties is borne in mind, it will be easily understood how the economic system was subjected to severe strain and plunged into stagnation during that period.[5]

There are a few other aspects of the exchange problem to be considered. Within the logic of the exchange system then prevailing, a decline in the relative demand of foreign currency was bound to cause depreciation in that currency, the spread of the external disequilibrium throughout the entire economic system being thus avoided. Moreover, the decline in the demand for exchange implied that the flow of monetary income provided by the export sector had no adequate real counterpart in the supply of imported goods, which was the very starting point of the disequilibrium itself. Such a situation could not, however, last forever; when the demand for foreign currency fell below supply, there was bound to be a fall in price of that currency, exporters would receive smaller cruzeiro amounts for the foreign exchange, and the monetary income from the export sector would fall. This reduction in income would counterbalance the contraction in the supply of imported goods and services, thus correcting the disequilibrium. It is true that the cheapening of foreign currency meant that importers would spend far less for imported goods—that is,

---

pletely different from those reached in the previous decade. This clearly demonstrates that the policy of protection of the coffee sector was followed without recognition of its ultimate consequences.

[5] Between 1937 and 1942 there was a reduction in per capita income of at least ten per cent—that is, identical with the growth in population. Data relative to the real product and income from 1939 are from *O Desenvolvimento Econômico do Brasil* (NBED-ECLA).

they would be buying their exchange at lower prices. It so happened, however, that the largest buyers of foreign exchange at that time were the monetary authorities themselves, who took up the whole mass of exchange with no outlet in current trade. The amount of income flow created by the enforced withholding of that foreign currency surplus was bound to be proportionately lower as the price of that currency fell. In summary, the value of those exchange reserves was approximately equal to the excess of income created in the export sector over the counterpart of imported goods and services. If the value of those reserves declined, there would be a corresponding decline in the excess of monetary income over the supply of imported goods.

But the problem did not end there. Even if it had been possible to avoid the increase in the flow of income from exports through a revalorization of the foreign currency, this still would not avoid the accumulation of monetary reserves. Under normal conditions a decline in the price of exchange necessarily increases demand for it, inasmuch as it cheapens the imported goods and improves their competitive ability. Thus the balance between supply and demand of exchange is reëstablished. Yet during the war years, however much exchange might be cheapened, the volume of imports does not increase inasmuch as the output of exportable goods and the availabilities of ocean transportation are controlled by the warring powers and are independent of the price system. In view of the conditions then prevailing, whatever the revalorization of the cruzeiro might be, the external demand for Brazilian goods would remain as it was, and the supply of imported goods would as a rule stay unchanged. Accumulation of reserves was therefore unavoidable. The only possibility of correcting such a situation lay in some discouragement of export producers through lowering of prices. However, if such a tendency has arisen, the foreign importers, under pressure of wartime needs, would have either increased prices in foreign currency or threatened to cut their exports to Brazil if the country insisted on enforcing such an exchange policy.

It is quite true that the rise in the price of exports after 1941 could have been avoided, insofar as the resultant inflation of exporters' income was concerned, with intensifying effects on the disequilibrium. However, even if the prices paid to the producer and middlemen in the export sector had been held to 1939 levels, disequilibrium would still have occurred to the extent that exchange reserves accumulated. Since the economy was operating to full productive capacity, even without bearing in mind the effects of a general decline in productivity, it was inevitable that pressure caused by disequilibrium between the level of monetary income and that of the supply of goods and services should lead to a rise in prices. This rise in prices in turn was reflected in the costs of the export sector, and hindered the carrying out of any policy aimed at maintaining the level of income in that sector. Hence there is no doubt that disequilibrium would still have occurred with or without monetary revalorization. Even had a revalorization policy been decided on, the disequilibrium which was bound to ensue would have made it difficult to enforce such a policy. Once a rise in domestic prices started, pressure against the exporting sector would have increased to such an extent that it would become impracticable to compel exporters to turn over their exchange at an arbitrary low rate set by the monetary authorities.

The situation which arose during the war years was of extreme complexity. In order to correct the disequilibrium spreading through the economic system—reflected in rapid and inordinate price increases—there was a need for action far wider in scope than mere exchange manipulation. It would have been necessary to start from the principle that the economy was being subjected to excessive strain and that there was a need for producing more than was currently required for consumption and investment within Brazil itself. That difference was equivalent to the accumulation of exchange reserves, which in turn indicated the amount produced but not utilized in Brazilian territory. Moreover, it should have been borne in mind that the government was increasing its expenditures for military purposes and thus reducing still further that part of the national product which was intended for meeting the needs of consumers and purposes of investors. Finally, there was a need for considering the general decline in productivity, owing to the disorganization of the coastwise shipping trade, the replacement of better quality fuels by less efficient types, the shutting down of equipment as a result of lack of spare parts, the replacement of mechanical equipment by sheer manpower, and so on.

Meanwhile, the flow of income continued to grow. The external sector generated a mass of buying power which increased in line with the rise in international prices. The government was distributing a larger mass of wage and salary payments. In the private sector the decline in productivity did not entail any reduction in payments to utilized production factors. To reëstablish equilibrium between this flow of income and the supply of goods and services, which had been curtailed, it would have been necessary to act on the economy as a whole so as to distribute the burden properly. Action might have been aimed either at directly reducing the flow of income —by reducing wages and other forms of payment—or "sterilizing" a part of the income which was being created. In a free enterprise economy the latter method is easier to apply and less unpredictable in its results. A cut in payments might have produced extremely discouraging effects either on the entrepreneurs or on the wage earners themselves. At a time when there was a need for boosting production, such a method would be counterindicated. On the other hand, "sterilization" of a part of the income implied merely postponing its utilization, something that is entirely acceptable at times of emergency, especially if the measure is accompanied by a series of direct controls on the distribution of essential goods.

It might be asked why Brazil did not endeavor to correct the disequilibrium through a series of measures aimed at freezing a part of the monetary income, a policy which was followed with a good deal of success in many other countries.[6] The reason may well be that it is not easy to introduce successfully measures of this type when the inflationary process is already in full course of evolution. Such process seems to have shaped up in Brazil faster than in most other countries. What was the reason for this?

When war broke out in 1939, the world economy was in the grip of a depression. Hence there was considerable unused productive capacity in most countries, and the number of unemployed was substantial in the United States, Great Britain, Canada, Australia, and even countries with less highly developed economies, in which the process of unemployment is not so marked. The tension caused by war caused progressive utilization of the idle productive capacity as a result of the rapid increases in government expenditures. It is estimated, for instance, that in Australia full utilization of existing capacity was not achieved before 1942. In other words, it was only after three years of war that the Australian economy began to feel real pressure from surplus demand. Similar processes took place in most of the other countries. The intermediate period acted as a kind of shock absorber, and gave the governments time to assemble the necessary apparatus for controlling the situation before disequilibrium became patent. Thus it was relatively easy to predict which sectors would be more sharply hit by the disequilibrium between demand and supply. In those sectors, as time went by, direct control systems were introduced. Furthermore, it was possible well in advance to in-

---

[6] If proper financing were available, the government would not cause any disequilibrium by increasing its expenditures. But this was not actually the case, as is shown by the persistent deficits during this period.

troduce administrative setups aimed at guiding the utilization of resources, and thus avoid too sharp disequilibriums at the more vulnerable points.

The Brazilian economy had, as we have seen, recovered by its own efforts during the 'thirties. Brazil, unlike the United States and a number of other countries, had by 1937 reached a level of per capita income higher than that for 1929. Furthermore, the 1938 crisis had minor effects in Brazil, for the simple reason that the external sector of the economy had not really recovered in the preceding period. Thus the decline in real income between 1937 and 1938 was only 2 per cent, and by 1939 the 1937 level had been regained. Hence the Brazilian economy had no breathing space before being subjected to the strain imposed by the war on practically every country in the world. The additional tension to which the economy was subjected after 1940 was automatically accompanied by a sharp rise in prices. The general price level, which had increased only 31 per cent from 1929 to 1939, rose by 86 per cent between 1940 and 1944. In 1942, the first year the economy was subjected to a more severe strain, prices rose by 18 per cent.[7]

Once disequilibrium has evolved into a rise in prices, any corrective policies are more difficult to enforce. The reason for this is that price rises are nothing more than a symptom that a pattern of income distribution is changing rapidly. Let us take a closer look at this process. The mass of income created in the export sector was suddenly left without a real counterpart when imports fell off. In 1942, for instance, the f.o.b. value of exports was 60 per cent higher than the c.i.f. value of imports, the balance amounting to 2,800 million cruzeiros. Furthermore, the economy continued to produce coffee in quantities

[7] As an index of the general price level from 1939 I have used the deflator implied in the territorial income, as calculated by the mixed NBED-ECLA group and published in *Desenvolvimento Econômico do Brasil, op. cit.,* Part I, Statistical Appendix, Table III.

larger than could be placed abroad or consumed internally. Coffee stockpiles accumulated in 1942 amounted to a value of 1,000 million cruzeiros. Adding to the above factors the government deficit of 1,500 million cruzeiros, there emerges a splendid base of operations upon which the banking system could expand means of payment, which did increase about 60 per cent between 1942 and 1943.[8] Between 1940 and 1943 the total quantity of goods and services available to the Brazilian population increased by only 2 per cent, whereas the flow of income rose by 63 per cent. This disparity gives an idea of the disequilibrium which arose between the actual supply and the monetary demand.[9] Such disequilibrium was conducive to a rise in prices. Once under way, a price rise tends to accelerate, inasmuch as one of the ways to protect real income is to reduce liquid assets to a minimum. A rise in prices is really nothing more than a valorization due to the pressure of demand upon all goods in course of production or already produced and in the hands of middlemen. This rise in prices tends to spread throughout the economy, and the form taken by the process is responsible for the resultant degree of income redistribution.

It can easily be understood that when a sudden process of price rises takes place, the entrepreneurs—precisely because of holding operating or other inventories, in the various stages of the production process—acquire considerable capital gains. Thus the correction of disequilibrium necessarily also entails a

[8] This abnormal expansion in means of payment reflects only too clearly the completely passive attitude of the monetary authorities. The banking system took it upon itself to rapidly multiply the inflationary pressure.

[9] For the basic data see *O Desenvolvimento Econômico do Brasil, op. cit.*, Part I, Table I, and Statistical Appendix, Table I. The same source has been used for the whole of the basic indexes cited in this chapter, for the period beginning with 1939.

redistribution of income to the benefit of some groups at the expense of others, provided the various mechanisms are free to act spontaneously. And as each one of those groups follows a different procedure in regard to utilization of income, such transfers make it difficult to foresee just how the population as a whole will be spending the total amount of available income. For that reason, once a fast price rise is on the way, it becomes extremely difficult to neutralize the surplus mass of income and to introduce direct controls at strategic points.

Fixing of the exchange rate was, as I have pointed out, one way of protecting the export sector against pressure by accumulated exchange reserves toward a valorization of the Brazilian currency and thus toward a fall in the cruzeiro prices of exported goods. Yet, by helping keep monetary income high, that defense mechanism unleashed other processes which had the opposite effect. The fast price rise necessarily affected costs in the export sector. From the time the exchange rate was fixed, the export sector found itself in a position to retain the whole of the price increase in the foreign market. If the level of domestic prices were to rise even more than that of export prices, it is evident that the export sector would face a relative decline in its real remuneration. In that event the freezing of the exchange rate would merely have avoided major losses to exporters. This, however, did not occur in the export economy as a whole; between 1939 and 1944, although the level of domestic prices went up by 98 per cent, export prices rose 110 per cent, although favoring various groups in a very unequal manner.[10] Every year of that period export prices were well above the domestic price level, showing that the

[10] The prices paid to coffee producers, for instance, rose by only 31 per cent between 1939 and 1943, whereas the general level of prices inside Brazil rose by 65 per cent. However, in 1944 the coffee producers regained and even exceeded the general price level.

export sector was able to take advantage of the fixed exchange rate to increase its relative participation in the aggregate income. Despite the fact that during the postwar period to 1949 domestic prices increased as intensively as those for export, the unbalance created in previous years persisted, even increasing in later periods.[11] This factor is of enormous importance in accounting for the transformations which occurred in the Brazilian economy in the 'forties. Whereas domestic and export prices increased rapidly during the entire period after 1939, import prices grew much more slowly. Between 1939 and 1944, for instance, import prices increased 64 per cent whereas the domestic price level rose 98 per cent. In the following period, the disparity continued to be marked. Between 1944 and 1949, import prices rose 36 per cent whereas the domestic price level increased 70 per cent.

The practical consequence of this growing disparity was the subversion of the relative price level which had served as a basis for Brazilian industrial development from the beginning of the 'thirties. If the evolution in the domestic price level in Brazil is compared with the import price level between 1929 and 1939, it will be seen that there was a relative rise of about 60 per cent in the price of imported commodities. On the basis of this price parity the Brazilian economy has been developing from the time of the depression until today. Such a parity does not necessarily imply that the price level within a country is high or low or, rather, that the currency is under- or over-valorized abroad. It is just as possible to prove that in 1939 the Brazilian currency was undervalorized abroad as it is to demonstrate that the situation was the opposite in 1929.

---

[11] Between 1939 and 1948 the internal price level approximately tripled and that of export prices quadrupled. Between the latter year and 1953 domestic price levels increased by 64 per cent and export prices by 84 per cent.

Between 1939 and 1949, the opposite process occurred and the price level within Brazil rose by comparison with the import price level. Hence there was a revalorization of the Brazilian currency, scarcely concealed by the exchange control system. A tendency arose toward the reëstablishment of the parity between internal and external buying power which had prevailed in 1929. It can readily be seen that a change of this kind would have far-reaching effects on the economic system. The parity of 1929 was reflected in an import coefficient of approximately 20 per cent. Actually, during the period between 1925 and 1929, the value of imports amounted to 22 per cent of aggregate income. During the 'thirties the development of the economy was based on the internal impulse which took place in the form of replacement of imports by domestically produced articles. In fact, as the economy grew, the import coefficient declined and was about 13 per cent by 1939.[12]

The import coefficient reflects the breakdown of the total expenditure of the population between imported and internally produced commodities. For a population formerly spending 20 per cent of its income on imported goods to change that percentage to 10, it is essential that there be a fundamental change in the relative prices of imported and domestically produced goods. A change in the level of relative prices would have to be caused either by a growth of domestic productivity far larger than that in the similar sectors of the countries providing the imports or by an alteration in the exchange rate— that is, a decline in the buying power of the currency abroad.

[12] The comparison is being made between one income series and another series on imports at constant prices, to avoid the faster rise in import prices causing an artificial increase in the coefficient. The data for this coefficient for the 1939–1954 period are to be found in *O Desenvolvimento Econômico do Brasil, op. cit.*, Part I, Statistical Appendix, Table XVI.

It can readily be seen that in view of the scarcity of capital and know-how in an underdeveloped economy, it would be inadvisable to ascribe the decline in the import coefficient mainly to improvement in relative productivity. The reduction in question actually occurred only because of a series of circumstances which favored the maintenance of monetary income and expanded the internal market, producing a rise in the price of imported goods. To modify this new price parity would be to endanger the entire economic structure based on it. This does not mean that the import coefficient is incapable of being modified. If importing capacity were recovered and grew faster than aggregate income, there would be a rise in the coefficient. But that rise would not have to be produced merely by changing the price parity to which I have referred. If import prices declined rapidly, the coefficient would increase rapidly; but in increasing, it would create further disequilibriums in the economy.

34. READJUSTMENT OF THE IMPORT COEFFICIENT

When imports were liberated in the postwar years and external supply became regular, the import coefficient underwent a sudden rise, reaching 15 per cent in 1947. To observers at the time this relative growth of imports seemed merely to reflect the compression of demand in previous years. It was in reality, however, a far more profound phenomenon. When the 1929 level of relative prices was reëstablished, the population endeavored once more to revert to the relative level of expenditures for imported commodities which had prevailed at that time. Such a situation was incompatible, however, with existing importing capacity. That capacity was practically identical with that of 1929, whereas aggregate income had increased about 50 per cent. It was only natural, therefore, that the urge to import displayed by the population (consumers and investors) tended to surpass to a great extent the actual possibilities of payment abroad. The solution which might be adopted for the correction of that disequilibrium was either substantially to devaluate the currency or to establish a series of selective import controls. The decision to adopt the latter solution was of much significance for the immediate future, although the measure had been taken in apparent ignorance of its true scope. This was a decision of basic importance to the intensification of the country's process of industrialization, as we shall see below. The industrial sector, more concerned with the problem of immediate competition from foreign producers, nevertheless assumed that the decision was detrimental to the interests of industry. On the other hand, the export sector, in the belief that it was a measure aimed at halting the rise in prices, felt that the decision had not been entirely unfavorable to it. The motives underlying the action of the Brazilian authorities seemed actually to have been the fear of an intensification in the rise of prices. With the devaluation of the currency, social unrest which was then gathering momentum was bound to increase even more.

What were the consequences of the said policy of maintaining an exchange rate which, once exchange reserves were depleted, would turn out to be incompatible with actual importing capacity? Disequilibrium was still prevalent, and it was therefore essential to bring it under some kind of control. The volume of imports would have to be reduced, and it was imperative to enforce a policy of selective buying abroad. It is worthwhile to draw attention to the fact that the government's immediate purpose—that of reducing or stabilizing price levels—was going to be overlooked as time went by. It would have been necessary to provide complete freedom to import finished consumption goods so as to increase the supply of those goods in Brazil and so that maintenance of the exchange rate might favor a decline in prices. Now, when the time arrived for distributing the available exchange, it became evident that such a policy could not be enforced. To cut down on imports of raw materials, as well as on semifinished products, fuels, equipment, and the like, in favor of the entry of finished consumption goods was impracticable. There were the threat of unemployment engendered by that policy and the magnitude of the interests bound to be thwarted. Thus the practical consequence of the exchange policy intended for fighting the rise in prices was a relative reduction in imports of finished consumption manufactures, to the benefit of capital goods and raw materials. In this manner the industrial sector was doubly favored: on the one hand, because the possibility of competition from abroad was reduced to a minimum owing to import controls; and on the other, because raw materials and equipment could be acquired at relatively low prices.

A situation extremely favorable to investments in industries connected with the domestic market was thus created. It was this situation that was responsible for the rise in the investment rate and the intensification in the process of growth during the postwar period.[1] Whereas the general level of prices went on rising within Brazil, capital goods could be purchased abroad at practically constant prices. Between 1945 and 1950, for instance, the price level of imports rose only 7 per cent, whereas that for domestically produced manufactures (producer prices) rose by 54 per cent. It will therefore be under-

---

[1] The average rate of annual growth of real product per capita (excluding the effects of variations in the terms of trade) was 1.9 per cent between 1940 and 1946, 3.0 per cent between 1946 and 1949, and 3.5 per cent between 1949 and 1954. The rate of savings was 13.9 per cent of income for 1946–1948, 16.0 per cent for 1949–1951, and 15.0 per cent for 1952–1954.

stood why imports of equipment grew 338 per cent between 1945 and 1951, whereas total imports increased by only 83 per cent. The industrial sector did not retain the whole of the benefits provided by the exchange situation. In increasing productivity, the industries transferred a part of the resultant improvement to the population as a whole through a relative lowering of prices. Thus between 1945 and 1953 the rise in prices of domestically produced industrial goods was about 60 per cent, whereas the general level of prices in the economy as a whole increased more than 130 per cent. Even so, the unbalance between internal prices of industrial products and prices of imported commodities remained substantial by comparison with the 1939 parity.

We may well ask what consequences might have been entailed to the Brazilian economy by the adoption of a devaluation policy in 1947, when the extent of the disequilibrium became apparent. Some Latin American countries followed that policy, and their experience helps us infer what might have occurred in Brazil. Devaluation was bound to mean, first of all, a reduction in the real value of reserves which the industrial enterprises had accumulated in previous years when there was no possibility of importing equipment. The actual possibilities of expansion of productive capacity would thus be reduced in the industrial sector. Second, there would be an increase in the income of exporters and producers connected with foreign trade. There would thus be greater incentives for investing in the export sector than in the sector linked with the domestic market. Such a situation would induce coffee producers to intensify the yield of their plantations and promote their expansion as well. Prospects would then improve for the supply of coffee, with an unavoidable repercussion on current and future prices. Consequently, the readjustment in coffee prices, which took place from 1949 on, would either have not occurred at all or would have been on a much smaller scale. On the other hand, the general rise in prices of imported articles would correct the disequilibrium between demand and supply of those items, bringing the import coefficient back to its proper level. Such a situation would not necessarily lead to either an increase or a reduction in importing capacity. It is undeniable, however, that it would have some repercussion on the make-up of imports. Foreign exchange resources actually utilized to import capital goods—and especially industrial equipment—would have been absorbed by imports of consumption goods, since a rise in prices would not be sufficient to eliminate, among the high-income groups, the demand for imported consumption manufactures. In 1938–39 those articles amounted to about 11 per cent of the total import value, whereas the corresponding figure in 1947 was more than 13 per cent. With the enforcement of selective controls, that percentage declined in 1950 to 7 per cent.

I have already described how the exchange policy adopted in the postwar years had as an unexpected effect a substantial favoring of investments in the productive sector associated with the domestic market, especially the industrial sector. Let us spend a little more time on the analysis of that problem. It would be wrong to surmise that the effect in question was merely a process of income redistribution in favor of some sector of the economy. A redistributive process of income in favor of entrepreneurs is capable of promoting economic development only within certain limits and under certain conditions. In a free enterprise economy the investment process has to go hand in hand with market growth. It is well known that the adjustment between the two growth processes occurs in a sporadic fashion, through cyclical rises and falls. But it would be an illusion to suppose that protracted inflation, by redistributing income in favor of the entrepreneurs, could intensify investment. The moment the market ceases to grow, the entrepreneurs—anticipating a reduction in profits—reduce their investments.

The income redistribution inherent in the situation in Brazil in the latter 'forties and early 'fifties was a more complex phenomenon. It was not, as might have appeared, a case of income transfer from the export sector to the producing sector linked with the domestic market. We have already observed that the export price index and the index of prices paid to the agricultural producer associated with the exporting sector grew more than the general price index for the economy during the entire period beginning in 1939. Neither was it an instance of income transfer from the agricultural to the industrial sector, since internal terms of trade for agricultural products vis-à-vis the general price index evolved throughout the period in a manner favorable to agriculture. Between 1939 and 1945 the relative situation of agricultural prices improved by about 30 per cent; this situation was sustained until 1949, when the sudden rise in coffee prices made possible an additional improvement of 20 per cent between that year and 1953.[2] It would be fitting to postulate that the redistribution was to the detriment of consumers as a whole. That hypothesis runs counter to the observation I have already presented, to the effect that the growth of investments—that is, of productive capacity—calls for a concomitant rise in consumer buying power. It is, furthermore, possible to try to demonstrate this phenomenon directly. If an index of the physical volume of total Brazilian output is drawn up,[3] it will be apparent that such output increased a little more than 100 per cent between 1939 and 1954. If on the other hand we measure the actual volume of consumption expenditure by the entire population, an increase of more than 130 per cent is obtained for the same period. It therefore seems evident that the Brazilian population managed during that period to raise consumption more than actual growth of out-

[2] See *O Desenvolvimento Econômico do Brasil* (NBED-ECLA), Statistical Appendix, Table XIII.

[3] Weighted index of production of goods and services, excluding the effect of modifications in the terms of trade.

put, and there was thus no possibility that entrepreneurs might have appropriated to themselves for investment purposes a part of the income which ought normally to have reverted to the benefit of consumers.

The benefits enjoyed by industrial entrepreneurs through low-price imports of equipment and raw materials really represent not the result of income redistribution in the static sense but appropriation by those entrepreneurs of a substantial part of the increase in the community's real income owing to the improvement in external terms of trade. The relative decline in prices of imported products, instead of benefiting every sector equally, was concentrated in the industrial sector for the simple reason that industry was the largest consumer of exchange. Let us consider this phenomenon from another angle. The relative decline in import prices implied, in the ultimate analysis, that the economic productivity of the entire series of factors utilized in the Brazilian economy was growing, inasmuch as with the same unit of work a greater amount of imported goods could be purchased. To get an idea of the importance of this fact, it should be noted that, measured by 1952 prices, real income in the Brazilian economy in 1954 was 237,000 million cruzeiros higher than in 1939, whereas the output actually achieved rose by only 209,000 million. There was, therefore, a 28,000 million cruzeiro increase made available to the community, owing to the increase in economic productivity referred to above.

This may explain why consumption in 1954 was 201,000 million cruzeiros higher than in 1939. Hence, practically the whole of the increase in real output was absorbed by consumption. Nevertheless, this did not prevent a rise in the rate of gross investments (investments over aggregate expenditure) between 1939 and 1954 from 12.9 to 14.3 per cent.

The exchange policy, by relatively lowering the price of equipment and by ensuring protection against foreign competitors, provided a possibility of this enormous increase in productivity being largely absorbed by the industrial sector. Thus the investment rate could rise without precluding a substantial increase in consumption. But for the powerful incentive to industrial investments, due to the circumstances involving the exchange policy, it is probable that a still larger part of the increase in economic productivity would have been absorbed by consumption. If the readjustment of the import coefficient had been effected, not through direct selective controls, but by means of monetary devaluation, it is obvious that imports of manufactured consumption goods would have been reduced to a lesser extent. It cannot of course be affirmed that consumption is necessarily reduced when imports of consumption goods shrink, inasmuch as the population, having no chance of consuming imported commodities, may boost consumption of domestically produced goods and services. It is quite probable, however, that investment opportunities would be reduced by larger imports of consumption manufactures. The exchange policy accompanied by selective control of imports therefore led, not only to concentration in the hands of the industrial entrepreneur of a substantial part of the income increase accruing to the economy, but also to expanding investment opportunities to the entrepreneur.

35. THE TWO SIDES OF THE INFLATIONARY PROCESS

I have already stressed the fact that acceleration in the rate of growth in the postwar economy of Brazil was fundamentally connected with the exchange policy and the type of selective control imposed on imports. By keeping the cost of imported equipment low while prices of domestically produced manufactures were rising, there was obviously an increase in the marginal efficiency of industrial investments.[1] It cannot be overlooked, however, that one of the factors affecting this process was the rise in prices of domestically produced manufactures. This is a matter of the utmost interest, well worthy of analysis. I have drawn attention to the fact that the additional capital available to industrial entrepreneurs for intensifying their investments did not result from a mere redistribution of income, and therefore did not stem from the inflationary process—that is, from the rise in prices. In other words, such capital was created through the general increase in economic productivity derived from the relative lowering of import prices. To attribute to inflation an increase in capital formation of the magnitude of that which occurred in Brazil between 1948 and 1952 is to indulge in a gross oversimplification of the problem, of no help whatsoever in clarifying it. The experience of other Latin American countries, in which inflation has been widely resorted to, demonstrates that such a process is incapable in itself of increasing capital formation persistently and effectively. Yet it would be wrong to overlook the role played by the rise in prices in Brazil in the postwar years. Two distinct problems are involved here: the reason for the persistent price increases, and the effects of such increases upon the economic process. Let us take the second problem first, for the sake of convenience.

A basic cause of the increase in capital formation was the rise in the marginal efficiency of capital—that is, the improvement of prospects for the industrial entrepreneur from the point of view of the profitability of new capital for investment. What lay behind such prospects of greater profitability for newly invested capital? Responsible were the rate of increase

---

[1] In other words, prospects of profitability of new capital invested in industry improved.

in the cost of equipment and the rate of increase in price of manufactures produced with such equipment. Once the exchange rate was fixed, the increase in the cost of equipment reflected the rise in import prices alone. If the level of domestic prices were to follow that of external prices, the cost of equipment would follow the entrepreneur's sale prices. Furthermore, whenever the level of internal prices underwent a relative rise (which happened as a result of the stabilization of the exchange rate), the cost of equipment would be reduced in real terms insofar as the entrepreneur was concerned. If prices had been stabilized as of 1947, the cost of imported equipment would always have been relatively low in Brazil, inasmuch as the balance between demand and supply of foreign exchange would have been obtained by means of direct controls. But when domestic prices rose, the aforementioned relative cost of equipment tended to fall still more. It is easy to understand the strong incentive to invest which resulted from the downward trend in the real cost of equipment. As the process became intensified, import controls had to be made stricter, since the unbalance between domestic and external prices increased. Furthermore, the entrepreneurs were increasing their share in the apportionment of exchange and thus securing a major part of the resulting increase in economic productivity injected into the economy through imports.

The continuing rise in the level of domestic prices was therefore the instrument which favored the appropriation by the entrepreneurs—mainly in industry—of a growing part of the increase in economic productivity which was benefiting the economy with the improvement in terms of trade. Thus, for inflation to play a positive role in the sense of intensifying investments and expanding the economy, something had to be redistributed whose origin was independent of the inflationary process. It is unquestionable, however, that inflation set in operation machinery which channeled into the hands of the entrepreneurs a growing part of the mass of income which improvement in terms of trade had generated within the economy. This process of transfer had to come to an end, because, once a certain composition of imports had been attained, the participation of capital goods and raw materials could no longer grow, at least on a short-term basis. Once this point had been reached, the relative rise in internal prices could no longer have any positive effect on the capital formation process through the stimulus to the importing of equipment. If it had not been for the sharp increase in importing capacity at the end of 1949 caused by the rise in coffee prices, that saturation point would have been reached in Brazil at lower investment levels than those achieved in 1951 and 1952. The decline in the rate of growth observed from 1953 on reflects in part the weakening of those stimuli.

In a previous chapter I mentioned the historic trend of the Brazilian economy toward increases in price levels, reflecting the process whereby the exporting sector transferred to the community as a whole its losses either in cyclical declines or in phases of surplus production. I have also indicated how such a process, tending to make prices rise permanently, rendered it difficult for the gold standard to operate. Let us now look more closely into some aspects of major interest in this problem of price level instability.

After the stage of major disequilibriums immediately following the war, there began a period of slackening of those disequilibriums and reversion to a framework of relative stability within a selective system of imports and control of exchange transactions. Thus, between 1947 and 1949, the cost of living index rose at an annual rate of less than 5 per cent, which amounted to a relative degree of stability (in the 1943–1947 period that rate of annual increase had been nearly 20 per cent). From 1949 on, however, a new rise in prices developed, which increased the cost of living by about 50 per cent between that year and 1952.[2] On observing the economic process more closely, we see that between 1949 and 1952 the volume of real output increased 28 per cent in the industrial sector but only 10 per cent in the farm sector. The rise in monetary income was 75 per cent in industry and 69 per cent in farming. These data seemed to indicate that the main factor of disequilibrium was to be found in the farm sector. This does not, however, reflect the entire truth of the matter. Although it is true that the physical production of the agricultural sector had risen by only 10 per cent, the real value of such production increased with the relative rise in export prices. Hence, if due account is taken of the fact that about one-third of the farm production is exported and that terms of trade improved from 30 to 40 per cent, it may be deduced that the real output of the farm sector had increased by approximately 20 per cent.

By comparing these data it will be seen that, insofar as agriculture is concerned, for each unit of real output 3.4 units of monetary income were created, as compared to 2.7 in industry. But that is not all. Whereas in the industrial sector an increase in monetary income is closely followed by an increase in production, with immediate effects on domestic supply, in the agricultural sector a corresponding increase in supply depends on expansion of imports. But as imports were placed under control so as to hamper the entry of consumption goods, there is no doubt that the increase in monetary income had to exert pressure on the supply of those goods. In a situation of selective control of imports, a large increase in monetary income due to a rise in export prices tends almost necessarily to evolve into a rise in the price level, because the supply of consumption goods cannot grow as fast as available income for consump-

[2] To measure inflationary pressure I preferably use the cost of living index. See *Anuário Estatístico do Brasil* for the index of cost of living for the working classes in São Paulo, and *Conjunctura Econômica* for the cost of living index in Rio de Janeiro.

tion purposes. In the first place, increased supply depends on imports, and these take time to obtain. Second, the need for screening the applications of importers and the preference granted to imports of production goods lengthens still further the time required to increase the supply of consumption goods.

The above remarks reveal some of the basic factors in the mechanism of inflation in Brazil. Inflation is a process whereby the economy tries to absorb a surplus of monetary demand. Such absorption takes place through a rise in the price level, and its main consequence is a redistribution in real income. Any study of the inflationary process concentrates on two aspects: the rise in the level of prices, and the redistribution of income. Yet it would be wrong to suppose that these are two separate elements. The very word "inflation" is inducive to such an error, because it stresses the monetary aspect of the process—that is, the expansion of monetary income. This expansion is, however, only the means whereby the system seeks to redistribute real income so as to reach a new position of equilibrium.[3] A situation may be conceived in which all social

---

[3] Viewing the process from another angle, it might be said that the rise in the level of prices is the way the system reacts against a redistribution virtually already existing when disequilibrium occurs. Suppose, for instance, that through the creation of means of payment the monetary income of one sector is increased. This automatically produces a redistribution of income to the benefit of that sector. If the benefited group were to increase its liquidity, then the redistribution might continue to take place as a purely latent phenomenon. However, if the inflated demand exerts pressure on the market and meets an inelastic supply, then a state of unbalance occurs which may be solved by a rise in prices. If the banking system provides the other sectors with funds to withstand this rise in prices—that is, to operate at a higher cost level —then the redistribution may be abortive. However, even if an inflationary spiral is formed, the group which started first will have an advantage, and that advantage will be the greater the larger the inflationary circuit.

groups develop defense mechanisms, aimed at hampering or preventing redistribution of real income as required by the introduction of some disequilibrium within the system. Such a situation, if carried to an extreme, might give rise to a sort of neutral inflation—that is, inflation without any apparently real effects. Prices would continue to increase without having any effect on the way in which real income is distributed.

It might be argued that if in a specific instance inflation had no real effects there would be no difficulty whatsoever in suppressing it, since none of the groups would have anything to lose as a result of stabilization. Such an observation is based on one of the mistakes which prevent many observers from grasping the true nature of the inflationary process. This mistake consists of a failure to conceive inflation in dynamic terms. In the kind of inflation we have called "neutral," real effects do exist, although they may be imperceptible to an observer analyzing the economic process by comparison of time spans of a certain magnitude. Thus a one-year period is large enough for all social groups taking the lead in distribution of income to complete the circuit of redistribution. At one year's end, the relative positions may be practically identical with those at the end of the previous year. It is only in this sense that we may state that such inflation has no real effects on distribution of income. Observing the process still more closely, we see that such effects do exist, but they are bound to annul each within the period of one year. An absolutely neutral process of inflation would be one in which all prices grew simultaneously and at the same rate. When we say "simultaneously," we mean that the period under observation has to be so short that no real effects take place during it. Such a rise in prices is an unmeaningful phenomenon to the economic analyst.

The difficulty in stopping the price rise in a neutral inflationary process lies in the fact that stabilization would entail the very thing against which the economic system is trying to create a barrier—that is, redistribution of real income. In any day or month some group will be winning the race for income distribution. That group would then be the beneficiary of the stabilization in price levels. Even if it were possible to set an average standard for income distribution over a period of one year, and the intention were to stabilize prices in line with such a standard—that is to say, by enforcing a series of price and wage readjustments—it would be difficult to satisfy every group. The average standard of income distribution during a one-year period would have to be quite different, dependent on whether the period were counted beginning in January or in June, and no one could tell in which month the rise in prices actually started. When such a situation arises—that is, one in which all social groups are prepared to defend themselves, and clearly realize their own position at each moment—stabilization becomes a difficult problem indeed. The rise in prices gradually displaces the system from one position of unstable equilibrium to another, without the creation of any process which might bring the system back to stability.

Clearly, inflation is fundamentally a struggle among groups for the redistribution of real income, and the rise in the price level is merely the external expression of that struggle. Let us now return to the problem of the flare-up of inflation in Brazil from 1949 on. Initial disequilibrium was unquestionably the result of the sudden rise in prices of export commodities—more specifically, those of coffee.[4] Technically, that rise cannot be described as an inflationary phenomenon, inasmuch as there was a concomitant rise in real income. The higher prices of coffee were paid in dollars, and could be transformed into a real supply of goods and services, the surplus demand being thus absorbed. If things had happened that simply, there would

[4] Prices of the remaining products also rose greatly with the outbreak of war in Korea. The rise in coffee prices, however, took place several months previously.

have been actual redistribution to the benefit of those deriving their income from export farming. Redistribution should here be understood in the dynamic sense: it is not a matter of income transfer between one group and another, but of an increase in the participation of certain groups in a larger volume of income. Such redistribution does not, however, take place automatically, inasmuch as the initial disequilibrium gives rise to a series of reactions of an inflationary nature which, within the context of the Brazilian economy, provide new opportunities for other groups to have a share in the increase in real income. As a matter of fact, the rise in export prices has an immediate effect on the real income of the groups benefited, since the exported product provides a larger mass of income. This increase in monetary income of some groups has a counterpart in the increase of the buying power abroad for the community as a whole. If, as occurred in 1949, there is a system of import controls in existence, the increase in buying power abroad cannot be utilized to expand the supply of goods and services on a short-term basis. Hence surplus monetary demand is created. The improvement in terms of trade, even though promoting an increase in real income because of an adjustment in time spans, introduces a disequilibrium of a monetary nature into the system. But that is not all. The increase in income available for consumption exerts pressure on the relatively inelastic supply of manufactured goods and creates an atmosphere of advance demand extremely favorable to the industrial sector. Industrial entrepreneurs resort to the banking system to secure funds for expansion. The banking system, whose liquidity had increased with the expansion of income in the exporting sector, provides the means of payment necessary to expand industrial and commercial activities. The expansion of monetary income in the sector connected with the domestic market likewise exerts pressure on the general level of prices. Because export prices are not dependent on the level of monetary demand within the country, the inflationary process tends to annul the gain in distribution of income afforded by the export sector through improvement in terms of trade.

The swiftness with which the inflationary process spreads in Brazil largely reflects the way in which the country's banking system operates. It might be expected that the inflationary effects of the unusual situation prevailing between the increase in monetary income in the export sector and the increase in imports would be cushioned by the monetary authorities, who could prevent the banking system—in a growing state of liquidity—from expanding credit. However, the banks almost always act in a completely passive manner. When the increase in monetary income is dammed up in the internal sector, exerting pressure on the price of manufactured goods, food, and services, the banking system provides the necessary means of payment. It would of course be wrong to suppose that the banking system itself is a prime mover in inflation, which, as we have already seen, does not originate as a monetary phenomenon. Inflation is the result of the action of certain groups striving to increase their participation in the real income. The improvement in terms of trade sometimes provides the exporting sector with such a possibility. In order for this improvement to be developed to the full, it is necessary that the income accruing to the export sector shall not be faced with a structure of supply rendered inelastic by an autonomous import policy. Once such resistance is encountered on the side of supply, the monetary symptoms of disequilibrium commence. Until that point, the increase in monetary income of the exporting sector is a mere reflection of an increase in real income, inasmuch as that increase has its counterpart in the inflow of foreign exchange.[5] Once the insufficiency of supply becomes manifest,

---

[5] The improvement in the terms of trade is a real phenomenon, just as is the increase in the output of the land. Favorable climatic conditions may provide an increase of 10 per cent in the coffee crop and thus

the surplus of monetary income emerges as an independent phenomenon. Consequently, since prices are not under control, they will necessarily tend to rise. Because a rise in price levels calls for expansion of the means of payment, at this stage of the process the monetary authorities can play an autonomous role. This role will, however, not be easy to carry out inasmuch as it will mean, in the ultimate analysis, protecting one group against the action of others. By restricting credit so as to avoid a rise in the price level, the monetary authorities will be ensuring a redistribution of income to the benefit of the agricultural export sector. As the industrial and commercial sectors participate much more actively in the banking system, it can hardly be expected that the latter will favor such a redistribution as a matter of active policy.

The rise in prices in the export sector—especially a sudden rise such as that which occurred in coffee at the end of 1949—entails at the outset greater profits for all those who have retained stockpiles. The middlemen (providers of services)—and soon the producers—see their monetary income growing rapidly. The rise in the price of coffee spreads from the international to the domestic market, where the local consumer will likewise have to pay more for the product. Hence, a first transfer of real income takes place from the entire consumer population to the exporting sector. Second, within agriculture the prices of the export sector tend to influence the sector connected with the domestic market. As the production factors linked with the export sector are benefited, a movement develops toward transfer of factors to the sector in which the

---

lead to an increase of the same size in the real income of the said groups. It so happens, however, that for the economy as a whole the rise in coffee prices will be a real phenomenon only if it is not accompanied by an equal rise in import prices. In the latter instance such a rise might benefit the coffee sector but would nevertheless still be a mere monetary phenomenon.

price rise occurred. Production associated with the domestic market thereby suffers—a fact which is all the more serious because the income of consumers will be growing as a result of the rise in export prices. Such a situation naturally leads to a resulting increase in the price of agricultural products intended for the domestic market. If the exporting sector, as in Brazil, comprises an extremely important sector of agriculture, it is perfectly natural that the factors connected with the domestic market will try to bring their rewards into line with the level established in the exporting sector, at least on a regional basis.

The way agriculture adapts itself to this double-market economy is to some extent responsible for the chronic instability of the Brazilian economy. When export prices rise, factors tend to be diverted from the domestic to the external sector. Hence, while consumer income is growing, the supply of agricultural commodities within the country tends to contract as a result of the displacement of factors. And since investments connected with the external sector require, as in coffee, a period of maturity of from three to five years, that transfer of factors may proceed for some time without having any effect on external supply. As long as the level of export prices remains high, there will be a trend toward displacement of factors into the external sector. When investments in this sector reach maturity, a situation of overproduction is often created. At this point, prices in the domestic market will again have risen enough to attain the level of export prices. When the latter fall, a contrary process of factor transfer commences, increasing production for the domestic market at a time when consumers' income is tending to contract. The primary sector of the Brazilian economy therefore contains an apparatus for increasing the disequilibriums which originated abroad. This again brings out the enormous difficulties faced by an economy such as that of Brazil in achieving a minimum of stability in its general price level. Trying to attain such stability without taking into account the nature and scope of the problem may be unwise from the viewpoint of growth of the economy. And in an economy of great potentialities and a low degree of development, the last thing that should be sacrificed is the rate of growth.

36. THE PROSPECTS FOR
THE NEXT FEW DECADES

Just as the latter half of the nineteenth century was marked by the transformation of a slave economy based on large plantations into an economic system based on wage labor, so has the first half of the twentieth century been marked by the progressive emergence of a system whose main dynamic center is the domestic market.

Economic development does not necessarily involve a reduction in the role played by foreign trade in the aggregate product. During the first stages of the development of sparsely populated regions with abundant natural resources—as can be seen by comparing the course of events in Brazil and the United States during the first half of the nineteenth century[1]—rapid expansion of the external sector permits a high degree of capital formation and paves the way for technical progress. As an economy undergoes development, however, the role played by foreign trade becomes modified. In the first stage, external induction is the main dynamic factor in the establishment of the level of effective demand. When external stimuli weaken, the entire system contracts through a process of atrophy. The

[1] See Chapter 18.

reactions which take place during the stage of contraction are not sufficient, however, to produce cumulative structural transformations in the contrary sense. If the contraction in external demand is prolonged, a process of disaggregation begins, along with a consequent reversion to forms of subsistence economy. This kind of interdependence between external stimuli and internal development was in full operation in the Brazilian economy until World War I, and to a lesser extent until the third decade of this century.

In a second stage of development, the role of foreign trade as a determinant of income level becomes progressively less important, although at the same time it does acquire greater significance as a strategic element in the capital formation process. Actually, in an extensive agricultural economy, increase in productive capacity is largely a mere result of the incorporation of labor and natural resources. Deforestation, extending plantations, opening roads, increasing herds, and rural building activities are all forms of capital formation based on extensive utilization of labor and natural resources. However, when the structural transformation of the system begins, with a relative increase in investments in the industrial sector and subsidiary services, the demand for mechanical equipment grows rapidly. The system therefore enters into a stage of intensive assimilation of more complex technological processes to which it has access through external interchange.

The intermediate stage of development is therefore marked by substantial changes in the make-up of imports and by a greater degree of dependence by the expansion process of productive capacity on foreign trade. Increased importing capacity is also a powerful stimulus to development of the economy in this stage. However, since external demand is no longer the main factor determining the level of income, growth may continue even in the face of the stagnation of importing capacity. Under such conditions, however, it is to be expected that development will be accompanied by powerful inflationary pressure, which increases as the transformations in the make-up of imports as a result of development become more intensive. Such transformations reflect the degree of dependency of the capital formation process on the importing of equipment.

The development of the Brazilian economy from the time of the 1929 world crisis fits well into this intermediate category. If the period is considered as a whole, the conclusion will be reached that the main factor determining the level of demand —and hence of development—has been investments connected with the domestic market. Nevertheless, it was only during that period in which there was increased importing capacity—1945 to 1954—that a truly rapid rate of growth was achieved. The most reliable statistical data available, from the industrial census of 1920 on, give a more precise notion of the rate of growth of the Brazilian economy. Between that year and 1929 the annual average rate of growth of the aggregate product was 4.5 per cent. Between 1929 and 1937 it fell to 2.3 per cent. For the next decade (1937–1947) there was a slight increase, to 2.9 per cent; between 1947 and 1957 there was a substantial rise, to 5.3 per cent.[2] For the entire period from 1920 to 1957, the rate of increase was 3.9 per cent, corresponding to approximately 1.6 per cent per capita. The rate of 1.6 per cent

[2] If it is assumed that the population increased at an average annual rate of 2.0 per cent during the first two periods, at 2.2 per cent in the third period, and 2.4 in the fourth, then the per capita growth rates were: 1920–1929: 2.5 per cent; 1929–1937: 0.3; 1937–1947: 0.7; 1947–1957: 2.8; and 1920–1957: 1.6 per cent. The estimate of the product during the 1920–1939 period was made by me. The basic series referring to this period are contained in *Estudio Económico de América Latina* (ECLA, 1949). The data for the 1939–1947 period are from *O Desenvolvimento Econômico do Brasil* (NBED-ECLA). For the 1947–1955 period they are from *Revista Brasileira de Economia*, Dec., 1956, p. 28. It has been assumed, on the basis of recent estimates, that the product per capita (excluding inventory accumulation) remained stationary in 1956 and 1957.

for annual per capita growth on a long-term basis is close to that achieved by Brazil, very roughly speaking, for the second half of the nineteenth century. This is fairly high, as we have noted, although somewhat below the long-term rate in the United States. Of the countries in Latin America, the only one for which sufficiently extensive series of statistics are available —Argentina—showed a somewhat lower rate for the first half of the twentieth century.[3]

The 1920–1957 period was marked by a substantial reduction in the relative importance of external demand as a determinant of income level. As a matter of fact, whereas the real product increased by about 300 per cent—that is, quadrupled —the quantum of exports rose by only 80 per cent. If it is remembered that in recent years the value of imports represented approximately 9 per cent of the aggregate product,[4] it may be inferred that in 1920 the figure cannot have been lower than 20 per cent. Thus, to the contrary of the patterns of extensive growth observed in previous centuries, the development during the period indicated was marked by substantial modifications

[3] The Argentine economy grew at the exceptionally high rate of 5.1 per cent a year during the 1900–1902 period. Despite the fact that the rate of population growth was the fastest of any country in the world during the period (3.3 per cent a year), the per capita increase was 1.7 per cent. During the 1929–1955 period, however, the per capita rate of growth of the product fell to 0.5 per cent, despite the fact that population increased at a rate of only 1.9 per cent per annum during that period. For the entire period the per capita rate of growth of the national product did not exceed 1 per cent. On this point, see Alexander Ganz *Problems and Uses of National Wealth Estimates in Latin America*, a study prepared for the conference of the International Association for Research in Income and Wealth (Pietersberg, Netherlands, 1957).

[4] In 1955 the gross national product reached a figure of 673 billion cruzeiros (see *Revista Brasileira de Economia, op. cit.*, p. 31) and the value of imports, including exchange premiums, was 60 billion (*Anuário Estatístico do Brasil*, 1956, page 237).

in the actual structure of the economy. A large part of the investments went to create productive capacity for satisfying a demand formerly met out of imports. Despite this, to the extent that the economy grew, with a reduction in the import coefficient, the make-up of imports underwent modification and an increasing share of those imports was directly connected with the process of capital formation.

Thus, although a sharp reduction in external demand no longer necessarily affects the level of employment in Brazil, its effects on the rate of growth are immediate. Even if an attempt is made to maintain the level of investment through a policy of public works, adverse effects cannot be avoided on the rate of growth of the economy due to changes in investment make-up.

Possibly the most important structural transformation that may be expected in the third quarter of the twentieth century will be a progressive reduction in the relative importance of the external sector in the process of capital formation. In other words, the capital goods industries—especially those producing equipment—will have to grow much more rapidly than the industrial sector as a whole. This new structural modification, which has been quite clearly seen to be shaping up during the 'fifties, will make it possible to avoid the effects of fluctuations in importing capacity being concentrated on the capital formation process. This is an essential condition before the economy can achieve the twofold objective of safeguarding employment levels and maintaining the rate of growth. Only thus can the economic system acquire greater flexibility and be in a position to take better advantage of foreign interchange, since it will thus be able to adapt itself more easily to changes in demand taking place in the international markets.

Viewed from a different angle, development during the first half of the twentieth century may basically be said to have been a process of articulation of the various regions of Brazil within a system with a minimum of integration. The rapid growth of the coffee economy between 1880 and 1930 on the one hand created substantial regional discrepancies in per capita income levels, but it nevertheless provided Brazil with a firm nucleus around which the remaining regions necessarily had to operate. This process of articulation commenced, as we have seen, in the south of the country. Owing to fortunate circumstances, the Rio Grande region—the most unusual region in Brazil from the point of view of settlement[5]—first benefited from the expansion of the internal market induced by coffee development. It is of interest to note that the expansion in sales by Rio Grande do Sul to the rest of the Brazilian market took place in the face of competition from the River Plate countries. Both Uruguay and Argentina substantially increased their sales to Brazil during the phase of great coffee expansion. Customs tariffs favored Rio Grande do Sul of course as it struggled in the first half of the century to supplant its southern competitors.[6] Articulation with the Northeast region took place through the sugar economy itself. In the latter instance the struggle for the expanding markets of the coffee region was waged, not against foreign, but against local, competitors. From the second half of the 'twenties on, southern Brazil became a more important market for the Northeast (except Baía) than that provided by foreign trade.[7] Finally, Amazonas became numbered among the regions benefiting from the great

[5] Rio Grande do Sul was hardly involved in the slave labor economy, and in the make-up of its population the Portuguese element was smaller than in the other regions of Brazil until the end of the nineteenth century.

[6] The last and most important chapter in this struggle to reserve for itself the market of the other regions in Brazil consists of the "battle for wheat production." Rio Grande do Sul is today a heavy exporter of wheat, rice, meat, lard, and wine to the other regions in Brazil.

[7] In 1954 coastwise exports from the Northeast (from Maranhão to Sergipe) were four times larger than exports abroad. In 1938 they had been only twice as large. See *Anuário Estatístico do Brasil*, 1956, pp. 240–241 and 281–282.

expansion of the coffee and industrial region, whose market proceeded to absorb the entire output of rubber besides making it possible for new lines of production—such as jute—to be introduced into the region.

Although by the middle of the century the Brazilian economy had achieved a certain degree of articulation between the various regions, the disparity in regional income levels had also increased sharply. As industrial development took the place of coffee prosperity, the tendency toward regional concentration of income increased. It is in the nature of the industrialization process that investments reach maximum efficiency only when they mutually complement one another—that is, when there is functional coördination into a greater over-all unit. In a free enterprise economy, such coördination takes place somewhat at random, and the probability of each individual's availing of a maximum of indirect advantages is greater as the number of agents acting simultaneously becomes larger.

The industrialization process started in Brazil concomitantly in almost every region. In the Northeast the first modern textile plants were set up after the tariff reform of 1844, and as late as 1910 the number of textile workers in the region was comparable to that in São Paulo. However, after the first trial stages were over, the industrial process naturally tended to concentrate in a single region. The decisive stage of concentration apparently occurred during World War I, when the first phase of speeding up industrial development occurred. The 1920 census showed that 29.1 per cent of the industrial workers in Brazil were situated in the state of São Paulo.[8] By 1940 that percentage had risen to 34.9, and by 1950 to 38.6. The pro-

[8] On this point, see the careful study by S. J. Stein, "The Brazilian Cotton Textile Industry, 1850–1950," in *Economic Growth: Brazil, India, Japan* (Durham, N. C., 1955).

portion in the Northeast (including Baía) declined from 27.0 per cent in 1920, to 17.7 in 1940, and to 17 per cent in 1950. Based not on number of workers but on installed motive power (secondary motors), the Northeast's share shrank from 15.9 to 12.9 per cent between 1940 and 1950.[9] Data on the national income seem to indicate that this process of concentration became intensified after the war; in fact, São Paulo's share in industrial output grew from 39.6 to 45.3 per cent between 1948 and 1955. During the same period, participation by the Northeast (including Baía) declined from 16.3 per cent to 9.6,[10] resulting in increasing disparity in per capita income levels. In 1955 the state of São Paulo, with its population of 10,330,000 inhabitants, had a gross product 2.3 times larger than the entire Northeast, whose population for the same year was 20,100,000. The per capita income in the São Paulo region was consequently 4.7 times higher than that of the Northeast.[11] This growing disparity between the living standards of the main population groups in Brazil may give rise to serious regional tension. Just as in the first half of this century there was a growing recognition of economic interdependence—as the various regions linked up around the rapidly growing coffee and industrial hub—in the latter half there may be increasing fear that rapid growth in one region is necessarily made at the expense of stagnation in others.

The tendency toward regional concentration of income is a

[9] For the data on the number of workers and installed power in the industries—according to the 1920, 1940, and 1950 censuses—see *Anuário Estatístico do Brasil,* 1956, Appendix.

[10] For the data on the national product per activity of origin, by states, for the 1948–1955 period, see *Revista Brasileira de Economia, op. cit.*

[11] The two other important population groups—the states of Minas Gerais and Rio Grande do Sul—are in intermediate situations. In 1955, per capita income in São Paulo was 2.1 times as high as that in Minas Gerais and 33 per cent higher than that of Rio Grande do Sul.

phenomenon observed throughout the world—for example, in Italy, France, and the United States. Once this process has commenced, it is practically impossible for it to reverse itself spontaneously. In a country as large as Brazil, it is to be expected that the process will tend to become extremely prolonged. The rise and growth of this kind of phenomenon are generally connected with relative poverty in natural resources in a particular region. In fact, where there are two regions coexisting within a single economy, integrated into the same monetary system, the one poorer in natural resources (especially land) will tend to present a lower rate of productivity per unit of capital invested. In monetary terms, it may be said that the subsistence part of the wages of the population tends to be relatively higher in places where the productivity of labor engaged in food production is lower.[12] The coexistence of two such regions within a single economy has extremely important practical consequences. Thus the flow of labor from the region of lower productivity to that of higher productivity—even though not attaining large relative proportions—will tend to exert pressure on the wage level of the latter, preventing that level from keeping up with rises in productivity. This relative reduction in the wage level is reflected in a corresponding improvement in the average rate of profitability of invested capital. As a result, even the capital generated in the poorer region tends to migrate to the richer one. Concentration of investments brings external economies, which in turn contribute to an increase in the relative profitability of capital invested in the more productive region. From the point of view of the region of lower productivity, the crux of the problem lies in the

[12] If the population of both regions had to produce merely the amount necessary for subsistence, a larger number of hours would have to be worked in the region with poorer soil.

relatively high prices of wage goods as a result of the relative poverty or inadequate utilization of the soil. Since the subsistence cost of manpower is relatively high, monetary wages tend to be correspondingly high in terms of productivity by comparison with those of the region richer in natural resources.[13] In such circumstances, there being no possibility of resorting to customs tariff or exchange subsidy measures to rectify the disparity, industrialization of the poorer region faces serious obstacles. As an awareness of the nature of this problem is acquired, regional tensions in Brazil—which had substantially dwindled in previous decades—may once again come into existence.

The search for a solution to this problem will probably be one of the main goals of economic policy during the next few years. That solution will call for a new form of integration of the Brazilian economy, different from that pure and simple articulation which occurred during the first half of the century, and which merely diverted into the markets of the coffee and industrial region products formerly placed abroad. A process of integration will have to be aimed at a more rational utilization of resources and factors within the over-all setup of the Brazilian economy. To the extent that the essence of this prob-

---

[13] To establish a balance between wages and productivity it would be necessary for wages in the south to be sufficiently higher to make up for not only the difference in productivity in the industrial sector but also the difference in productivity in the food-producing agricultural sector. However, the existence of surplus labor in the less-developed regions and the flow of this labor toward the more-developed region exercise continuing pressure tending to increase the unbalance. The cost of transportation and other factors prevent the transfer of labor from reaching the volume required to cause structural changes, but it is sufficiently high to affect the evolution of real wages in the region of higher productivity.

lem is grasped, there will be an elimination of certain misconceptions—such as that the rapid development of one region must necessarily entail as a counterpart the slackening of development in others. The decline of the Northeast is a longstanding phenomenon which long preceded the process of industrializing southern Brazil. The basic cause of that decline lies in the inability of the system to overcome the forms of production and utilization of resources which were established in the colonial period. Articulation with the southern region, through cartelization of the sugar economy, prolonged the existence of the old system, whose decline had commenced in the seventeenth century, inasmuch as it contributed to the preservation of the ancient single crop system.

This system is by its very nature antagonistic to any process of industrialization. Even though in specific instances it does amount to a rational (economically speaking) form of use of the soil, single crop farming is compatible with high per capita income levels only when the population is relatively sparse. When the population is heavily concentrated—as it is in the humid belt in the Northeast—single crop farming makes it impossible to achieve higher forms of organizing production. Actually, in the densely populated regions, high per capita capital density—an essential for increased productivity—is achieved only with industrialization. Industrialization, in turn, is invariably accompanied by rapid urbanization, achievable only if the farm sector responds with adequate supplies of food. If all the good farm land is concentrated in a rigid single crop system, the major demand for food will have to be met out of imports. In the Northeast, the major demand in the cities tends to be met by means of food imports from the south, thus contributing to an increase in the disparity between nominal wage levels and productivity, to the detriment of the poorer region. However large the relative advantage of sugar production in the Northeast[14] may be, it must be borne in mind that that sector employs only a small part of the population, and that industrialization will be impracticable if the urban populations depend for their food partly on goods brought in from southern Brazil. The regions in question being a part of a single monetary system, what determines industrial profitability is the ratio between productivity per worker and monetary wages per worker. And, since the monetary wage is dependent on the cost of foodstuffs, the advantages of the Northeast in terms of cheap labor are lessened as the supply of food produced in the region becomes more inadequate.

The process of economic integration in the next few decades, although calling for the disruption of archaic forms of utilization in certain regions, will also make it necessary for an over-all vision of the utilization of Brazil's available resources and factors to be achieved. The increasing supply of food required by industrialization in the urban zones, incorporation of new land areas, and interregional transfers of labor—these are all aspects of the same problem of the geographical distribution of factors. To the extent that this redistribution proceeds, the incorporation of new land and natural resources will permit a more rational utilization of the labor available in Brazil through a lower rate of capital investment per unit of production. Furthermore, capital investment in the infrastructure will be better used in view of the lesser dispersion of resources. It

[14] The relative advantage of sugar is based on a comparison at the enterprise level between the income produced per hectare planted with sugar cane and that from any alternative crop. However, in a region with a large labor surplus the greater productivity at the enterprise level may be completely in disagreement with greater social productivity—that is, bearing in mind investments made not only directly in the agricultural sector but also in the overhead of the economy of the region.

may be expected that if this integration proceeds, the average rate of growth of the economy will tend to increase. Assuming that the long-term annual rate of 1.6 per cent increases to 2.0 per cent, per capita annual income in Brazil by the end of the present century will have reached a figure of 620 dollars at present levels.[15] If, furthermore, it is assumed that the rate of growth of the population on record between 1950 and 1960 (3 per cent per year) is maintained, by the end of the century the population will have increased to 225 millions. Even if this occurs, Brazil will still stand out at that time as one of the major world areas in which there is sharp disparity between the degree of development and the aggregate potential resources.

[15] The gross national product per capita in 1950 was approximately 230 dollars. This calculation has been made on the basis of the year in question.

Index of Names

omy of Pará organized by, 96, 141; Order declines with persecution, 97; Maranhão colonists enemies of, 97

Jute, 264

Labor, native, 10 n. 6, 14 n. 5, 43–44 and n. 2; capture and trading of Indian slaves first stable economic activity, 44–45; role of, 51; Jesuit fathers oppose, 74, 141. *See also* Manpower problem; Slavery

lavra, 82

Laws of the Indies: prohibits non-Spanish ships in Spanish-American ports, 12 n. 1

Lisbon earthquake (1755), 89; eliminates Lisbon as entrepôt under French occupation, 99

Low Countries: Portuguese products shipped to Flanders, 8; expansion of sugar market, 8–9; Spanish, 15 n. 1; Austrian, 15 n. 1

Madeira, sugar production on, 2 n. 1, 7 n. 1; Madeira River, 148 n. 5

Manpower problem: 19th-century slaves, 127 and n. 1; serious problem in 3d quarter, 134; need, 134–135; low freight rates and spontaneous emigration from Europe to U.S., 135; expanding market, 135–136; problem of exports, 137; Vergueiro's idea, 137–138, and temporary servitude, 138; immigration from Italy, 140 and n. 6; rubber and, 143; elimination of slave labor, 148 ff. *See also* Labor, native; Slavery

Mantiqueira Mts. (Minas Gerais), mining economy, 85

Maranhão, state of, 64, 73–74 and nn. 2, 3, 75; islanders from

Azores to, 72; soil, 73; disorganization of markets, 73; Indian hunting, 74; poverty, 75; Jesuit penetration, 75; autonomous center, 96, 97; linked with sugar and mining economies through cattle breeding, 97; prosperity in last quarter of 18th century, 97; Pombal's attention to, 97; colonists enemies of Jesuits, 97; trading company responsible for development of region, 97; cotton and rice, 97–98; exceptional prosperity, 98; then economic trouble and decline in per capita income, 104; internal convulsions, 104 n. 4; rebellion, 106 n. 7; cotton once profitable, 122; manpower drainage, 129; integrated with Pará, 141

Martinique: settlement of, 19; difficulties from tobacco prices, 25; no head taxes, 55 n. 5

Maté, expansion in production for export, 158 and n. 4

Massachusetts Bay Company, 20 n. 4

Mato Grosso: cattle-breeding economy, 84; mining economy, 85; internal convulsions, 104 n. 4; population transfer to, 145, to Triângulo Mineiro, 145; population increase, 159

Methuen Treaty (1703), 38 n. 5; destroys manufacturing development, 87; landmark in economic development of Portuguese and Brazil, 88; grants Portuguese wines reduction in duty in English market, 88; no real basis for survival of, 89

Mexico-Peru axis, Spanish defense system along, 4, 61 n. 1

Minas Gerais: internal convulsions, 104 n. 4; supplying coffee market